PRAISE FOR *RELATIONAL CHILDREN'S MINISTRY*

Dan has it right. His observations and practical advice can help church ministry leaders immeasurably.

—**JACK D. EGGAR,** president/CEO, Awana

This is perhaps the most sobering and inspiring book on children's ministry to date. An essential read for anyone working with children in the church today.

—**DR. GARY M. BURGE,** professor of New Testament, Wheaton College

Dan reminds us that real spiritual growth happens through relationships, and gives practical help and direction on how to realign ministries to this mission.

—**MINDY STOMS,** Promiseland director, Willow Creek Community Church

Amid all the stories about young people leaving the church, this book offers great encouragement for revitalizing the formation of the young.

—**VINCENT BACOTE,** associate professor of Theology, Wheaton College

Dan does an excellent job of saying what most of us are thinking, but then takes it a step farther with compellingly clear guidance to implement effective plans in our ministry.

—**HEIDI M. HENSLEY,** children's pastor, Bayside Church

This book challenges the status quo, providing powerful insights and encouragement to take your ministry to the next level.

—**DAVID KIM,** founder, SproutBox

Dan reminds us that children's ministry is a vital part a local church and that discipleship of the next generation is nonnegotiable.

—**ED RAMSAMI**, pastor, HeronBridge Community Church,
South Africa

Jesus Christ has called us to make disciples who will mature in the Christian faith and reproduce their kind. Dan understands that children and youth comprise a fertile field where we can work.

—**LYLE W. DORSETT**, Billy Graham Professor
of Evangelism, Beeson Divinity School

Dan is on a mission to challenge children's ministry leaders "to disrupt what they have been doing for years to make sure they're truly leading the next generation toward a lifelong relationship with Jesus."

—**RICHARD ROSS**, PhD, professor of student
ministry, Southwestern Seminary

Dan's experience, wisdom, effective communication, and discipleship savvy converge in a great children's ministry book. A solid guide for practitioners of community-oriented discipleship.

—**GREGORY C. CARLSON**, chair and professor of Christian
ministries, Trinity International University

Finally, someone is offering solutions to the exodus of kids and teens from the faith community. This book is a must have.

—**DAVID RAUSCH**, creator of GO! Kidmin Curriculum, Mooblio

Dan invites pastors, parents, and any interested party to discuss questions which demolish some of our cherished assumptions. Out of this comes a stronger model of relationship and growth for children.

—**PETER WORRALL**, associate professor of education,
Moody Bible Institute; author, *Twenty Things
We'd Tell Our Twentysomething Selves*

Dan is a voice to be reckoned with. The ideas he shares in this book will empower families and church leaders to transform our kids into lifelong disciple makers.

—**STEVE CARTER,** teaching pastor, Willow Creek
Community Church; author, *This Invitational Life*

This book will help catapult the kidmin community into deeper dialogue and to a more effective and biblical way of relationally engaging and discipling kids and families today and for years to come.

—**MATT MARKINGS,** vice president of ministry resources, Awana

Dan is honest, real, and vulnerable about the importance of relationships in transforming the lives of children and youth. He helps everyone from the newest kid influencer to the veteran to keep first things first.

—**PHIL JACKSON,** MDiv, pastor, The House Covenant Church;
founder/president, Firehouse Community Art Center Chicago

Dan's commitment as an equipper of church leaders and communicator of the truth is best captured through his passion to faithfully live in the tension of proclamation and demonstration of what he desires to see in others developed.

—**KABWE M KABWE,** pastor, Grace Baptist Church, Zambia

Dan has written a must-read book for parents and all who have the precious opportunity to influence a child.

—**NANCY MATOSSIAN,** family and children's ministry
coach, FAM Network, a division of HomeWord

If you want an easy, comfortable, feel-good book, don't read this one. If you want a book that challenges your thinking, encourages your soul, transforms your children's ministry, and transforms you at the same time, grab Dan's book right away.

—**KEITH FERRIN,** author, speaker, blogger, storyteller

Dan guides church leaders back to the center, where kids and families can grow together in vibrant faith.

—**MATT GUEVARA,** executive director, International
Network of Children's Ministry

Dan concisely delivers a model and vision for what churches can do to meet the unique needs and demands of this generation of children.

—**NANCY J. KANE,** L.C.P.C., associate professor,
Moody Bible Institute

Dan has done a great service for all of us who work in our churches' ministry with children.

—**SCOTTIE MAY,** associate professor of Christian
formation and ministry, Wheaton College

RELATIONAL CHILDREN'S MINISTRY

RELATIONAL CHILDREN'S MINISTRY

TURNING KID-INFLUENCERS INTO LIFELONG DISCIPLE MAKERS

DAN LOVAGLIA

ZONDERVAN

Relational Children's Ministry
Copyright © 2016 by Daniel M. Lovaglia

This title is also available as a Zondervan ebook.
Visit www.zondervan.com/ebooks.

Requests for information should be addressed to:

Zondervan, 3900 *Sparks Dr. SE, Grand Rapids, Michigan 49546*

Library of Congress Cataloging-in-Publication Data

Names: Lovaglia, Dan, 1975-
Title: Relational children's ministry: turning kid-influencers into lifelong disciple makers /
      Dan Lovaglia.
Description: Grand Rapids: Zondervan, 2016.
Identifiers: LCCN 2015038335 | ISBN 9780310522676 (softcover)
Subjects: LCSH: Church work with children.
Classification: LCC BV639.C4 L68 2016 | DDC 259/.22—dc23 LC record available at http://
      lccn.loc.gov/2015038335

Art direction: Juicebox Designs
Interior design: Kait Lamphere

Printed in the United States of America

16 17 18 19 20 21 22 23 24 25 26 /DHV/ 15 14 13 12 11 10 9 8 7 6 5 4 3 2 1

To my family and the family of God,
for today and long into the future.

My gratitude pours out to my wife Kate and sons
Avery and Aaron for sharing an honest life with me,
one keystroke and chapter at a time.

To each of my parents, grandparents, and relatives, thank
you for sacrificially gifting me with grace and truth to
become the person I was uniquely created by God to be.

Thank you to the kid-influencers who impacted my faith
trajectory and keep traveling the unscripted discipleship adventure
beside me—if only every name and story could be included.

To my many mentors in life and ministry, your faithful
presence, patience, and persistence continues to make me
a better person in every relational sphere of life.

To the disciple-making community, thank you for opening your
hearts and hands to know, love, and serve children of all ages
so they will come to know, love, and serve Jesus Christ.

CONTENTS

FOREWORD

IN EVERY GENERATION, God raises up movements and leaders with a key message for that generation. *Relational Children's Ministry* is the message for this generation, and Dan Lovaglia is the messenger to deliver it. Today, while the children's ministry movement is strong, the need to help children and families commit their lives to God as his disciples has never been greater. This book is the most useful book I have seen on this topic, combining practical suggestions for doing excellent children's ministry with helpful suggestions on how to be a heathy leader. Dan provides some of the finest content on the day-to-day practice of children's ministry, all of it integrated into a discipleship model that transcends your typical vision for children's ministry. As I read this book, I thought, "This is a message for *every* church leader."

Dan knows that in the church today, you cannot focus solely on working with children; you must also come alongside the parents. We have a favorite saying at HomeWord: "One of the major purposes of the church is to mentor parents so that parents mentor their children and the legacy of faith continues from generation to generation." Dan teaches you how to make that happen. He knows that when you reach the family, you reach the world. His insights on family ministry are fresh and right on target.

Dan also reminds us that good, healthy ministry is all about building relationships. The apostle Paul wrote to Timothy, "We not only gave you the gospel of God, but our very lives as well" (1 Thess. 2:8). Relationships were Jesus' discipleship method, and they've always been the most effective tool for real-life transformation. Our job, as Christian educators, is to bring young people the gospel in a practical life-changing way, and as Paul instructs and Jesus modeled, we do this by building relationships with the children and families we serve. Kids won't always remember the words we taught them, but they will never forget the loving relationships that brought them the words of the gospel.

I believe Dan Lovaglia is one of the key leaders for this generation, helping the church to develop healthy, biblical models for children and family ministry. Dan lives out his faith in his own family. He has grown as an influential leader working at Willow Creek Community Church and now is multiplying that impact through the ministry of Awana. When you combine his convictions with his leadership experience, the result is a powerful and compelling book. In the final chapter, Dan describes Awana's impact over the generations and how it is continuing its work today. Dan has been instrumental in transforming this ministry to the "new Awana," one that is helping lead the way in reaching a new generation with the gospel.

I'm glad you are reading this book. I believe it will help you better minister to children, and it will affirm you in your calling to make a difference in the lives of kids and their families. As Jesus once said, "Whoever welcomes one of these children in my name, welcomes me" (Mark 9:37). Thank you for welcoming Jesus into your life and for investing into the lives of children.

—*Jim Burns,* PhD, President, HomeWord

ACKNOWLEDGMENTS

WRITING A BOOK is hard work, and as you will soon discover, I believe work inevitably comes with weeds. Fortunately, we till the soil together. Many thanks from me are due.

My family—Kate, Avery, and Aaron—cheered me on week after week to bring these pages to life. This is as much their story as it is mine. I'm honored to be able to share snippets of our faith journey. Through laughter and tears, our unscripted adventures with God and each other are formed. If you get a chance, ask them how much they love crossing the Golden Gate Bridge.

At my age it feels a little weird to thank my mom, but I must. She had every reason to keep children's ministry and the church from changing the trajectory of our lives. Fortunately, God's grace was always one step ahead of her. The fact that she grabbed on to a relationship with Christ and never let go is remarkable. The immediate and extended family, both biological and spiritual, that we enjoy today is in large part because she models the Lord's hospitality like no other.

The rest of the pages that follow bring to light individuals God used in miraculous ways, often without them realizing it, to further his redemptive work in human hearts and the world for eternity. Tracking down the kid-influencers, role models, mentors, and ministry colleagues led to wonderful reconnections. Almost all of the names used are actual first names of people I know, love, and admire. (In case you are tempted, please resist pinging them on Facebook.)

I am also particularly grateful for my ministry mentors and friends, Nancy Kane, Scottie May, and Pat Cimo, for inviting me to embrace Christ more than any other Kingdom endeavor I could pursue. Thank you to Judson Poling for stretching me as a writer and to Dave Rider for calling me out as a relational leader.

A special thank you to Matt Markins and Nancy Raney at Awana for kicking me out of the nest. A safe place to stumble and soar is not easy to find. Each of them brought ideas and perspective to ensure the heart of this book gets into readers' hands and applied in ministry with kids, families, and church leaders. I could not have tackled this without the many teams at Awana. Zac Wendland is a master visual storyteller and Lisa Bohn strategically cuts through clutter with focus and ease. Nicole Bunger finds remarkable ways to use design to communicate creatively. They, and so many others, diligently supported the creation of this resource in ways they will never fully know.

When you are as relational as I am, the list of contributors to commend gets long fast. Thank you to my editors, Ryan Pazdur and Harmony Harkema, and the entire team at Zondervan for sharpening the content, believing in this project, and keeping my fingers from rambling (I'm sure you'll thank them too!).

And to my readers, children's ministry dreamers and practitioners, thank you in advance for carving out space and time to grow in relationship with God for the sake of yourself, kids, and families. Disciple-making communities of kid-influencers need you fully engaged.

AUTHOR'S NOTE

DURING A RECENT SUMMER, right after I started a new role in the parachurch ministry where I work, I headed to my church's annual dads' camp with my younger son, Aaron. Each morning we get time alone by the river; loosely structured time to read the Bible, pray, and journal (or drift off to sleep!). This year, like most years, I had a significant face-off with God. I couldn't help but ask, "Who did you create me to be, and what have you called me to do in this world?" While wrestling with him, the following words began to flow from my pen as I wrote:

> You are mine.
> You belong to me.
> No one can touch you or harm you.
> No one can strip you away from me
> or claim you as their own.
> You are deeply loved and appreciated.
> It is my joy to tell the world that I love you
> and rescued you when you were just a boy.

As I sat in my oversized Adirondack chair, a cool wind whistled through the trees. The sun warmed my face. I looked for a long time at the profound words I had just penned.

What do you want to say, God? What story do you want my life to tell?

I sought God's guidance. I opened myself up to be used by him. And now, after a series of surprising events, you are reading this book.

Yes, I am *that* author. The "I never planned to write a book" variety. I *wanted* to, but finding my voice took a long time. By God's providence and with the timely nudge of trusted family, friends, and ministry colleagues, this book has come to life.

Children's ministry in and through the local church changed my life. This thread runs through my discipleship story. Deep convictions reside in me about how Jesus calls children of all ages to follow him. It moves me that God brings kid-influencers into their lives to serve as guides, side by side on the same discipleship journey. I cannot shake this vision. We need Christ-centered communities that hang on God's every word and walk side by side with him and one another, families of faith that transcend generations.

Where relationship in Christ is central, the church's mission will always prevail. For the current discipleship trajectory to get reset and redirected, I needed to have my bell rung. Apparently I'm not alone in this. Many children's ministry leaders believe that something disruptive in children's ministry is needed so lifelong discipleship becomes the norm rather than the exception. This personal journey has taken many twists and turns over the decades, but it is finally time for me to speak up and share my story.

PART ONE

RISE ABOVE THE STATUS QUO IN CHILDREN'S MINISTRY

CHAPTER 1

ARE WE JUST SPINNING OUR WHEELS?

Our greatest fear should not be of failure but of
succeeding at things in life that don't really matter.
Francis Chan[1]

What good is it for someone to gain the whole world, yet
forfeit their soul?
Mark 8:36

©imagedepotpro/www.istock.com

MY FAMILY AND I live about forty miles outside of Chicago in the midst of a river valley. It was a difficult adjustment when my wife, Kate, and I moved to the suburbs from the heart of the city. Almost two decades later, we have experienced a lot of life and a lot of change. I never thought I would say this, but I really do love it here. It's good for my heart, relationships, and ministry. There are lakes and forests and wildlife all around. There are horse farms, fishing holes, and herds of deer. It's not exactly in the middle of nowhere, but it's close.

Over the years I have particularly grown to enjoy the two-lane route between our home and the rest of civilization. Despite the fact that Illinoisans are typically cast in a negative light as "flatlanders," where we reside is quite hilly. About ten years ago, when I was serving as a full-time children's ministry pastor, I got stuck in bumper-to-bumper traffic on the way to church. It was winter. Visibility was limited. It was cold. It was icy. As the trail of cars ahead of me slowed down at the bend in the road, we were all at a standstill. When it came time to start creeping forward, my vehicle could not move an inch. The wheels kept spinning, but the car didn't move.

No one likes getting stranded on the side of the road. It's frustrating. It

21

derails momentum and holds you back from where you want to go. To be completely honest, I experienced multiple seasons in pastoral ministry where I wondered, "Are we just spinning our wheels?" Having clocked countless discipleship hours with children and families on behalf of this and future generations, it regularly occurred to me how difficult it is to see clear progress from one day to the next. Maybe we were moving forward in our mission; then again, maybe not.

There is but one integral mission of the church passed down throughout history. It gets expressed in many ways in a wide variety of settings. It encompasses many dimensions of spiritual life in relationship with God through faith in Christ. Still, the essence of the calling and vision is the same. It's true for people of all ages, infants through adults. It applies to anyone who humbly stands before God the Father for the forgiveness of sin and life everlasting.

Just before ascending to heaven, Jesus spoke these powerful words to his closest followers: "All authority in heaven and on earth has been given to me. Therefore go and make disciples of all nations, baptizing them in the name of the Father and of the Son and of the Holy Spirit, and teaching them to obey everything I have commanded you. And surely I am with you always, to the very end of the age."[2]

Go. Make. Disciples.

It's easy to say, but difficult to do.

It's even harder to measure.

Defining it is challenging, but necessary in order to focus our attentions on following Jesus fully. Our children's ministries and churches will drift without a discipleship direction.

Discipleship is the lifelong transformation of someone who decides to trust Christ for salvation and become like him in every way. It happens individually in the context of community through the cultivation of God-honoring attitudes, convictions, practices, and relationships.

More than mere beliefs and behaviors, the core operating system of an individual is replaced upon entering a relationship with Jesus and the body of believers. This is the heartbeat of active faith. *Attitudes* reflect the posture of the mind and heart *toward* God, the truth of his Word and other people. *Convictions* demonstrate an internal commitment to biblical truth, to living it out privately and publicly. *Practices* encompass the spiritual disciplines for cultivating (i.e. stimulating or reinforcing) Christlike *attitudes* and *convictions*. And finally, *relationships* foster interpersonal connections with God and others that nurture biblical *attitudes* and *convictions* in community.

This operating definition of discipleship is the thread woven throughout this book. The supporting tenets bring light to how people relate to God and each other. Children's ministry can be part of changing lives and the world when Christ stands at the center.

Everlasting character formation takes place as the person of Christ becomes fully evidenced in and through the Holy Spirit as he takes up residence within a child of faith. In other words, believers are made new from the inside out. Like dye penetrates cloth, discipleship reflects the total and eternal saturation of a human soul. Relational children's ministry must find ways to bring lifelong discipleship of this kind into the context of churches and homes and schools and sports teams—anywhere kids and kid-influencers are found.

This mission was entrusted to the original disciple-making community to faithfully pursue together so that anyone, anytime, anywhere could be given the opportunity to come to know, love, and serve Jesus Christ fully. For centuries, the body of Christ around the globe has held fast to this unifying vision as central to the family of God. Ministry models and methods for multiplying disciples who passionately love God and people continue to be created and implemented. Programs and products promising to support Christ-centered character formation and community are on shelves and online in abundance. Still, the nagging question continues to be raised: "Are we hitting or missing the mark when it comes to lifelong discipleship and disciple making in the way of Jesus?"

Spiritual formation is the task of the church. Period. It represents neither an interesting, optional pursuit by the church nor an insignificant category in the job description of the body of Christ. Spiritual formation is at the heart of its whole purpose for existence. The church was formed to form. Our charge, given by Jesus himself, is to make disciples, baptize them, and teach these new disciples to obey his commands (Matt. 28:19–20).

James Wilhoit[3]

Take a step back and look around on any given weekend or weekday, whenever and wherever the church community gathers. Explore with fresh eyes what people experience. What is happening with infants and toddlers? How about five-to seven-year olds? What is their faith formation environment like? What is being taught to third and fourth graders about God, his Word, and his people? In middle school and high school, how are kids being shaped by their encounters when faced with overlapping and often conflicting worlds and worldviews? Where are parents and other kid-influencers in this mix? Are they engaged or disengaged? Who is encouraging and equipping them as they guide others? What you discover may surprise you. It sure surprised me.

In many church and children's ministry settings, wheels are spinning without much forward movement or momentum. That's why I've written this book. It's for kid-influencers like me who are passionate to reach and disciple children in a manner worthy of the One they are called to follow. It's for those in ministry who, like me, wonder if all the well-meaning work we do from week to week is actually making a difference today and for all eternity. It's for disciple makers who feel like they are doing a lot for God without becoming the people God created them and others to be. We do not need to look far to discover that kids and parents are hurting, both inside and outside our church families. Church leaders are divided on priorities, and we are no longer sure what matters most. The landscape of the world is changing rapidly. There are signs all around that something in our ministry is missing, but it's difficult to see the horizon when you are standing still in the middle of the forest.

IS WHAT'S GROWING GOOD ENOUGH?

A pear tree never produces limes. Fig trees never grow olives. And a malnourished tree never bears anything of value. The seed and state of the root determine the fruit. This principle is true for farmers, and it's equally true in ministry. Whatever gets planted grows from the potential that is contained in the seed. And whatever grows will only flourish if the roots take hold and continue to be nourished over time. Typically when we plant a seed we expect a certain result. Plant corn; get corn. Plant zucchini; get zucchini. But what happens if you plant an unknown seed in uncertain soil? Your results may vary.

Let me explain. A church might say, for example, that its ministries are doing great because of strong attendance or giving patterns. So they create sub-ministries and programming that is attractive to particular audiences, then hope for the best when it comes to lifelong discipleship. Participants of all ages come and go, but the desired discipleship trajectory wanes. The church only tracks what can be counted from week to week: the people and the money. I learned this the hard way when I had to confront the keepers of our church database about someone who had moved away but had been entered as present for the prior six months. No one was intentionally padding the numbers. Everyone just assumed that the girl was still showing up every week with her single mom and sister. No one was really paying attention to her as a person—she was just another number and a name in a database. Another time I found myself in a heated debate over congregational survey results. We were considering whether or not to offer weekly spiritual growth classes. The respondents indicated that they placed a high value on offering electives yet simultaneously indicated that they *would definitely not attend*. Perhaps you can relate. Sometimes ministry seems to be more about crazy making than disciple making.

Lifelong discipleship arises from a deep conviction that God is the one who starts and sustains what is needed for growth. So we begin by prayerfully leaning into him about why the church exists and what approach the community will take to make disciples. In almost every church context, concern is inevitably expressed for the next generation of believers, and how to best offer ministry to kids and families. Leaders consider several factors before crafting children's ministry environments and experiences. Curriculum is written or purchased. Teachers are recruited and trained. Parents are expected to drop off their kids and are challenged to take their role as spiritual champions at home more seriously. Seeds are planted, and good things are expected to grow.

But what do you do when your ministry is overgrown? When you see growth, but little fruit? You sense that the fruit is misshapen or missing, but you aren't sure why and you don't know what to change. If you are reading this book, you are likely involved in some type of children's ministry in your church. Perhaps you are a volunteer, or you are charged with some role of leadership. Either way, there is likely a current of concern inside you; you can't help but wonder if today's reality is going to lead to adult disciples who love and follow Jesus for life.

I routinely come back to one of my favorite verses, one that struck me early in my ministry. In 3 John 1:4, John writes to the church and says, "I have no greater joy than to hear that my children are walking in the truth." That verse resonates deep in my heart, as I hope it does in yours. There is almost nothing better than seeing people come to know, love, and serve Christ because God used me to know, love, and serve them along the way. Still, as I look back on several decades of following Jesus and pastoring, I'm not sure what grew was always good. Like everyone, I have regrets. I am increasingly aware of cracks in the spiritual foundation of my ministry, in my family, and in myself. As much as I desire to walk in the truth and desire the same for others, that desire must be coupled with an intentional pursuit and not just wishful thinking.

So as you think about the kids you serve and the kid-influencers around you, can you honestly say you are content with the ministry you are doing? Or is God challenging you to something beyond the potentially good things you are seeing today? What's holding you back from leading through the challenges your children's ministry and church are facing?

If you're like most leaders, it's probably time to step off the ministry treadmill. You need to get clarity from God about what changes you and he would like made to your children's ministry. A day of solitude with the Lord could be the most strategic meeting you have as a children's ministry leader. It's also worth pulling together a team of faithful leaders and parents (and kids too!) to check your ministry's disciple-making pulse. If you're courageous enough to ask hard and honest questions on the front end, I believe God will give you the courage to make constructive changes moving forward. I pray the principles and practical applications in this book help too.

BECOMING MINDFUL OF WHAT'S MISSING

You've probably heard some of the disturbing statistics about children and teenagers walking away from church and Christ. They are everywhere. The state of the union, spiritually speaking, is not easy to read, and the forecast looks quite grim.

> History will judge us by the difference we make in the everyday lives of children.
> **Nelson Mandela**[4]

Spend a brief window of time immersed in media or the retail shopping world, and you will come to appreciate how fast the world is moving. We say kids are growing up too fast, but in fact they are being exposed to adult realities at younger ages. Parents live in one reality while their kids navigate another. Teachers, coaches, and spiritual leaders come alongside to help in whatever ways they can, but without the help of parents in the home, many of these well-intentioned efforts fall short. The common denominator in all of this—in homes, schools, and churches—is that there are no silver bullet solutions.

As I have served in churches and children's ministries over the years, I've seen faith-related fruit grow in the lives of kids, parents, and leaders, but something is still absent much of the time. The missing ingredient seems to be the sustaining power of lasting and loving relationships.

It's relatively easy to measure attendance patterns, judge success by how teachers impart information, or determine fruitfulness by what kids say they are learning. Or we can focus on the way children behave (or misbehave) and whether parents seem pleased. But these are not the best barometers of growth and fruitfulness in ministry. How can we tell if the seeds of trust, love, authenticity, and honesty are planted and growing? Attributes such as these must be intentionally sown and cultivated, and we must clear away any impediments. The most transformational environments and experiences build in and build upon life-on-life interactions. This is why children's ministries have a unique opportunity. They can be fantastic environments for spiritual growth when the context and catalyst is Christ-centered community.

Children's ministry leaders are crying out: *We created outstanding programs. We taught great information. We saw good behavior. We showed up faithfully. We sent home support. We gave so much. What did we miss?* If we want to better understand where we have missed the mark in our discipleship, we must have an honest talk with those who grew up in our care. David Kinnaman's research in *You Lost Me* and Chap Clark's insights into today's teens in *Hurt 2.0* both make a similar point here: we are missing the transformative power of relationship.

According to David Kinnaman, "The relational element is so strong because relationship is central to disciple making—and as we've said, the dropout problem is, at its core, a disciple-making problem."[5]

Chap Clark writes, "Adolescents have suffered the loss of the safe relationships and intimate settings that served as the primary nurturing community for previous generations traveling the path from childhood to adulthood. . . . They need adults who are aware of the power of small, deliberate, and consistently authentic applications of relational concern, care, and nurturing."[6]

These two books point to a common thread running through the church and culture. Honestly, my shelves are lined with resources seeking to address the root of the problem. American historian Henry Adams, speaking of the for-better-or-worse reality of impacting another person's life, said, "A teacher affects eternity; he can never tell where his influence stops."[7] This adds color commentary to the strong caution given to Christian educators in James 3:1: "Not many of you should become teachers, my fellow believers, because you know that we who teach will be judged more strictly." It's painful to discover that one's teaching and influence has not produced the intended results. But that's a perfect posture and starting point. Yes, it's hard and humbling to ask, "Where did we go wrong?" And it's even more difficult to face this reality when relatively few are volunteering or lending a hand. My goal here is not to place blame. It's to encourage you, to point you to a better way, a better future in discipleship.

GETTING TO THE HEART OF RELATIONAL CHILDREN'S MINISTRY

Any time there is a drop in development, a disruption is needed to shift direction. Innovation depends on the reality that what once thrived will fall by the wayside. Remember when you thought nothing could possibly replace vinyl records, cassettes, or CDs? Now you can carry around thousands of MP3 songs in your pocket. And for those who hate keeping a collection of albums, you can subscribe to online services and apps that will stream unlimited music right to your device for a nominal monthly fee. The music industry experiences disruption all the time these days. Similar disruptions are happening in travel, hospitality, technology, education, and more. When the status quo is no longer meeting people's needs, it's time for change. So what kind of disruptions do churches and children's ministries need in order to refocus, to get back to the heart of disciple making?

[Reaching our youth is] about implementing those beliefs and traditions with a greater understanding of the goal of Christian parenting: to lead our own children to a lifelong and intimate relationship with the one who made them and loves them more than we could ever comprehend.

Brad Mathias[8]

I believe that as kid-influencers of all kinds are used by God to know, love, and serve children, these children will increasingly come to know, love, and serve Jesus Christ. This in turn will overflow into the lives of their peers, parents, and others who cross paths with them as fully devoted disciples of Christ. My point is that the hard work of disciple making is not something any one person is accountable for in the family of God. It's the responsibility of the community. Everyone has a role and responsibility. Children's ministry that integrates multiple spheres of relational worlds is needed because discipleship is not a fabricated program wherein we check off a list. It is inherently relational, requiring investment in the lives of people. For this to become normative, church and children's ministry leaders need to be willing and even challenged to take constructive steps to refocus their ministry approach with a different goal in mind: building long-term relationships with kids and families.

NOW IS THE TIME TO TAKE CONSTRUCTIVE STEPS

Do you recall at the beginning of this chapter when I mentioned getting stuck on the road at the bottom of the hill in the middle of winter? I never told you how I got unstuck, did I? Well, as I looked in my rearview mirror, I noticed someone from our church. Though I recognized him, we had never met face to face. I exited my car while everyone honked at me (as if I were not aware I was inconveniencing them). I walked to his vehicle, introduced myself, and explained my situation. Without hesitation he said, "I'll give you a push." I reentered my car, waited for a little tap on my bumper, and soon I was back on track. How did I stop spinning my wheels? I had to get out of my box, take a step of faith, forge a new relationship, and work together to find a solution.

You see, with multiple cars lining up behind me, the problem had quickly become larger than something I could fix alone. I needed help, and thankfully someone from my church came to the rescue. How does this relate to children's ministry? I'm convinced that we must do our ministry steeped in community. In this context, God provides the resources needed for his purposes to prevail. It takes a team to solve the problems we face today.

If you are like me, you need a nudge from time to time. You need accountability to keep moving ahead. You need others who can share your struggles and joys. And you may have a hard time moving forward with solutions when the how and why are unclear. But I have good news for you. This book is laid out so you can start at the beginning, by taking a look at several core underlying questions and issues. Next, we move into several chapters that offer alternate approaches to the most common models of ministry, ways of shifting your ministry focus toward lifelong discipleship. Finally, there are a few chapters that provide you with action steps to take toward constructive change, both personally and with other leaders in your setting.

Choosing to pick up this book was the first constructive step. But as you keep diving further in, I believe it will be important for you to engage in three additional steps as well. You must be willing to:

Rise above the status quo in children's ministry by facing the disturbing realities about discipleship with kids and families.

Relate intentionally to kids and families by being disrupted by Jesus and putting five life-giving discipleship invitations modeled by him into practice.

Realign ministry for a new trajectory by hitting three "reset buttons" in ministry to ensure lifelong discipleship is embedded.

Rise above. Relate. Realign. Turning kid-influencers into a community of lifelong disciple makers is possible but will require perspective, persistence, and patience. It's time to stop wondering and waiting to see if children are growing and becoming fruitful disciples. We need to take a fresh look at what we are doing and align it with the biblical, revolutionary, time-tested ministry approaches taught by Jesus. Whether you are tasked with leading an afterschool tutoring ministry, a church Sunday school, a midweek outreach and discipleship program, a homeschool co-op, a recreational sports league for children, or just one family in a neighborhood, you can take steps to reevaluate and build up a relational children's ministry approach, in whatever environment you oversee.

QUESTIONS FOR REFLECTION & DISCUSSION

1. What motivated you to read a book on relational children's ministry?

2. How important to you is ministry with kids and families? To the church or ministry leadership supporting you?

3. How would you describe discipleship to someone who is considering a decision to trust and follow Jesus? What would you say to a child? To an adult?

4. On a scale from 1 (not confident at all) to 10 (very confident), how confident are you that children's ministry in your setting is producing lifelong discipleship in kids and families? Explain.

5. What concerns you most about the direction children are heading in relationship to Christ and the church community?

6. Would you say kid-influencers in the home or church have a bigger impact on the discipleship trajectory of a child? Which did you choose and why?

7. If you could make one constructive change to children's ministry, what would it be and why?

8. Who is someone you will commit to talking to and praying with about what you're discovering as you explore relational children's ministry?

CHAPTER 2

MINDING THE DISCIPLESHIP GAP

If you board the wrong train, it is no use running along the corridor in the other direction.
Dietrich Bonhoeffer[1]

Start children off on the way they should go, and even when they are old they will not turn from it.
Proverbs 22:6

©Tommaso Tagliaferri/www.istock.com

SEVERAL YEARS AGO, I had a long layover in London and visited the city for a few hours. My travel companion and I, wanting to make the most of our first time in Europe, took the express train to Paddington Station to grab a bite and see some sights. Grand visions of fish and chips, red double-decker buses, and the changing of the guard at Buckingham Palace swirled around in our jet-lagged minds. To my surprise, it all worked out as planned. We navigated the public transportation system. We correctly adjusted our watches and internal clocks to the time zone change. We even exchanged currency to avoid getting stranded in the heart of the city and missing our early evening flight. Yet as fun as our layover adventure was, there is one moment that stands out vividly in my mind today: crossing the street.

I should add that this was my first time on UK soil. Truth be told, it was my first time outside North America, and I was keenly aware that being in a foreign land demands heightened sensitivity to cultural differences. While exchanging currency and asking for directions, I listened carefully to overcome my unfamiliarity with thick British accents. In the train station, I paid close attention to every "mind the gap" warning so as not to stumble over the threshold or off the platform onto the tracks. And having watched movies set in England, I was *acutely* aware that drivers in England favor the left side of the road.

So, puffed up with good advice and a bit of naiveté, I confidently charged out of the train station. Coming to the street ahead, I kept telling myself, "Look to the right to see if a car is coming. Look to the right first." And that's what I did. What I was not prepared for was the man on the motor scooter who nearly sideswiped me into the nearest hospital. My plan was sound in theory, but as it turns out, I was standing on the curb of a one-way street.

Had I looked to my left, I would never have stepped into oncoming traffic. But I failed to heed the signs. I ignored my surroundings. I didn't pay attention to the specific situation right in front of me. I should have stopped and simply taken a step back to look around.

TAKING A STEP BACK

For fifteen years, I served in associate pastor roles focused on guiding kids and families in the area of lifelong discipleship. I've learned that working with children and teenagers is a bit like travelling in a foreign country. There are similarities between the way we think and live, yet the world of children and teens is still so different from my adult world. Lest you think me uneducated and ignorant, I should add that I have done my best to keep up with current trends in the areas of children's ministry, student ministries, and family discipleship. I have personally worked with believers of all ages, walks of life, and stages of spiritual growth. The Lord has allowed me to come alongside diverse people and ministries representing a wide range of denominational affiliations, and socioeconomic and cultural backgrounds. No matter whom God places in my ministry path, it truly delights me to be used by him to equip followers of Jesus. Still, we need to be aware that ministry to children and teens isn't easy. And we need to keep our eyes open or we'll inevitably get knocked aside by something we didn't see coming.

THE DISCIPLESHIP GAP IS DISTURBING

Children's ministry leaders, churches, and parents are eager for discipleship to be passed on from one generation to the next. Through kid-friendly programs and best-laid discipleship plans, they follow the Proverbs 22:6

Disturbing Statistics
Tell Us a Bigger Story

 "Millennials" are young adults presently in the 18-29 age range. Many walk away from the church, but never drop their relationship with God.

3 of 5 Millennials who grew up in the church have dropped out at some point.

1 of 9 lose their faith in Christianity.

2 of 10 feel lost between the "church culture" and society.

4 of 10 wander away from the institutional church.

3 of 5 disconnect either permanently or for an extended period of time from church life after age 15.

principle: "Start children off on the way they should go, and even when they are old they will not turn from it." Children touched by God's grace and great ministries have high hopes for a future of faith while sitting through Sunday school classes and youth group Bible studies. Still, many walk away after getting out from under the wings of their churches and homes. The facts and figures surrounding lifelong discipleship do not line up with our expectations of effectiveness, especially during the faith-testing "twentysomething" years.[2]

Since these doomsday scenarios are a dime a dozen, instead of citing statistics that point to the problem, children's ministry leaders need to focus on solutions that tell a different story. They, and the kids and families they serve, have more discipleship resources available than at any other time in human history. The technological age has made it possible to distribute a wide spectrum of products under the banner of whatever philosophy and program resonates most. If a church is looking for plug-and-play curriculum, it's available in print or digital download format from a host of providers. If a children's ministry leader wants to embrace an entire ministry model with an accompanying library of content, purchasing and implementing it is just a click away. It does not take long for your eyes to glaze over while you're searching online for just the right Bible study for kids and families. Attending a resource expo at a conference provides a more personal touch, but still, the options are endless. There are so many competing models and methods out there. Let's try to simplify and focus our attention on some broad categories to consider.

In 2006, educator Michael Anthony compared four modern approaches to working with kids in his book *Four Perspectives to Children's Spiritual Formation*. This is a great text for those who are interested in taking a deeper dive into how educational theory and spiritual formation overlap and are expressed in ministry. The chart below provides an adapted summary of the four technical models outlined by the author.

These four models, and the methods that flow from them, are not directly in competition with one another. Children's ministry leaders typically choose models based on their particular background, philosophy of ministry, gifting, personality, or setting. Sometimes these models are in place simply because they were inherited from a previous children's ministry leader. While a balanced combination of all four models would seem to be ideal, it's unlikely to find it in practice. During his research, Anthony discovered that

Four Children's Ministry Models

Media & Motion
Taste and see that the Lord is good. Psalm 34:8

Media-Driven Active-Engagement models leverage sensory experiences to move the heart and hands toward participation in God's story.

Reflection & Response
Teach us to pray. Luke 11:1

Contemplative-Reflective models emphasize character formation as cultivated beyond simply transmitting biblical information.

Drama & Discovery
Do not merely listen to the word. James 1:22

Pragmatic-Participatory models provide opportunities for faith in action to be encountered in Scripture and lived out.

Mind & Memory
Rightly divide the word of truth. 2 Timothy 2:15

Instructional-Analytical models believe biblical knowledge is the foundation for developing godly beliefs and actions.

"It's often difficult to get successful ministry practitioners to articulate just why their programs are successful."

Michael Anthony
Perspectives on Children's Spiritual Formation

Adapted from *Perspectives on Children's Spiritual Formation* "it's often difficult to get successful ministry practitioners to articulate just *why* their programs are successful."[3]

What is common to all the discipleship resources targeted at kids and families is their sincere desire to stem the tide in response to the disturbing data. But the source of the problem is just as uncertain as the solutions proposed. As I have worked in the children's ministry community to identify the problems that keep us from effectively discipling children, I've seen four common scapegoats emerge, each addressed by different models of ministry. These four scapegoats are *cultural shifts*, *cowardly parenting*, *content-shallow resources*, and *careless church leadership*.

ARE CULTURAL SHIFTS TO BLAME?

Some children's ministries establish their discipleship focus around the idea that cultural shifts are the primary reason kids are not growing in their faith. Are kids walking away from the church and/or their foundation of faith because of changes in the broader culture? What role does technology and the media play? Is there a correlation between the level of dysfunction in the home and the strength of a child's commitment to Christ? What impact does living in rural, suburban, or urban environments have on kids' and families' faith? Children's ministry leaders have many good questions to ask here. And for some it feels like the primary culprits are the media tycoons and video game developers who sabotage the home from the inside out. Others turn their attention to the educational system and extracurricular activities that prey on the family calendar. The state of politics and debates about prayer in schools get plenty of hits.

So is this the reason? Undoubtedly, cultural shifts are impacting lifelong discipleship. But there is more to the story.

IS COWARDLY PARENTING TO BLAME?

What happened to the good old days when every family had a Bible at home and actually read it (or so we thought)? How can kids commit to walking with Christ when they're in sports every night of the week? Why are parents so lazy when it comes to helping out at church? I have yet to talk with a children's ministry leader who isn't bothered when parents treat their program as a babysitting service. The belief that parents should be the primary spiritual influencers in their homes and children's lives is on the rise, and with good reason. In some cases this scripturally sound belief comes across as an accusatory attitude, pitting parents and churches against each other. In many cases, families and churches are just doing the best they can with the resources God has provided. Unfortunately, they have difficulty speaking the same language and seeing one another as allies rather than competitors.

ARE CONTENT-SHALLOW RESOURCES TO BLAME?

"Why is this only available on digital download and not DVD? What is all this extra stuff in the box? We just wanted the reproducible curriculum."

Children's ministry leaders do not want to spoon-feed God's Word to hungry children. At the same time, they want curriculum and resources that are well-designed and practical for ministry. Why is so much of what's out there too complicated to follow? Or too simplistic? Why do we end up doing so much prep work every week? Especially when we only have a handful of kids showing up, and they're bored with the content? Anyone who works with children and desires to develop an appropriate learning experience understands the tensions associated with packaged curriculum. Some resources provide too much information; others give too little. Some curriculum companies create full-service programs; others only supply individual products that must be reconfigured or supplemented.

The best resources available rarely show up ready to use off the shelf. Sadly, children's ministry leaders can get caught up in blaming the curriculum for not being "pre-customized" or contextualized to each unique ministry context. Sometimes this is because they feel the spiritual depth of the materials is not sufficient. In other cases, the critique is pointed at the means of delivery, that it's not compatible with the needs of a particular church environment. To move past this and embrace a vision for lifelong discipleship, children's ministry leaders must step away from looking for perfect plug-and-play content solutions. We need to utilize curriculum, to be sure. But we want to find material that can be implemented, adapted, and strengthened in a variety of ways.

IS CARELESS CHURCH LEADERSHIP TO BLAME?

Why does the church leadership treat our children's ministry like a Sunday morning daycare center? What kind of solid discipleship ministry can we possibly have without a budget? If only we had more presence in the pulpit, the children's ministry would never be short on volunteer leaders. Why do my teachers prepare their lessons in the parking lot on their way into the building every week? Children's ministry leaders certainly want to work with other church leaders and ministries in the church. Yet sadly, there is often a silo mentality between different ministries, and sometimes the children's ministry feels like the second-rate program in the church's ministry lineup. It's crucial for those in charge of what is happening with kids and families to be in close alignment with the rest of church leadership. Having a common mission, vision, and values and a prayerful plan in place can go a long way to ensure lifelong discipleship takes root in the lives of kids and families. Sometimes all it takes to get everyone working side by side toward one God-honoring goal is to take initiative and lead stakeholders through constructive conversations. It's an honoring way to move past questioning motives and into courageously leading for a greater cause together.

Given these four scapegoats—cultural shifts, cowardly parenting, content-shallow resources, and careless church leadership—which one is living in your back yard these days? Identify which one(s) cause the most frustration and finger pointing in your church or children's ministry. Talk about them with your ministry team and colleagues. Get the issues out in the open. It's an important first step to attempting wise solutions. As a leader, you can name and contain the problem. Just don't feed it, or the scapegoat will never go away!

You may not struggle with the four scapegoats I've outlined in exactly the way I've described, but trust me—the sentiments expressed here are quite common. And what leaders who buy into these scapegoats share is a desire to see children grow as disciples of Jesus. They just have different solutions to very different problems. They employ models and methodologies in good faith. Leaders genuinely want to do whatever it takes to adjust the lifelong discipleship trajectory of kids and families. Most leaders I know sacrificially invest day in and day out because they truly love the people God has entrusted to their care. They are willing to carefully examine the scary statistics because they've also seen the real-life examples of kids' lives changed.

HEARING FROM THOSE WHO MAKE IT THROUGH

Let's agree that the journey of discipleship in the footsteps of Jesus has no finish line. When we work with children, we need to understand that while we may not see the adults they eventually become, that's okay. We love them in their current stage of life knowing it's just one day in their lifelong adventure of following Christ.

The reality of the dropout problem is not about a huge exodus of young people from the Christian faith. In fact, it is about the various ways young people become disconnected during their spiritual journeys. The conclusion is that most young people with a Christian background are dropping out of conventional church involvement, not losing their faith.[4]

There is a powerful video curriculum that accompanies Kinnaman's *You Lost Me* that vividly portrays the stories behind the research and the statistics. The words and stories of these young people—those of the Millennial generation—gripped me. Their honesty, authenticity, and integrity moved me. The fact that they would go on record to share how the church both helped and hindered them along the way was refreshing. Some have made it through the discipleship gap; others are still fumbling along. Watching these segments marked me; these real people's church experiences gripped me.

And then it hit me.

Their story is my story.

The church *found* me.

And then . . .

It *almost* lost me.

I was introduced to the terms "God," "church," and "Jesus" for the first time when I was eight years old. My parents had divorced a few years earlier. My father had just completed inpatient treatment for alcohol and drug addiction. And my mother, a devout atheist and feminist, was working to make ends meet at a local hospital. As is common for children in homes broken by divorce and fractured by dysfunction, I was shuffled from house to house and from childcare provider to childcare provider. The stories and memories still bring tears to my eyes, although I am fully aware that God shielded me from far worse.

Just after I entered third grade, I moved into a new apartment with my mom in a nice part of town. We were unable to afford the best amenities, but the location provided great schools and hope for the future. With both parents at odds but still in the picture, I had no idea what the road ahead would bring.

We were living in northern California, and my mother decided to enroll me in a daycare operated by a local church. I still remember my mom's words to the folks in the office that day at Oak Tree Daycare.

"If you tell my son about God, church, or Jesus, I will burn your building down," she said. My mother was always up for a fight. She had led a very hard life from the start and had grown up in a religious family. Looking back, it makes perfect sense to me that she wanted to protect her boy from the trials she had gone through in her childhood home, many of which occurred in the name of Christianity. I remember the superintendent's simple and stunning response: "So we'll plan on seeing Danny on Monday after school, then?" There was no way at the time that my mom could have known the woman in charge of the daycare had a similar story, and was navigating her own family through all kinds of dysfunction. The big difference was that she had found a rock solid faith and a family of God to call home.

My mom ended up signing on the dotted line. Oak Tree was a startup effort by a small Baptist church across the street from my new grammar school. It had opened its doors a few months prior and was launching its first afterschool program. The location was perfect, and the price was right. Today, if I could find childcare within walking distance of my home for a dollar per hour, I would pay for all the kids on my block to be there!

The leaders of this children's ministry had a very clear mission. They would let nothing stop them from reaching kids and families with the gospel of Jesus Christ and equipping them for lifelong discipleship. And they did it with great intentionality by providing a safe haven for kids after school where they could do homework, get a healthy snack, and play until mom or dad showed up (always in that order, of course). Within a few months, I decided to follow Christ as the forgiver of my sins and the leader of my God-given life. To my surprise, it didn't feel strange or weird, like getting struck by lightning. I just knew that my relationship with Jesus had changed me. I was different now.

Day after day, week after week, I came home from daycare and shared with my mom the Bible stories and songs I was learning. I'm sure it helped her to see that the daycare was doing more than just that as well. Someone was holding me accountable to do my homework, and my grades were improving. Each afternoon or evening when my exhausted, single mom would pick me up from Oak Tree, the staff would greet her and encourage her to keep going. Their loving support and gentle reminders that I was thriving went a long way toward winning her trust. In time, albeit reluctantly at first, my mom began driving me to church on the weekends so I could go to Sunday school and church with families of friends I made after school. I loved learning about Jesus, and I loved that my mom was willing to let me pursue my own discipleship path.

The daycare center and the church it was attached to became my extended family during a very tumultuous time in my life. To this day, I love that God used a metaphorical oak tree to save, shelter, and strengthen me into a lifelong relationship with him. Trees grow and bear fruit wherever their seeds take root, and that was exactly what happened in my life. Soon, those seeds were spreading to my mother's heart as well. About a year later, God graciously allowed my mother's heart to soften. She had grown close to the leader of the daycare center and eventually made her own decision to follow Jesus Christ. A couple of years later, we both went public with our faith by being baptized together.

Fast-forward through the pages of my childhood and into the story of my own family. My wife, Kate, and I have enjoyed nearly twenty years of marriage and full-time ministry together. We have two wonderful sons. Avery and Aaron are making their way from boyhood to manhood in lockstep with Jesus, their parents, and a church family that adores them. I do not need to look very far back to be reminded that I, along with so many of my family members and friends, are trophies of God's amazing grace. My mom frequently reminds me that God is in the business of restoring the years that were swallowed up (Joel 2:25) and of the faithfulness of the Lord to answer her prayers for me as she released me into his hands (1 Sam. 1:27–28). When a former atheist starts honoring God for who he is and what he has done, you know a life has been changed.

Now, knowing my children's extended family walks daily with God brings me so much comfort as a dedicated disciple and dad. I look back on my years moving into and through adolescence, and I can picture the faces of high school and college students, pastors, Sunday school teachers, afterschool care providers, Bible club leaders, athletic coaches, music instructors, discipleship mentors, and more who served as surrogate biological and spiritual family members for me along the way. If you've never taken time to reflect on your spiritual family, I encourage you to think back on the key relationships God placed in your path. He undoubtedly used each one to help you become the kid-influencer and children's ministry leader you are today.

SO WHAT MAKES THE DIFFERENCE?

As I noted earlier, there are many ways to diagnose the problem of sustainable, lifelong discipleship. And people give many answers. Changes in culture, bad curriculum, lack of support from church leadership, limited family involvement—these are just the top four I hear. But Kinnaman contends that "the dropout problem is, at its core, a faith-development problem; to use religious language, it's *a disciple-making problem*."[5] This perspective resonates with me.

To use Kinnaman's terms, I could have easily grown up to be a *nomad*, a *prodigal*, or an *exile* (see p. 44).[6] My experience at home was definitely far from ideal. My experience at church was generally positive, but there were many times when imperfect programs and people let me down in unthinkable ways. I have metaphorical battle scars from both environments. Wounds still exist in my soul that could have easily defeated me, yet through many dark nights, my faith in God and my long-term commitment to follow Christ has remained steadfast. The presence of the Holy Spirit played the most significant role in all of this, of course. Yet the Spirit works through means, and one of the primary means through which the Spirit has enabled me to persevere has been the existence of a bridge of life between my home and church family.

What made the difference in my discipleship journey from childhood into adulthood was the *way in which* I was invited to receive a remedy for what ailed me. The people who loved me and surrounded me during those years made a huge difference in my ability and willingness to stick with Jesus through thick and thin. God placed his disciples in that church community and challenged them to invest in me as a person, not just as another name or number in the database. They sang the songs and used the curriculum, *but they also made sure I was known*. They took my questions seriously. They resisted the temptation to always provide answers, encouraging me to dive into God's Word myself. They also opened up doors for me to serve, modeling for me the sacrificial nature of Jesus. They reached past the curriculum and the ministry program and spoke directly into my life. Why? Because they saw themselves as lifelong disciple makers. They saw what they did as more than

The World of Nomads, Prodigals, and Exiles

Nomads

Walk away from church engagement, but still consider themselves Christians.

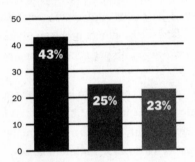

43% Think going to church or being with Christian friends is optional.

25% Say faith and religion just aren't that important to them right now.

23% Say they used to be involved in their church but don't fit there anymore.

Prodigals

Lose their faith, describing themselves as "no longer Christian."

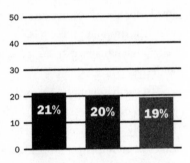

21% Say Christian beliefs just don't make sense to them.

20% Say they had a negative experience in church with Christians.

19% Say their spiritual needs cannot be met by Christianity.

Exiles

Still invested in their Christian faith but feel stuck (or lost) between culture and the church.

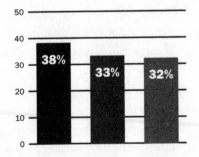

38% Say they want to find a way to follow Jesus that connects with the world they live in.

33% Say that God is more at work outside the church than inside, and they want to be part of that.

32% Say they want to be a Christian without separating themselves from the world around them.

childcare or teaching, more than moral instruction or entertainment—they had a vision of me (and them) following Jesus for the rest of my life.

The presence of faithful Christ followers has always had a huge impact on me. The transparency of men and women who model faith in intentional and unintentional ways reminds me God is real and in the business of really changing human hearts. Hebrews 10:24–25 raises up a sense of authenticity, community, and urgency for followers of Christ of all ages: "And let us consider how we may spur one another on toward love and good deeds, not giving up meeting together, as some are in the habit of doing, but encouraging one another—and all the more as you see the Day approaching." There is beauty and mystery in the phrase, "let us consider," for this can play out in so many ways. How can we build one another up and hold each other accountable to a life of love? What can we do to encourage and not discourage? Why not keep meeting even in moments when we would rather run and hide? What might happen if we held fast to the hope that Jesus is coming back for disciples who are ready?

Notice that there are no quick-fix answers to these questions. Passages like this one offer starting points that lead us to so much more. It was this kind of open-ended, yet structured discipleship, that grounded my beliefs and shaped my story.

Like Jesus with his closest followers, I was granted the opportunity to apprentice with godly men and women who were fully devoted to spiritual practices and relationships as part of the church family. Throughout this book I want to share some of those stories and point to people like Mrs. Anderson, Steve, and others that God used to help me make it through particular discipleship crossroad situations. I can testify firsthand that change happens when kids and families are equipped and encouraged to engage in Scripture and prayer on a regular basis. It also happens when authentic community and compassionate serving are practiced. The spiritual leaders and role models in my life guided me and others toward an intimate relationship with Christ, the family of believers, and my family at home.

Without being pushy, they appropriately spurred me on along the way. Their obvious desire was that I would come to *own* my faith instead of *borrowing* from other people's beliefs. When I was confused or conflicted because of something at church, they made sure to stand by my side in the midst of imperfect programs and people. Timeless spiritual practices and relationships, when coupled with intentional equipping by committed kid-influencers, really can change the trajectory of a child's life. And this, I believe, is what will lead to fruitful, lifelong discipleship for this and future generations.

> Ultimately, how our kids turn out is between them and God. The Holy Spirit will guide them at each turn if they allow him to control their lives. But to simply say, "How my children turn out is up to God" and not give our own careful thought and attention to it is to abandon our God-given responsibility, whether we're a parent or a ministry worker or a church volunteer.
>
> **Larry Fowler**[7]

NOW IS THE TIME TO REALIZE THE WAY FORWARD

Sometimes the future is easy to see. Sometimes it's not. I annually serve pastors and church leaders in Zambia, Africa. In my work with them I have come to appreciate a phrase that Kabwe, my friend and colleague in ministry, uses frequently: "What is the way forward?" He and other leaders in this setting appreciate the importance of identifying where things are at today so tomorrow will lead to a brighter, more hopeful future.[8] When we end our training sessions, it's typical for whoever is leading the meeting to call everyone's attention to establishing appropriate next steps. It's "leadership 101" but its necessity is often underrated. How to proceed can't be left unclear. Some instances require a quick conversation and call to action because what is on the horizon is fairly easy to decipher. There are also times when finding the way forward requires lengthier deliberation because the complexities of the issues require greater levels of wisdom, patience, and courage. It's marvelous to watch the community come together around a common, albeit complicated, problem so that a way forward will serve God's grander purposes for his family of faith.

When I first read books like *You Lost Me* by David Kinnaman and *Revolution* by George Barna, it was a wake up call for me as a parent and a pastor. If you've read these, you'll know what I mean. I feared that what I had been doing in the past needed to change for different future results both at home and at church. Sure, there was a sizeable list of success stories from the children's, student, and family ministries God had entrusted me to lead over the years. There were thank you notes on Facebook from former students and cards in the mail from parents from time to time. Yet despite the evidence of spiritual succession in my wake, I had this nagging sense that this was a global problem that would not go away.

I hope that in this chapter you've come to see that the discipleship gap—our failure to make lifelong disciples of Jesus—is a complex problem. There are no simple solutions or easy answers. We point at scapegoats without asking hard questions of our ministries and ourselves. Something *is* missing. Disrupting the status quo sounds noble until it's time to negotiate toward a preferred future. Will you be bold enough, humble enough, to raise the questions? Will you embrace, stand upon, and champion the principles and practices that will lead to lifelong discipleship?

The optimal discipleship trajectory for relational children's ministry is clear—children are formed into disciples of Jesus when a loving community of Christ followers love them and model for them what it means to follow Jesus. This isn't just a matter of the right curriculum or resisting cultural trends. And while engaged families are essential, it takes the entire church to make it work.

Kids and families need children's ministry leaders who are wise and willing to disrupt what they have been doing for years to make sure they're truly leading the next generation toward a lifelong relationship with Jesus. Church leaders who decisively recognize the need to contextualize for the spiritual sake of their congregation and its surrounding community must step up. Together, children's ministry leaders and families have a shared responsibility to steer the discipleship of kids toward a new trajectory. By recruiting kid-influencers who will "mind the gap" and serve families, God will be able to guide his children to safe passage through the discipleship narrows. When these kid-influencers begin to identify what contributes to the discipleship gap in their children's ministry, they will be facing reality courageously. When they open up their minds and hearts to learn from Jesus' timeless discipleship approach, they will be able to invite kids and families into lifelong discipleship faithfully. And when they determine what needs to be adjusted in children's ministry to reach and disciple effectively, they will be using discernment as they implement seismic shifts wisely.

Relational disciple making is not a radically new idea, but building it into our programs and ministries will require radical intentionality.

QUESTIONS FOR REFLECTION & DISCUSSION

Using the questions below, set aside time (20–45 minutes) to be reminded of your own discipleship story, calling as a kid-influencer, and current approach to children's ministry. This reflective work will serve you and those you serve as you seek to put relational disciple-making principles into practice. Commit to sharing your thoughts with a close friend, mentor, or children's ministry team member.

1. When did your discipleship journey as a follower of Christ begin? Who did God place in your path of life that spiritually influenced you most?

2. How would you describe the discipleship trajectory of the children in your church? What will the foundation of faith be like for participants in the programs you provide?

3. Which "scapegoat" do you think contributes most to the discipleship gap facing children today and why?
   - Cultural Shifts
   - Cowardly Parenting
   - Content-Shallow Resources
   - Careless Church Leadership

4. What vision for the future motivates you to serve faithfully as a kid-influencer in children's ministry today? How are you minding the discipleship gap?

5. What is one change you and your church can make today to refocus on relational children's ministry and lifelong discipleship with kids and families?

PAIN POINTS IN TODAY'S CHILDREN'S MINISTRY

The Christian ministry is the worst of all trades, but the best of all professions.

John Newton[1]

Therefore, since we are surrounded by such a great cloud of witnesses, let us throw off everything that hinders and the sin that so easily entangles. And let us run with perseverance the race marked out for us.

Hebrews 12:1

©Dirima/www.istock.com

NO PAIN, NO GAIN, RIGHT? I know that many people, like me, harbor a love-hate relationship with exercise, especially running. My friends range from casual joggers to ultra-marathoners, and they will all boast about how life-giving running is for them. They tell me tales of pressing past the proverbial wall, overcoming physical limitations, and reaching a euphoric state.

This has never happened to me. Never. But I still run.

When I run my mind wanders, my body gets tired, my clothes get sweaty, and my muscles stiffen up. I slam into the same invisible wall my peers press through, and I end up pushing it uphill with me. The discipline of exercise requires a conscious choice and a concerted effort on my part. I choose to continue because the benefits outweigh the cost of not doing it. In addition to physical fitness, exercise cultivates self-control and perseverance. It also ensures I will be able to serve my family and the world around me with greater mental focus and longevity. Running is never my first choice. But even though it's painful, I'm committed to keeping it as part of my regimen.

Running to stay fit and running a ministry have more similarities than you might think. Pain points are a natural part of discipleship and leadership. And how we handle the inevitable pressures will impact the kids, parents, and leaders we serve, for better or worse.

WIDE-EYED WONDER MINISTRY

I never planned to serve in children's ministry. To be honest, I never sought to pastor in a local church. My plan, after graduating from Bible college, was to get married and become a missionary to teenagers in Australia. It seemed like a self-sacrificing cause at the time: uproot for the sake of Christ, teach English as an inroad to evangelism with high school students, travel the world with my bride—and probably learn to surf too! The Lord clearly had other plans.

Through a series of God-guided surprises, I started as a full-time youth pastor two months after completing my degree. Instead of lugging my wide-eyed enthusiasm to another continent, Kate and I shifted it to the suburbs of Chicago. I was responsible for leading middle school, high school, and college students, and for shepherding a community of parents and adult leaders while attending to an ever-increasing list of *Other Pastoral Duties as Assigned*. Maybe the writing was on the wall, but after a few very full ministry years, I desperately needed a break from the barrage of constant frustrations. A relatively small number of disappointed kids, discouraged parents, and dissatisfied church leaders tipped the scales and nagged at my self-worth. Issues like unclear church-wide vision, limited financial resources, volunteer burnout (and dropout!) and cumbersome curricula that promised to be ready "right out of the box" just made matters worse. No matter how hard I tried, the challenges never went away.

At one point, my perspective got so derailed I knew something had to give. One Friday afternoon, I stopped by a local deli to pick up a party platter of sandwiches for a youth leaders' meeting. A stack of store brochures caught my eye as I waited for the man behind the counter to pull my order together. In that moment, time seemed to stand still. All I could focus on were three words: "Franchise Opportunities Available." I daydreamed about opening a delicatessen for about half a second. I didn't have aspirations of becoming a small business owner, but I was clearly disillusioned with ministry. I could tell the state of my soul was in trouble.

That moment was a turning point for me. Within the year, God saw fit to make some radical shifts in my life, both personally and professionally. He allowed me to learn some key lessons about ministry and myself that I could not have learned any other way. The Lord also let me face several hurdles, formulating insights and gaining experience to better navigate and push through the ministry issues that had plagued me for years. A new way of discipleship gripped my heart.

After a nine-month hiatus during which I healed up from round one of pastoral ministry, I thought for sure I was ready to take things to the next level. I joined a church staff as pastor of student ministries *and* children's ministries, adding to my previous responsibilities. Equipped with an accredited degree, an official ordination certificate, a well-articulated ministry philosophy, key leadership lessons from past failures, and the know-how to establish a solid mission, vision, values, and strategy, I forged headlong into the unknown. But I soon learned I was just as challenged at my new church as I had been at the previous one. I sought high-level counsel from children's and student ministry experts to help me. I read their books. I attended their conferences. I took copious notes. I listened to their sessions in the car to and from work. I reached out to them through email and phone calls, and some even called me back. I established two core leadership teams, one for children's ministry and one for student ministry. I kept tabs on my schedule to keep from burning out. And I maintained close communication with my senior pastor, other ministry leaders, my volunteers, and families. I even rallied pastors from around the area for networking and citywide events.

In short, *I* was doing everything and doing everything right in my own eyes. *I* was on a mission, and *I* was dragging people along with me.

RUNNING RAGGED

Outward success was hiding deeper problems in my heart and life. My naiveté and underlying arrogance were the true barriers to ministering in God's way. Even though I was working with teams, it felt like no matter what ministry approach we tried, success was limited. We significantly ramped up the levels of teaching, worship, activities, small groups, events, and serving. Child attendance, volunteer retention, and parent involvement all increased, especially in the children's ministries. The plan looked great on paper. It even looked good to our visitors. We experienced substantial spiritual and numeric growth in some areas. In others, however, it fell short of what we hoped. Our children's ministry leadership team worked hard together week in and week out. The volunteer teams grew as the number of children we served kept increasing. Our small pastoral staff, core families, and new additions were excited about the ministry. But we still had some nagging questions.

Were evangelism and discipleship really happening? Were transformational relationships between kids and God happening at home and in church? We knew what we wanted to be true, and we kept busy in ministry, but *we had no idea if what we were doing was really working.* The harder we ran, the more walls we hit—and the more ragged we became.

I know I'm not the first ministry leader to face this. And I highly doubt I will be the last. Jon Tyson, entrepreneurial pastor and author of *Sacred Roots*, explains a subtle shift he made in the midst of great ministry success:

> The slow-spreading hue of stress began to color everything we did. And we were doing a lot—programs and kids' care and small groups and all the stuff we knew had worked before. We launched outreach projects, pastoral care, justice ventures, and team trainings. Yet the more we seemed to do, the less we could truly give. The process was so slow you would not have been able to observe it at any given moment, but the end result was there: the joy was gone. It wasn't any one thing in particular but everything combined that led us to replace wonder with work, people with programs, organization with power, and dreams with duties.[2]

Finding balance between ministry as a Holy Spirit-created community and a human-led organization is difficult. A pure desire to serve God and serve people can easily take a turn for the worse when the management of ministry tussles with the passion for making disciples.

For two thousand years, three verses have served as the genesis for discipleship ministry efforts. The Great Commission in Matthew 28:18–20 records Jesus Christ extending his authority and presenting his followers with explicitly simple instructions:

Go.

Make disciples.

Baptize them.

Teach them to obey.

Jesus bluntly charged his faithful followers to lean into his unlimited power and eternal presence. He sent them out to continually initiate and multiply disciples all over the world. Yet even with this focused starting point, our discipleship ministries can spin out of control rather quickly. Misguided children's ministry, devoid of Jesus' authority and abiding presence, can default to The "Not-So-Great" Commission:

Go . . . and go . . . and go.

Make programs.

Administrate all things.

Don't lose any kids.

Every week several hundred thousand church congregations gather for worship services in America. The global number is even greater. Many provide specialized children's ministry programs that desire to teach the Bible, present the gospel of Jesus Christ, and lead kids toward lifelong discipleship. Paid directors lead some; volunteers lead others. Some have elaborate permanent facilities while others set up and tear down weekly. Some adapt published curriculum for their context, and still others create relevant materials from scratch. Time commitments for serving, annual budgets, ministry models, and teaching philosophies all vary from one church to the next. Each of these factors makes for more and more complex ministry. A lot of churches and children's ministries end up "going and going and going" and "doing and doing and doing" with very little disciple making actually happening.

Despite the different variables in children's ministry, one pressing reality remains constant: *kids . . . of all ages . . . show up . . . for church . . . e-v-e-r-y week.*

Children find their way inside wherever doors are open. Based on attendance trends and the state of families, the same adults rarely bring the same kids every week, but children are always present. Senior pastors and elder boards generally recognize the importance of having something available for families if they want to build their congregation. Church leadership often looks to someone with a specific passion for reaching and equipping kids to lead the charge.

You probably already know this, but it takes a lot of creativity to keep children engaged. It takes even more coordination to manage all the supplies and make sure each child goes home with the right parent (or whoever dropped them off!). Weekly children's ministries are exhausting and exhilarating. Yet for too many churches, the flywheel of children's ministry unintentionally trades in "reach-teach-multiply" discipleship for "come-eat-leave" consumerism. Parents hand off their child before the church service, children get corralled into large and small groups for Bible-based teaching and activities, parents pick up their children after the church service. The cycle continues week after week, year after year.

We must work hard to keep this from happening.

You can raise the lifelong discipleship bar for yourself, your leaders, and your church by evaluating your susceptibility to "come-eat-leave" children's ministry. If you buy into the biblical "reach-teach-multiply" vision, it will take open discussion and purposeful planning to implement disciple making in step with Jesus' commission. One step you can take is to ask, "What would be missed in people's lives and in our world if the doors of our church closed?" You and the leaders around you need to know if consumerism is taking root and discipleship effectiveness is deficient.

The apostle Paul illustrates the dangers of doing ministry without a clear focus or purpose in mind. He writes in 1 Corinthians 9:24–27 (emphasis added):

> Do you not know that in a race all the runners run, but only one gets the prize? Run in such a way as to get the prize. Everyone who competes in the games goes into strict training. They do it to get a crown that will not last, but we do it to get a crown that will last forever. Therefore *I do not run like someone running aimlessly*; I do not fight like a boxer beating the air. No, I strike a blow to my body and make it my slave so that after I have preached to others, I myself will not be disqualified for the prize.

All children's ministries are susceptible to running ragged, without a disciplined goal or focus. Unsuspecting leaders can steer things off course with misdirected vision and values. My teams have often caught me rushing around, flailing my arms in the air, trying hard to hold things together. Discipleship with children is a marathon, not a sprint. Disciple making is a race with eternal implications. We must resist the temptation to just keep busy in order to keep church leaders, parents, and kids happily occupied.

This is why children's ministries and their leaders must learn to recognize the pain points that are common to all ministry endeavors. Without understanding the underlying problems and why they're happening, we won't be able to find lasting solutions.

YOU'RE NOT ALONE: FOUR INEVITABLE MINISTRY PAIN POINTS

Blisters and sore muscles rarely stop runners. They are considered minor issues that just come with the territory. Severe shin splints, on the other hand, are another matter altogether. Pain is an indicator that something needs attention. I have a friend who loves to train and compete. He says, "I press through stress and pause at pain." Sometimes pain highlights a surface-level concern; other times it's a symptom of a deeper problem. My friend needs to know how bad things really are so he can make wise decisions moving forward, whether that means proceeding with caution or stopping completely.

Every athlete encounters physical and mental strain, and a healthy level of stress is actually good for us. It stretches us and pushes us beyond our limits so that we grow and develop. Yet when stress is unexpected or overly severe, potentially debilitating problems take root. Church leaders, regardless of tenure, often have similar complaints about programmatic problems. In children's ministry, there are core issues that rise to the top of the list year after year.

So what's our typical response?

Desperate leaders rustle through resource catalogs and scour myriad webpages looking for turnkey solutions. Conferences provide additional perspective and help. Children's ministry networks bring peers together to encourage each other and share ideas and similar struggles. More than once I have heard pastor Andy Stanley wisely remind leaders, "There is a difference between problems to solve and tensions to manage." The programmatic problems in today's children's ministries are often unavoidable, but they *are* predictable and manageable.

I have identified four of the most common pain points, problems that will never be fully eliminated this side of heaven. Learning what they are is an important first step for kid-influencers if they hope to rise above them and develop an effective children's discipleship ministry.

PAIN POINT 1: FATIGUED LEADERS

Passionate, gifted, well-equipped kid-influencers are necessary for a children's ministry to succeed. Children need a safe environment shepherded by mentors who know, love, and serve them in the way of Christ. Typically churches kick off their ministries in sync with local school calendars. Churched families expect something will be offered for their kids and an endless supply of loving leaders will be present (especially during fall, winter, and spring months). And although regular attendance by families tends to drop off dramatically when school is out, don't forget summer!

This never-ending cycle of children's ministry leads to the expectation that children's ministry leaders will maintain a sufficient number of qualified volunteers to accommodate year-round ministry. It's a lot to shoulder, and like the Israelite brick makers under Pharaoh, the go-to solution is to make more bricks with the same amount of straw. Just make it happen; minister more with the leaders you *do* have. If they get tired, find a way to motivate them. If they try to quit, do whatever it takes to keep the ministry engine running.

Some children's ministry pastors have found creative ways to proactively deal with leader fatigue. They set up community building, training, and celebration gatherings. They create rotation calendars so volunteers can serve according to their preference of availability: weekly, bi-weekly, every six weeks, bi-monthly, bi-annually, annually, and even quinquennially! (Just kidding, but you should look that last one up.) One of my favorite ideas is the concept of "Summer Serve." By inviting others to serve a few times in children's ministry outside peak attendance months, it gives school year leaders a break to rest up between ministry seasons and creates a built-in recruiting opportunity for new children's ministry volunteers. Whatever solution you try, know that the relational tensions being managed are between very real scheduling needs and the value of sustainable volunteer ministry.

SCHEDULING NEEDS ← → SUSTAINABLE MINISTRY

The need for quality leaders drives many of the decisions in children's ministry. How many leaders will it take to run this program or teach this curriculum? Do we have enough kid-influencers to facilitate small groups, or do we need to go to a large group model? What impact will another request for volunteers have on the other ministries in the church? Will the church leadership view children's ministry negatively because it always needs more people to serve? These questions directly impact how churches go about implementing and staffing children's ministry in their unique settings.

The temptation is to start with questions that set a bare minimum: How few leaders can we have and still keep the doors open? Is there a way for us to lower what we expect of those who work with kids? Will children really notice if our only requirement for serving is a pulse? We do this because we are fatigued. And fatigued leaders get this way for a reason. Usually it's a combination of their choices and the demands placed on them. Children's ministries frequently burn out volunteers by not placing them in meaningful roles with clear commitments. The need to fill open positions sometimes trumps pre-qualifications like spiritual gifting, desire, and experience. Or a gifted leader signs on the dotted line, but the ministry does not provide opportunities for him or her to get spiritually recharged along the way. The best children's ministries pay attention to the fact that the question is not *if* their leaders will tire, but how they will try to prevent exhaustion and what will they do *when* it inevitably sets in.

STRESS TEST
The Leader's Need for Speed

The speed of the leader drives the speed of the team. Fast is fun; frantic is costly. If your calendar is completely full, it's difficult to walk well with God and others.

- How sustainable is your current pace as a ministry leader?
- How well are the kid-influencers you serve able to keep up and keep from burning out?
- How fatigued are you and the disciple makers around you?

It's your responsibility to care for yourself over the long haul. This will have an impact on those around you. Find someone who can help you objectively review your commitments and ministry approach for the sake of yourself and those you lead.

PAIN POINT 2: SCARCE BUDGETS

"Yvonne, check this out!" I called over my volunteer children's ministry coordinator to look at what turned out to be a makeshift closet.[3] Our church's repurposed parsonage served as the staff office, volunteer central between weekend services, the Sunday school room for second and third grades, and the midweek space for kindergarten through fifth grade, new member classes, weekly men's Bible studies, and special student ministry events. There was quite a bit of storage available in the basement, although everything needed to be raised several inches off the ground due to regular flooding. The old cabinets throughout the house were filled with ministry odds and ends that had accumulated through the years: colored construction paper, staplers, blank cassette tapes, half used bottles of glitter glue, old hymnals, buckets of broken crayons, foil serving dishes, and miscellaneous plastic utensils. Rarely did we find anything of great value when rummaging around, until today.

I had hit the jackpot!

We had wrestled for weeks as a children's ministry leadership team over how to spend our limited funds. Every sub-ministry in the church was going through the same exercise. There was not much in the way of funding to go around, so we needed to prioritize and be frugal. The rooms definitely needed a facelift, so we were able to work out a deal with one of the commercial painters in the church. He donated several gallons of mis-tinted paint and invested time leading a team of volunteer high school students, who gave the place a facelift. We dodged a financial bullet, and it only cost us a few pizzas and some extra carpet cleaner. We were also able to get quite a few contributions from local businesses that could benefit from offloading surplus items and getting a tax credit. I was impressed by the creativity and tenacity these faithful leaders exhibited as they successfully solved one problem after another. After all our debating was done, there was just one big-ticket item left to tackle: curriculum.

Finding children's ministry curriculum options is not usually a big issue. There are tons of high quality resource providers out there with many solid product lines to choose from. The issue isn't availability; it's flexibility and affordability. Finding fantastic curriculum that works for one age group is easy. Finding a curriculum that works for a variety of settings and group sizes is next to impossible, and the best options typically come with a higher price tag. Of course, you can always write your own. But writing materials from scratch is a huge time commitment. So before you ask questions like "Is it user-friendly?" and "Does it line up with our beliefs and values as a ministry?" the first question that knocks options off the table is, "Can we afford it?"

"What did you find *now*, Dan?" Yvonne asked.

"Do you know what is behind the shower curtain in the bathroom by the main offices?" I asked.

As it turned out, the church had subscribed to a quarterly curriculum for several years prior to my arrival, and most of it was still stacked to the ceiling in a bathtub. Because our children's ministry had a scarce budget, I told my leadership team our spending policy was to *utilize and expend all current resources*. I challenged them to repurpose whatever we could find in cabinets, drawers, closets, totes, *and bathtubs*! We knew this would require ingenuity on our part. We knew it would stretch us as wise stewards. We knew it would cause us to redefine our high standard of excellence. But we had no idea that stumbling upon an archive of lightly used resources would impact our perspective on children's ministry and our approach to spending the way it did.

As we looked at the older curriculum materials, my team and I uncovered a relational tension we had not considered before, a tension around financial pressures. We believed great environments for kids required big budgets. But good experiences aren't always improved via financial means. Like too much salt in soup or paying for a large drink when refills are free, at some point spending more money does not make your ministry better. The pain point of scarce budgets can be misleading. Instead of running at a healthy pace with God's presence and provision, children's ministries end up hobbling around holding up "The grass is greener over there" signs. Some churches get so caught up in having the best thing on the block that they lose sight of the biblical goals of their ministry. There is a myth that ministries need to be on par with the Magic Kingdom and led by Mickey Mouse or children will stay away. Yes, there will be kids who, expecting something epic, get turned off by church because of silly crafts and poorly presented Bible lessons. On the other hand, the presence of caring adults and teenagers who invest time, eye contact, a listening ear, and genuine love will lead to relational connections that can have an eternal reward. Don't forget: kids are drawn to Christ *by* Christ. That's more powerful than anything you can buy. We all want great environments where our children learn to live and love well. And we all want them to have consistently good experiences along the way. But there are many ways to help this happen without breaking the bank. We manage the tension between "good" and "great" because we believe God will meet us in the middle as we honor him and serve people.

If you are struggling with financial challenges, pray. Then find a way to keep the focus off the budget and back on the children and their families. Financial challenges will always be a reality in ministry. Scarce budgets can be overcome in community with God's help and by relying upon one another. Your goal isn't just a cool program with great crafts and games, it's lifelong discipleship in the lives of kids.

STRESS TEST
Budget Busters

Contentment is the inner disposition of "enough." Unfortunately, when it comes to time and money, the cup never seems to be full. Leaders need to decide how to spend resources well, a difficult discipline to master when anxiety about finances creeps in.

- How frustrated are you by the amount of money your ministry is allotted?
- In your children's ministry, what factors apart from money would ensure kids have great experiences with God and others?

- Who do you need to talk to about getting the resources you need so children will have the optimal opportunity to come to know, love, and serve Christ?

Environment is important, but it's not everything. Spending money won't buy solid relationships between kid-influencers and kids. Rather than focus on scarce budgets, you can find creative ways to accomplish the God-honoring ministry goals that matter most to you.

PAIN POINT 3: COMPLEX PROGRAMS

When my new employer handed me a clipboard, I had no idea what I was getting into. It was my first day, and suddenly I was leading kindergarten and first grade classes in a very large children's ministry. My boss said to me, "Whoever holds the golden clipboard is in charge. Be careful who you give it to, but make sure someone responsible always has it." I still remember the serious look on her face, like she was Gandalf entrusting the precious ring to Frodo in J.R.R. Tolkien's *Lord of the Rings*.

At first, I thought nothing of it. Then I discovered what she meant. She was right. The clipboard wielded power. It gave me knowledge, perspective, and authority. It was my connection to the outside world, a quick reference source to make sense of what was happening in front of me. It provided important insights week in and week out. It was a scratchpad for key decisions, scheduling requests, supply challenges, content questions, volunteer issues, and safety protocols.

In the right hands, the clipboard could be used to solve the problems of the world. But in the wrong hands, it would bring an end to modern civilization.

Ok, so maybe that's an exaggeration. But if you have served in children's ministry, you may know what I'm talking about. When my boss handed me that clipboard, she might as well have given me a master key to the Pentagon. Why was the clipboard so significant in our ministry? "The clipboard" represents the one critically important function that ties every ministry together.

Whether you use one or not, clipboards symbolize a core function shared between event managers, wedding coordinators, shift supervisors, party planners . . . and children's ministry leaders: *administration*.

In our ministry, the clipboard cut through organizational complexities. It brought order to the controlled chaos of the ministry. Better than any name tag, the clipboard identified who was in charge and, when used properly, it would tell that person exactly what was supposed to be happening at any given moment.

For our ministry, God gifted us with the best clipboard carrier ever, and I gladly handed it to her every week. Meghan was in high school at the time, but she had served as volunteer administrator for years.[4] She and her family served in various roles at the church every weekend. They adored the kids and loved our leaders, and we worked with Meghan and her family to make sure the planning on the front end was executed well on the back end. There were a lot of children to keep track of, and that meant we needed a lot of leaders. Meghan was great at details, keeping track of who showed up and recording notes about everything. She helped the greeters welcome kids, kept track of attendance, portioned out Goldfish crackers for snack time, stocked bins with lesson supplies, wrote personalized thank you notes to leaders, redistributed each child's craft masterpiece, and made sure every kid went home with their appropriate guardian.

It was more than a normal human being could manage. I still thank the Lord for wiring Meghan the way he did and giving her the capacity to administrate at such a high level. Because Meghan handled all the administrative details, it freed up the rest of our team to serve in other roles across the ministry. And most importantly, it allowed us to be flexible when a crisis developed—which happened *every* week. Volunteers would call in sick at the last minute. (During my first weekend, I got seven "Sorry, I can't be there" voicemails!) The curriculum would get lost in the mail. I'd find one of my leaders prepping in the parking lot just before class. Supplies ran out. The senior pastor's message would last an extra twenty-two minutes. Week after week, we'd find a new problem to tackle. But with Meghan working behind the scenes, covering our administrative details, we had the time and energy to address these crisis situations.

One of the best things I've learned through doing children's ministry over the years is that things work best when you keep them simple. Overly complex programs drain energy from the ministry. Every layer of complexity brings with it additional potential to distract the attention of those serving away from the people they are called to reach, disciple, and serve. Over time, as ministry structures become more and more complex, more and more of your "ministry energy" gets redirected back into keeping the program running and not into the lives of the children.

Simplicity is the goal. The purpose of children's ministry is never the program itself—it's bringing glory to God and serving children and their families. Complex programs do not make ministry meaningful; they create ministry madness. So how do you achieve this simplicity? How do you avoid becoming too complex? The setting, values, and culture of a particular church each play an important role in deciding how to go about structuring ministry. Implementing something that works can easily evolve into an ongoing administrative nightmare. The relational tension we must manage is between structured creativity and significant impact. Children's ministries function best when kids, parents, and leaders can engage naturally *and* a compelling, God-honoring vision is being pursued.

Churches must be prayerfully mindful of these two things: the people they serve and the approach God is calling them to take to minister effectively. For children's ministry to be fun and filled with truth, it needs structured creativity rooted in God's Word. Any nourishment flows through that system and brings life to all that grows. For a ministry to make a difference in families and the world, it needs outreach and discipleship components that lead to significant impact. Unfortunately, rarely (if ever) is there a philosophy, program, or product line that is a perfect fit for every church's children's ministry. The key is that whatever approach or curriculum you adopt, you need to get everyone involved. Get the senior pastor and the rest of the church leadership on board with the plan. Make sure your volunteer leaders and the families and children in the ministry are aware of what you are doing—the goals, the structure, the purpose, the mission and vision for the ministry. Again, there is no one way to do all of this. Wrestling between too simple and too complicated will be a constant pain point in every children's ministry. Learning to contextualize and adapt so the program and the curriculum serve your people—that is the goal. How to do this will be addressed more specifically in later chapters.

STRESS TEST
It's Complicated

Board games can be creative and complex without being need-lessly confusing. Naturally, more parts and moving pieces make things more complicated. The same is true of children's ministry programming.

- What in your ministry would the kids, parents, and leaders consider "nice to have" versus "need to have"?
- What aspects of your programming could be removed without decreasing engagement or discipleship effectiveness?
- How seamlessly could you step out for a weekend or for several weeks without "everything" (or so it seems) falling apart?

Both creativity and simplicity are necessary when it comes to working with children of all ages. Becoming people who love God and others as followers of Christ is foundational for disciple-making ministry. Invite someone you trust to evaluate the complexity of your programming with you. Then cut through the clutter so you can build on a solid core.

PAIN POINT 4: SHALLOW CONTENT

Have you ever heard children or teens say, "Church is boring"? Chances are, if your children and teenagers are saying it, adults are probably thinking it too. If your idea of "going to church" means going to a building once a week to sing songs, listen to sermons, and interact superficially with strangers, then I can see why it's not very appealing. Over the years, my oldest son and I have spent time talking about this tension. Avery is a pastor's kid. He knows the ins and outs of church. He knows the building and the people. A few weeks ago I picked him up from youth group and asked him the question every parent asks on the drive home from church: "So, what did you learn?"

Avery rolled his teenage eyes at me.

"It was stupid," he said. "We talked about David. Again."

Avery went on to rehearse every story in King David's life he had learned over the past fourteen years . . . all of them . . . in detail. Then he summed it all up:

"We never go any deeper. We talk about the same stories, week after week, year after year. I don't get the point of going to church. It's just like school but on the weekend."

It's important for you to know my family and I are involved in a solid evangelism and discipleship ministry. We love our church community. We know how much work goes into making sure the teaching is engaging and applicable. My wife and I have both worked in the children's ministry as volunteers and staff. We have ministry degrees focused on Christian teaching. But we are also parents. And when it comes to our son Avery, we know we are responsible for teaching him and giving him the opportunities he needs to go deep with God and his people.

Young Life founder Jim Rayburn once said: "It is a sin to bore a kid with the Gospel of Jesus Christ." For many years, this mindset revolutionized the church's approach to children's and youth ministries. Today, there are countless programs and resources available to make Christian education and discipleship more attractive to kids: large group dramas, small group activities, Bible-based object lessons, interactive story books, Scripture memory games, DVD curricula, mobile apps, and more. Still, despite the resources available, the Word of God is still presented poorly, whether through speech or action. Sometimes the truth is last in a swirl of constant activity. At other times it's presented without application to life, or divorced from the context of a relationship with the child. Kid-influencers are called to disciple children in the truth, and this means sharing the love of Christ with children in compelling, challenging, and personal ways. We use words, but we also disciple children by example. We want them to encounter God's Word, to be loved by God's people, and to exit on the other side saying, "Give me more. I want to dive deeper."

We want children to enjoy church as a *community*, not an event. As kids get older in the faith, the fun factor is fleeting. We want them to hunger for God's Word and to love being with God's people. But we can't jump to quick solutions. We need to unpack the problem and seek to better understand it before we can promote a new way forward. So let's take a closer look at what is happening in children's ministry today.

According to recent Barna Group research, roughly one third of Americans highly value attending church. Another third couldn't care less. The final third lands somewhere in the middle. Of the third that says church attendance is very important, the majority indicate that they go to learn about God or they see it as a place for their kids to learn about God. Among the other two-thirds who are ambivalent or don't value church attendance, if we dial into the specific responses of the Millennial generation we get reasons like this:

Church is boring
I can teach myself
I just go because I always have
It is filled with empty rituals
Leaders don't practice what they preach
God seems missing
Doubts and questions are discouraged
I feel judged[5]

Does this discourage you? Don't let it, because it gets worse.

Awana, the ministry I work for, is a 65-year-old global children's ministry.[6] In 2013 and 2014 we commissioned two significant marketplace studies. The first took a comprehensive look at how Awana is perceived in the United States. The second study was more general, looking broadly at children's ministry passion areas, pain points, and possible solutions. It was helpful to see how the church at large in America viewed the legacy ministry of Awana. The study confirmed, clarified, and corrected some of our key assumptions. When we looked at the latter study and saw the gap between the intended purpose and the reality of children's ministry, we were stunned.

When you consider the ministry you lead, why did you get involved in the first place? Are you seeing the results you hoped to see? How's it all going, really? These core questions about motivation, effectiveness, and satisfaction fueled our study. We wanted to hear firsthand from the children's ministry leadership community. And we did. We were met with a surprising level of candidness about the highs and lows of working with kids as part of a local church. To serve the leaders and ministries we listened to, Awana published *The Gospel Truth About Children's Ministry: 10 Fresh KidMin Research Findings.*[7] It gives voice to the passions and challenges kid-influencers carry with them each day in their desire to reach and disciple children. It also points to what matters most in children's ministry. It lays out what every kid-influencer can focus on so kids and families will come to know, love, and serve Christ.

What would you say is the most important purpose or objective of children's ministry? What one or two essential ingredients for effectiveness would you include? If you said, "Share the gospel, make disciples and teach the Bible," you would be right on target with the collective voice of hundreds of children's ministry leaders.

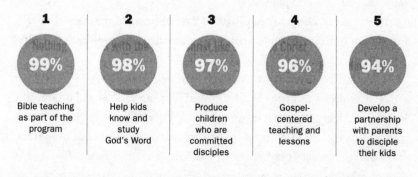

The Top Five
What Children's Ministry Leaders Say Matters Most in Programming

1	2	3	4	5
99%	98%	97%	96%	94%
Bible teaching as part of the program	Help kids know and study God's Word	Produce children who are committed disciples	Gospel-centered teaching and lessons	Develop a partnership with parents to disciple their kids

At first glance, we were encouraged to discover that the five highest-ranked responses are right on target with the mission of the church. While children's ministry leaders list things like serving, worship, small groups, having fun, and cultural relevance as important, nothing tops the charts above evangelism, discipleship, and Bible teaching. Sounds good, right?

Well, that's what the leaders *say* is important to them. But when you ask them how things are actually going, you'll hear a different story, as we did.

Children's ministry leaders were asked to rate how well their ministry was fulfilling what they believed to be the primary objectives or goals of their children's ministry. Across the board, they indicated clear gaps between their intended outcomes and the reality they saw in the lives of those they served. This seems positive from a particular perspective. Effective children's ministries recognize their need to constantly be improving. Mature leaders are fully aware that a 100 percent success rate is never going to happen. What matters most is keeping the right priorities in order, right?

While we appreciated the honesty and sincerity of the responses, what stood out to us were the things that leaders told us were getting shoved to the side. While plates and people keep spinning in ministry, what's at the core is off target from what everyone says really matters. The study found that "The Top Five" were important in theory but children's ministry leaders did not believe they were fulfilling these key ministry purposes. Evangelism fell short by 7 percent, discipleship by 14 percent, love for God's Word by 9 percent, and partnering with parents by 21 percent. On and on down the list, gaps could be identified. Disciple-making relationships fell 11 percent short of ideal, cultural relevance fell 14 percent short, and ministry/serving for kids fell short by 15 percent. A major discipleship disconnect became more and more evident in the responses.

In every area, children's ministry leaders self-reported that they were falling short of fulfilling what they believed mattered most in children's ministry.

In every area, that is, except one.

"Having fun" turned out to be the *only area* with a positive fulfillment rating. Children's ministry leaders ranked "having fun" as important, but it still landed as #10 on the list of priorities. On one hand, it's encouraging to hear that most leaders feel that their ministries provide a fun experience for children. No one is saying we should remove the fun-factor. Apparently a lot of valuable fun is being had and there is some truth to the fact that we want to see smiles enter and leave the room week after week. Having fun is not the problem. The problem is that having fun is not the most important purpose of a children's ministry. We can have all the fun in the world, but if children are not meeting Christ and discovering how to worship God, read his Word, share their faith, love people, and follow Jesus moment by moment, we aren't accomplishing the fundamental mission of our ministry as their church family.

Anyone who works with kids is familiar with the tension here. Let me put it this way: there is a tension between presenting exciting content (having fun) and introducing kids to engaging truth (connecting the Bible to real life). As kids grow, fun isn't the driving factor that keeps them rooted in faith. When push comes to shove, they will walk away from the church because discipleship and daily life remain disconnected. When the church family seems irrelevant or unsafe or misguided, children will seek out truth in community elsewhere.

A quick search on the web will surface plenty of things kids find intriguing. But what they consider "exciting" is very subjective, based largely on personal preference and individual tastes. What is exciting to one person is boring to another. And what is exciting to someone on Monday might not be exciting on Tuesday. The truth is that there will *always* be something more exciting than your children's ministry. That's not a reason to kill the excitement. But it cannot be your primary (or even secondary) goal. Your goal is engaging children and students with God's truth. God's Word is the cornerstone of all you do, and the purpose of God's Word is not to bring a superficial excitement or a one-time emotional response. God's Word should lead to long-term life change. Children's ministry leaders need to balance out the tension here. On the one hand, we don't want to bore kids. So we must seek to engage interest without being shallow. One of the best ways to do this is by matching biblical truth to personal experience through a meaningful relational environment. We walk with God and one another.

So what did we conclude from our study? Both kids and church leaders are telling us, "Something's not working." And right now, whether we intend this or not, "having fun" seems to be winning out over discipling kids in following Christ and making disciples. Adults highly value fun and make it happen for children's sakes; yet kids are still noticeably disconnected. The next generation is walking out the door because after the fun times fade away, they are left with nothing but shallow content and superficial community. If discipleship and disciple making are really our priorities in ministry, then something must change.

STRESS TEST
Diet and Depth

There's a myth in ministry that blockbuster productions yield the most fruit. If numbers are the measure, it's probably true. If discipleship is the desired outcome, dizzying lights and dynamic communicators won't make a difference if substance is lacking.

- How prevalent is biblical content in your curriculum for kids and families?
- What do you do to equip kids to wrestle with faith instead of spoon-feeding them snippets of God's story?
- How are parents and leaders challenged to grow as disciples while being involved in your children's ministry?

Healthy meals aren't always exciting, but they give you the energy you need for life. Kids, parents, leaders—and you—need spiritual nourishment, not just weekly doses of faith-centered fun. Carve out time to review what is being taught and caught by those involved in your children's ministry. Adjust as necessary so you maintain a steady diet and depth of God's grace and truth.

NOW IS THE TIME TO PRESS BEYOND THE PAIN POINTS

There is an African proverb that says, "If you want to go fast, go alone. If you want to go far, go together." On every journey there are unforeseeable challenges and dangers. Serious runners know the importance of staying in a pack or running in pairs. Getting up early to run when it's still dark is far easier if you run with someone supportive. When storm clouds turn to rain, it's easier to run if you share the experience with a drenched friend. Running with others helps you push past your exhaustion and your discouragement, past that moment when your mind starts giving in and the body starts giving out. Sticking together helps strengthen your motivation and your perseverance. We all need a cause and likeminded companions who come alongside us to push past those shared pain points.

As I look out over the countless children's ministries I see today around the country and around the world, I believe it's time for children's ministry leaders to move past a "pain management" model. We can no longer keep running the same programs that give us the same results while children grow bored and drop out. With intentionality and persistence, we must rise above status quo to bring new life to children's ministry. The goal is to take on and live out the mission that Jesus gave to us. We want to engage children in God's Word together with God's people to make disciples of Jesus.

This won't be a quick fix. It will require some painful changes. It will require perseverance over several years. But it's worth the cost. Consider these timely words from Paul to Timothy, his child in the faith:

> But you, keep your head in all situations, endure hardship, do the work of an evangelist, discharge all the duties of your ministry. For I am already being poured out like a drink offering, and the time for my departure is near. I have fought the good fight, I have finished the race, I have kept the faith. (2 Tim. 4:5–7)

In the same way, we are charged to press on toward a goal beyond our temporal obstacles and focus on our final destination. The pain points in children's ministry will never disappear completely. Believe me, change is possible! In the pages that follow, we'll see that relational children's ministry is a model that is biblical, faithful to the mission of Jesus, and one that builds upon the strengths of the past. A new focal point will help us press past the pain toward a new faith trajectory.

QUESTIONS FOR REFLECTION & DISCUSSION

1. How has your experience in children's ministry changed over the years? How has reality been different from what you dreamed serving kids and families would be like?

2. In what way(s) are you "running ragged" as a ministry leader these days? What factors inside and outside your control impact your priorities and pace the most?

3. How "fatigued" are the leaders in your children's ministry? How well do you balance the schedule and make sure the ministry is sustainable?

4. Regardless of budget size, there never seem to be enough resources to go around. How do you make sure kids in your ministry have good experiences when they show up? What creative ways have you found to wisely steward what you have to make great environments for ministry?

5. How satisfied are you with your current ministry program? If you could change one thing to make it more impactful, what would it be and why?

6. What content challenges do you face in your ministry context? Would you say you err on the side of fun or boring? Why?

7. What distractions are keeping you from effective children's ministry? What steps are you willing to take to rise above the pain points for the sake of kids and families?

8. Why do you think relational children's ministry is worth exploring?

PART TWO

RELATE INTENTIONALLY TO KIDS AND FAMILIES

CHAPTER 4

JESUS' DISRUPTIVE APPROACH TO DISCIPLESHIP

When Jesus walked among humankind there was a
certain simplicity to being his disciple.
Dallas Willard[1]

Sitting down, Jesus called the Twelve and said, "Anyone
who wants to be first must be the very last, and the
servant of all."
Mark 9:35

©Marcus Lindstrom/www.istock.com

S HOTGUN. I CALLED IT."

If you have older kids, you've probably heard this phrase before. I'm not sure where my sons learned to compete for the front passenger seat, but as soon as they were old enough to sit up front in the car, fights over who called "shotgun" first became a daily occurrence. On more than one occasion I found a full blown wrestling match happening in my front yard before school. Apparently front seat privileges matter.

At first I tried to make everything fair by encouraging them to take turns. But I still ended up with one child sulking in the back seat and the other proudly gloating next to me. Then, for a while I made them both sit in the back to avoid the issue altogether. Well, as it turns out, "riding shotgun" is a cultural phenomenon that transcends the generations. The phrase comes from the late 1800s when stagecoach drivers needed protection for precious cargo. Someone was assigned the sidekick role and they were appropriately armed to make sure nothing bad happened on the journey. The purpose of the shotgun rider was clear: safeguard the driver and the payload. Today "riding shotgun" is about selfish enjoyment. It's about having status and holding it over others. It's about who gets to be first. It's about who gets to be in front with the driver.

Sadly, I've experienced something similar to this childish behavior in leadership, both personally and professionally. "Riding shotgun" is all about who gets to be closest to the leader. It's about having the status and significance that comes from being in charge, out in front, leading the way. And it can be a real problem in children's ministry leadership ranks.

Children's ministry gets off track when other agendas overshadow loving relationships with God and others. Status and significance come from being created and saved by God, not from big pastoral staff teams or church facilities. High attendance numbers and attractive spiritual events don't always reflect what's going on behind the scenes. It's not the size of your ministry but the state of your heart that matters most. When the allure of favoritism starts to creep in, it's time to take a step back. Romans 2:11 plainly states, "For God does not show favoritism." James 2:8–9 teaches us that favoritism plays no part in loving one's neighbor. Corporate ladder climbing is not what discipleship, ministry, and servanthood are about. Relational children's ministries need leaders who embody childlike faith at their core.

The gospels record a debate between Christ's closest followers: "Who is the greatest?" In Matthew 18 the disciples are arguing with each other, jockeying for position in the kingdom, and they ask Jesus to step in and settle the score. Instead of picking his favorites, Jesus has a sit-down with his disciples, a teaching moment. He explains that prominence and privilege in the family of God don't work the way they are thinking. Instead, he does something unexpected. Jesus invites a child over and explains that this child—a person with no rights, authority, or power in that culture—is the first to enter the kingdom of God. He is encouraging them not to value what the world values, to pursue humility over hierarchy. He also raises the value of children in that culture, helping them to see that children matter to God, that children have something to teach us about knowing and relating to God. He makes it clear that being childlike in faith isn't optional; it's optimal.

And there is one additional point we learn from Jesus' example. It's that caring for children, loving children, and doing ministry with children is a very good thing. It's precious to God. Jesus' illustration flies in the face of how status and significance are defined in the world. It reminds us that who sits in the front seat, being up front and in charge, getting all the attention, is not what matters.

The work of making disciples who progressively reflect Christ's character and way of life is serious business. Petty attempts to be first, to make your ambition the priority, are childish. But being humble in service to God and others demonstrates childlike faith and models what it means to be one of Jesus' devoted disciples.

Don't miss something that is easily overlooked here. Did you notice how Jesus responds to the disciples? Does he give them a lengthy dissertation? Or a list of things to do? Instead of answering their question, "Who is the greatest?" directly, he brilliantly exposes how their hearts and minds are at odds with God's heart and mind. He uses an object lesson, full of God's truth, to engage them. He shows them what matters most and leaves it to the learners to make the application to their own lives. And we should not forget that this teaching is based on prior relationships and experiences they've had together. It's his presence and his relationship with the disciples that make his teaching all the more powerful, getting the message through the hardness in their hearts. This is just one of many times where the disciples are stopped in their tracks by something Jesus says or does.

If I were asked to characterize the way Jesus approached discipleship I would say that he was intentionally and relationally *disruptive*. In the context of relationship, where there is a foundation of trust, respect, and love, he challenges and disrupts the assumptions of his followers. And I believe that his model gives us a template for a relational children's ministry that engages children in God's truth. If you and I want to effectively relate to kids and families, we need to understand what Jesus did and learn to put his methods into practice as kid-influencers.

But before we can do this with others, we have to experience this disruption ourselves.

DISRUPTED FIRST: A DISCIPLE MAKER'S PREREQUISITE

We often use the phrase *discipleship* or *making disciples* to describe the goal or mission of the church or to talk about our focus in ministry. But what does that mean? Discipleship is the lifelong process of transformation in a person who trusts Christ for salvation. It's the natural and necessary consequence of being saved by Christ. We become a follower of Christ and seek to become like him in every way. It rightly permeates our attitudes, convictions, practices, and relationships until we reach full maturity in Jesus Christ.

This spiritual journey is unique, unparalleled to any other experience known to humanity. How can I say this with certainty? Because in discipleship sin is being eradicated from a person's heart—our hearts. We are seeking to grow in our knowledge and affection for God. We make choices and decisions, but we do this relying upon the power of the gospel and the work of the Holy Spirit. God's unconditional love changes us, and at one level, this is all very simple—yet at another it's very complicated.

What do I mean? Well, imagine the look on Nicodemus' face in John 3 when Jesus talked to him about being born again. It's probably the same look that little kids and junior high students have in church when this story comes up. Here we have a highly educated religious adult who comes to Jesus under the shadow of nightfall to discuss matters of eternity. Patiently, the Lord responds to Nicodemus by disrupting his understanding of how things work in God's kingdom. He invites him to learn something new, that there is a work God is doing that Nicodemus does not yet understand, a work of salvation. This clandestine encounter, and disruptive answer from Jesus, sets Nicodemus on a new trajectory for the rest of his life.

> Only a disciple can make a disciple.
>
> A. W. Tozer[2]

Nicodemus was not the only one radically changed for eternity. Look at Peter. Or Matthew. Or the Samaritan woman at the well. Think about the Roman centurion. Mary. The apostle Paul. Go down the list of individuals in the New Testament who encountered Christ. Jesus brought disruption into their lives, a disruption that had to happen before they could minister to others. Christ met people where they were at, engaged with them in a way that was particular to their questions or struggles, and then invited them into a relationship with himself and with God's family. In order for us to become relational disciple-makers, we must have a face-to-face encounter with God through faith in Christ first.

I know some of you are saying—"Of course! Isn't that obvious?" But it's not. Though I can't offer statistics on this, I know that children's ministries are filled with people who dearly love kids and want to have a significant role in ministry. Yet, they do not personally know, passionately love, or purposefully serve Jesus. Or they may know him in their head, but their love relationship with him is stagnant and practically dead. They attend church and do all the right things, but they are not seeking to be a disciple of Jesus.

Let me make this clear: becoming a disciple of Jesus is a pre-requisite to disciple making. If our lives are not significantly disrupted by Jesus' call, the rest of what I say in this book won't matter. Discipleship is relational, and we cannot pass along to others what we have not experienced ourselves. It's my sincere prayer that this section will stop you in your tracks if there's any doubt in you as to whether you've been disrupted by Jesus yet or not. Take seriously the opportunity to explore Jesus' *convicting call*, *challenging example*, *consistent presence*, and *clear invitation* over the next several pages. If not for you, what you discover may help you introduce him to someone else who has yet to meet him.

DISRUPTED BY JESUS' CONVICTING CALL

"Truly I tell you, unless you change and become like little children, you will never enter the kingdom of heaven" (Matt. 18:3). Imagine standing with the disciples when they heard this for the first time. You'd probably be confused. Is Jesus really saying that we should be like kids? What does that mean?

Several years ago I found myself stepping out into the unknown. I had agreed to help lead a mission team that was serving at an orphanage and HIV/AIDS hospice center in Johannesburg, South Africa. This was my first overseas missions experience in Africa, and it was like no other serving trip I have experienced. For a week we showered love on infants, toddlers, and preschoolers who were waiting to be adopted. We cared for adults who could no longer care for themselves. It was humbling to play with, read to, and feed kids who had never experienced a life outside the foster care system. It was heart wrenching to be with people who did not have anyone.

As much as we invested in their lives, we found that the Lord used them to bless us as well. It doesn't matter if you are young or old, rich or poor, healthy or sick; we all share a common hunger for God, to be restored in relationship with God and his people. No, we didn't need to travel halfway around the globe to learn this. But that's where God spoke to us, convicting us of this truth, and I am grateful that he did.

I share this personal story because I believe that there is much that we can learn about God and his kingdom by working with children, if we are willing to learn. Throughout human history children have ranked as second-class citizens. Sadly this is still true globally today.[3] Yet Jesus unashamedly redefines and restructures the order of things, helping us to see the world from God's perspective. I find that most kid-influencers are familiar with the passage in Mark 10:13–16 where Christ indignantly stops the disciples from keeping the kids at a distance. It's a moving witness to think about the Lord scooping up children in his arms and blessing them. Here we see him unconditionally expressing the Father's love for children as a reminder of the love God has for each of us. Christ reflects God's heart of love and he calls every disciple to do that as well.

I also share this experience because sometimes I find adults reducing children's ministry to a glorified form of babysitting consisting of silly games and stories to bide time while adults do more important things. We need a wake up call. We cannot ignore the truth that Jesus sees every disciple as a child. And this means that every child is a full-fledged disciple as well. We are mistaken when we think of discipleship as something relegated to adults. Discipleship is for children of all ages, infants through adults. It's learning to love and relate to our heavenly Father and to each other as followers of his Son.

In this scene from Mark 10, we should also notice that after welcoming the children, Jesus offers one of those convicting "drop everything and follow me" calls. In fact, Jesus regularly invited people to overturn their lives in response to God. And while we may not all be called to move to another country or sell all we have to live with the poor, we should expect that following Jesus will be costly. It will require that we change. Once an individual turns away from their sin toward God, they are on a journey of repentance. This means that their course in life has been disrupted and is now heading in a new Holy Spirit-guided direction. This may not lead everyone to be a kid-influencer involved in children's ministry, but it will lead each of us into humble trust and dependence on God. It will also lead us to do radical things for the sake of God's Kingdom. We must have the heart of a child from start to finish.

DISRUPTED BY JESUS' CHALLENGING EXAMPLE

You can't just take a "quick glance" at the gospels. If you sit down and read, you'll discover what millions of others have found—Jesus is remarkable in every way! The way he interacted with people, how he prioritized decisions, what he chose to spend time doing, who he loved, and who he challenged—he always went against the grain, doing the unexpected.

If there was one thing that irritated Jesus, it was the hypocrisy of the religious leaders. Jesus regularly called out those whose words and actions did not align with their motives. He taught his disciples that the inside and the outside need to be aligned. Because Jesus was God, his message and ministry methods were always in sync. And as his followers, we need to look at our own lives, to make sure we are following his example and living out what we believe.

> Now that I, your Lord and Teacher, have washed your feet, you also should wash one another's feet. I have set you an example that you should do as I have done for you.
>
> **John 13:14–15**

There are several places in the New Testament where we are specifically called to follow the example of Jesus. And one of the most powerful is found during the Last Supper in John 13. The disciples are aware that something is up. Their beloved rabbi keeps reminding them that his betrayal and imminent death are on the horizon. Their response? They are in denial and they can't believe it. Then, during the Passover meal, Christ speaks to his followers and seeks to prepare them for what is about to come. He focuses on key truths, speaking of the past, the present, and their future in relationship with God. He draws attention to the bread and wine, pointing them to the meaning behind the elements and asks them to remember his life, death, and resurrection regularly until he returns. The entire scene is filled with meaning and powerful truth. But what happens *after* dinner is astounding.

> . . . Jesus received attention because he paid attention. He saw and was interested in what people were doing and saying and in their needs, and in helpful sympathy he empathized with them. His works prepared the way for his words.
>
> **Herman Horne[4]**

The teacher and leader who has been with them for three years, the one they love and respect, stoops down to serve his followers. And he does it by taking on the most menial of jobs, a task worthy of a slave. He washes their feet. Perhaps they had simply forgotten to do the customary foot washing before dinner. Regardless of who should have done the washing, Jesus took the initiative and seized the opportunity to teach by his example. He humbled himself before the disciples and took on the role of the evening's forgotten servant. In doing this, Jesus demonstrated to them that love is not about selfish fulfillment; it's a gift that serves and sacrifices. He showed them this love, and then challenged his followers to go and do likewise.

DISRUPTED BY JESUS' CONSISTENT PRESENCE

Jesus' promise in Matthew 28:20 to *always* be with his disciples probably meant more to them than reading these words means to most of us today. When you spend time with someone and share life together in close proximity, your relationship deepens. And they must have wondered, how can you be with us if you are not physically present? Today, we have the blessings of knowing God intimately through his Word and prayer, and as part of his church community, but we can no longer be face-to-face with the Lord like the disciples were. We have our connection to Jesus through the Holy Spirit and we can know that wherever we are, whatever we are doing, Jesus is present with us by his Spirit. Today, Christ's consistent presence still disrupts people as they encounter him through reading the Bible and through interactions with his disciples. God's Spirit is still actively involved in connecting people to Jesus. And as those who represent him, physically, as the body of Christ, children's ministry kid-influencers play an essential role in sharing the love of Jesus with others.

Every relationship needs time and proximity to grow and develop. My sons were blessed to have met all of their great-grandparents. We even have an amazing five-generation picture that includes my sons Avery and Aaron with their *great-great*-grandmother! Yet even though my sons met their great-grandparents, it would be a stretch to say they knew them well. They met them in person on occasion, heard the family legacy stories retold, checked out the faded photo albums, and they believe these relatives truly loved them. But their relationship with their great-grandparents pales in comparison to the relational depth they experience with their immediate grandparents. My wife is from Canada and my relatives are spread across the United States, so it takes intentionality and planning to spend time with our extended family. Over the past decade I have learned that proximity and time play a key role in developing depth in a relationship.

We all know this intuitively, but it takes time to get to know someone. It takes time to find out what they care about most, to experience their character coming through firsthand or to learn what they believe about matters of life and faith. And the same is true in a discipleship relationship with Jesus. The gospels show us that Jesus hung out with ordinary people in everyday ways. He spent time with the disciples on the seashore and in fishing boats. Christ regularly visited with people in their homes, frequented dinner parties, and reclined while conversing over lengthy meals. He went on long walks with his friends, prayed with them day and night, joined them for weddings, and wept with them at funerals.

Through his consistent presence, Jesus gave people immediate access to God. Christ was intentional in how he chose to relate to people. He related to people unconditionally, lovingly, patiently, boldly, and even controversially. He would even tell people that seeing him was the same as seeing God himself (John 10:30; 14:8–10).

The good news is that the immediate presence of Jesus is still a reality today through the Holy Spirit. God is actively engaged in the daily life of each and every believer through the Holy Spirit, who resides in every believer. Whether it's with two, two hundred, or two thousand people, the Holy Spirit resides at the heart of all Christ-centered community (Matt. 18:20). Today, because the church is the body of Christ (1 Cor. 12:12–27), this community of devoted disciples is the Lord's hands and feet in the world. Our presence represents God to the world, and our words and actions communicate God's truth and love to those in need. Relational children's ministry is an expression of this reality. Disciple-makers remain consistently connected to Jesus so that they can faithfully reflect his consistent presence. But this isn't automatic. Before kid-influencers can point children to Christ, they need to be disrupted by Jesus themselves. They need to experience his consistent presence in their own lives.

One great way to dive deeper into this is to gather some close friends or children's ministry colleagues to spend time in the presence of Jesus together. It can be difficult to step away from the busyness of life and ministry, but taking time to slow down is critical for getting on the same page as God the Father and those you serve alongside. If it's been awhile, take some time away. Let Jesus disrupt you today.

DISRUPTED BY JESUS' CLEAR INVITATION

"Follow me." You can't be much clearer than these two simple words. The gospels record Jesus speaking this particular phrase twenty times throughout his ministry. Some people followed. Some fell away. Others flat-out resisted. This powerful two-word invitation is at the start and heart of discipleship and disciple making.

In his "follow-me" approach to discipleship, *Jesus was committed to creativity and simplicity for the sake of eternity.* This was true of his lifestyle, his teaching, and his relationships. Christ cut through the complexities of people's inner and outer worlds by drawing them in and redirecting their trajectory. He pulled them closer to God and one another by graciously confronting them with eternal truth. Jesus used parables and object lessons to creatively and simply present the nature of God. He spoke of mustard seeds and yeast, and used bread and wine as metaphors to communicate truth. He used object lessons, placing a small child in the center of a circle of debating adults. And Jesus masterfully raised powerful and poignant questions: "Who do you say I am?" (Matt. 16:15–16) and "What do you want me to do for you?" (Mark 10:35–37, 50–52). He spoke to the crowds, but his words were also for specific individuals—he communicated to both *at the same time.*

I have been following Jesus for over three decades, and I have dedicated my life to pointing other people to do the same. Yet if you shine a spotlight on my life at any given moment of the day, you'll quickly learn I have not mastered this yet. My guess is most of you would say the same. The notion that any of us can represent the loving compassion and matchless wisdom of Jesus is breathtaking and heart-stopping. Even if we can't do it perfectly, we are still called to this high standard. The apostle Paul laid down the gauntlet in 1 Corinthians 11:1, saying "Follow my example, as I follow the example of Christ." He was fully aware of the gap between his life and the life of Christ, yet he still called others to follow his example. He communicated his teaching and instruction using his own life as the context and recorded the struggles faced by the early church, its disciples, and key leaders. Likewise, relational children's ministry is about representing Jesus, but it's not about achieving a state of sinless perfection in our ministry—it's a ministry rooted in the gospel of God's grace. Through the grace of the gospel, we bring a message of life transformation through which people meet Jesus and are called and transformed by him. The life change we experience as disciples is ongoing and comprehensive.

The beauty of following Christ is that we share a common starting point, finding forgiveness at the foot of the cross and hope in the resurrection. We all begin here, and it's from the cross and resurrection of Christ that we get the strength to follow Jesus each day. We share the same goal—to be like Jesus in every way, to live and love as the Lord did. And we are all commissioned to multiply this transformation by sharing the message of good news and living out Christlike lives, as salt and light to the world.

Christ invites us to be his disciples. It's audacious. It's disruptive. Choosing to respond can be scary. But choosing not to respond is even scarier. This calling is a matter of life and death.

> We are overwhelmed by the magnitude of the words follow me because we are awed by the majesty of the "me" who says them.
>
> **David Platt[5]**

"Follow me" is the invitation Jesus places before each one of us. Pastor and author John Ortberg sums up the ministry of Jesus by saying, "His life and teaching simply drew people to follow him . . . He made history by starting in a humble place, in a spirit of love and acceptance, and allowing each person space to respond."[6] This is the challenge we, as kid-influencers and children's disciple makers, face every day. While no two children's ministries will be exactly the same, we are all seeking to follow the same invitation to follow Jesus. We all need to be committed to being simple and creative for the sake of eternity. And before these "follow me" principles can permeate your church or your children's ministry, they must penetrate your own life and the lives of those around you. When they do, your personal encounter with Jesus will prepare you and your ministry for a new kind of discipleship in the way of Christ.

Are You Disrupted?

Jesus' *call*, *example*, *presence*, and *invitation* transform human hearts daily. Before transitioning to a model for ministry, take a look inside. What does God have to say to you? Where do you most need to grow? What's holding you back? Open yourself up to being disrupted in new ways as a relational children's ministry leader, but as a disciple first.

FIVE LIFE-GIVING DISCIPLESHIP INVITATIONS TO DISRUPT YOUR MINISTRY

As we look at the discipleship call of Jesus, we discover five life-giving invitations he has for us. Jesus models a relational discipleship approach that is inherently disruptive, yet extremely effective. I have found that following five principles based on the ministry of Jesus can lead to a renewed discipleship trajectory. Individuals can benefit from these principles. Families can benefit. Ministry leadership teams can benefit. And for those of you, like me, who are kid-influencers and children's ministry leaders, the next several chapters will focus specifically on how to utilize these five invitations as the basis for a relational children's ministry.

Jesus' Relational Invitation

- Draw people into an unscripted adventure with God.
- Wrestle with messy faith together.
- Establish unconventional community.
- Model Christ's life-transforming mission.
- Equip for dynamic discipleship.

While these principles may seem to be sequential steps, they actually happen fluidly throughout a person's discipleship journey. They flow out of Jesus' encounters with would-be disciples and bring a clear focus to our understanding of his discipleship approach. In the pages that follow, begin to brainstorm and think creatively about how this invitational model might be used in your own faith community, especially as you seek to reach children and families with the gospel of God's grace and invite them on the journey of lifelong discipleship.

Jesus' Five Discipleship Invitations

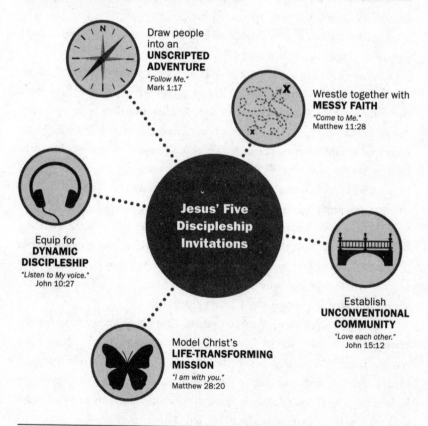

Draw people into an **UNSCRIPTED ADVENTURE**
"Follow Me."
Mark 1:17

Wrestle together with **MESSY FAITH**
"Come to Me."
Matthew 11:28

Equip for **DYNAMIC DISCIPLESHIP**
"Listen to My voice."
John 10:27

Jesus' Five Discipleship Invitations

Establish **UNCONVENTIONAL COMMUNITY**
"Love each other."
John 15:12

Model Christ's **LIFE-TRANSFORMING MISSION**
"I am with you."
Matthew 28:20

INVITATION 1: DRAW PEOPLE INTO AN UNSCRIPTED ADVENTURE

"Come, follow me," Jesus said, "and I will send you out to fish for people."
Mark 1:17

In my experience, traveling is more of an art than a science. It does not matter if I'm heading down the street or to another state; something unexpected always happens. Construction leads to detours. Restroom breaks lead to delays. An unanticipated encounter leads to a split-second decision and a change of plans. You can choose your destination and take your first step, but after that it's up for grabs. A checklist can help you prepare for a trip, but you need a compass to keep you on course.

The first principle modeled for us is this: *Jesus compellingly drew people into an unscripted adventure with God.*

One way of reading the book of Acts is to see it as the unscripted adventures of Christ's closest followers. Having walked with Jesus for three years, they didn't always know where they were headed, but they knew that each day would bring something new. And they knew that after being with Jesus, their lives would never be the same. There is a particularly memorable scene in Acts 16:25–34 where we find Paul and Silas singing . . . in the middle of the night . . . before a captive audience . . . in prison! As a kid, I never thought this story seemed odd when I was coloring activity sheets about it in Sunday school. But as an adult, I see it has greater significance. Paul and Silas didn't know what that day would bring. They didn't plan to be thrown in jail, but they still knew how to act like Jesus when they got there. There was no "what to do when the unexpected happens" checklist for them. They simply followed the compass of Christ's character.

Wrongful imprisonment turned out to be a common scenario for the apostles. They also witnessed several dramatic, supernatural events. Jesus warned them that situations like these were on the horizon. He recruited them from their ordinary lives to join his extraordinary life. And that night in Acts 16, as Paul and Silas sat in jail, more than just the floor and walls were shaken. The Philippian jailer's heart shifted. Thinking he would be executed for losing his prisoners, he learned not a single one had left. Struck by the reality that something supernatural was happening, that not one prisoner had sought to escape, he humbly asked, "What must I do to be saved?" Paul and Silas didn't respond with a list of religious rules for him to keep. They gave him just one simple instruction: "Believe." On that day, his unscripted adventure with God as a disciple of Jesus began.

The first principle we need to grasp is that most of discipleship happens in the unscripted, unplanned moments of life. I believe we need to recapture this understanding, because in my experience far too many churches try to manage and even control the adventurous journey being led and orchestrated by the Holy Spirit. Instead of responding to the work God is doing, we seek out a method that plans every moment and teaches children how to respond in every situation—how to follow the script. Often, this is a call to live a good, moral life, or what we need to think or do to avoid hell and get to heaven.

But this approach just doesn't work. Why? Because what is true of traveling is also true of following Jesus. You are probably familiar with the saying, "If you want to hear God laugh, tell him your plans." As soon as we attempt to set an agenda for our lives, life itself gets in the way. When we try to create a definitive list of do's and don'ts, a valid exception to the rules suddenly surfaces.

discipleship = faith > formulas

To be clear, not all plans are evil. We should develop structures for our ministries and have plans and schedules in place to lead programs effectively. Being unscripted doesn't mean you "wing it." It means our focus and emphasis is no longer on achieving the perfect program or teaching kids how to be perfect, moral people. *Relational discipleship is marked by faith over formulas.* Jesus never said, "Come believe these 10 things about me, and that will make you my disciple." He simply said, "Follow me" (Mark 1:17). Jesus didn't answer every question people asked. Instead, he stirred up new ways of thinking by asking questions himself in response. He broke down walls by talking to people he wasn't supposed to talk to. Jesus led a disruptive life, but he never deviated from pointing people toward loving God and loving others. There was something captivating about Jesus that inspired people to follow him, even though the future was unclear.

We cannot script out our own lives, much less create a script that will cover every possible circumstance we might face in life or in ministry. A relational focus means we make our plans, follow our checklist, and then leave room for God to disrupt lives. Discipleship is what happens in those disruptive, unplanned moments.

INVITATION 2: WRESTLE WITH MESSY FAITH TOGETHER

Come to me, all you who are weary and burdened, and I will give you rest.
Matthew 11:28

Before my wife and I were married, we had several months of pre-marital counseling. Getting engaged was serious business, and the coaching we had together as a couple took our relationship to a new level. We weren't forced to do the counseling. There was no mandate or requirement for us to complete it to be married. But week after week we willingly entered into a relational wrestling ring, talking candidly about ourselves in the presence of our counselor. Each week, we spent personal time alone in study and reflection before coming together to talk about the next topic. Nothing was off limits. We talked through our expectations and our future goals. We covered family planning and finances. We explored how our families of origin impacted the way we thought about marriage and how it could help or hinder us in growing as a couple. You name it; we wrestled through it.

At first I found myself overwhelmed with the amount of effort it would take for our relationship to succeed. One day, I realized this process would actually end up saving us a lot of work and effort in the long run. By having these difficult conversations, we were learning how to use the relational tools we needed to persevere over the long haul. By God's grace, I'm proud to say that for the last two decades, Kate and I have stayed committed to one another. We continue to enter that relational wrestling ring out of love for each other, not obligation. Jesus calls us to do the same in our relationships with him and with one another.

Jesus graciously challenged people to wrestle with messy faith together. This second principle is critical to walking with Christ without expecting an easy road ahead.

Not long after Jesus rose from the grave, something surprising happened to two of his disciples on the road to Emmaus. In Luke 24:13–25, these disciples encountered a stranger while they were walking along. The death of Christ was fresh on their minds, as was the recently discovered empty tomb. These followers of Jesus were absorbed in matters of the heart, wrestling with their experiences and what they knew to be true. And Jesus stepped right into the middle of their discussion. Verse 15 says he "came up and walked along with them." The presence of Christ made all the difference in how the disciples related to God and each other in the midst of trying times and emotions. Their faith got messy, but it didn't fall apart.

These two disciples had lots of questions. They were confused, and there were no easy answers to their questions. Their faith in God had to be messed up before it could grow and develop. But they didn't run from it. They stuck it out and walked along the road with Jesus as he explained what had happened, showing them how the Old Testament Scriptures had predicted everything and showing them how a suffering Messiah was God's plan all along. Fortunately this walk with Jesus didn't end there. The eyes of their hearts were opened. They recognized that something was stirring within them. The fire of the Holy Spirit enlivened them from the inside out while they were in the presence of Jesus.

While we can't be physically present with Christ, we can experience his Spirit's presence when we are with other believers. This has a tremendous impact on us when we feel safe enough to struggle with matters of faith that don't always make sense.

Learning to love others is always a process. It's shaped by trial and error. Adults experience this reality in marriage and in friendship, and especially as parents caring for their children. In our home, we are especially mindful of the relationships we are cultivating in our immediate and extended family. We pay attention to the way our sons interact with each other as siblings and with us as parents. In our home we uphold values like honesty, patience, responsibility, and forgiveness. We value these Christlike virtues because we want to honor God and show Christ's love to each other.

I suppose we could try to cultivate these virtues in our family by handing out long lists of things we value and rules to memorize. And while some of that might help in the short term, it would ultimately not lead us to the goal. Our goal is not to simply teach certain behaviors and have our children parrot the responses we want from them, it's to foster an attitude of the heart that results in ongoing acts of love.

---

discipleship = relationship > regulations

Relational discipleship is marked by prioritizing relationship over regulations. The goal of Jesus in calling his disciples was not just outward obedience to the rules. He never said, "Obey me because you have to;" he invited people to "come to me" (Matt. 11:28). It was in relationship with him that they found life for their weary souls. His ministry was marked by freedom from obligations and a renewed emphasis on the heart, on the inward motivation behind our choices, affections, and behaviors. To be clear, God gives us commands to live out and there are plenty of red-letter sections of Scripture where the Lord calls us to demonstrate our devotion through obedience. And yet adherence to the rules is never the goal in itself. Our obedience is marked by our affection for Jesus. It's rooted in love and gratitude for God. And as Jesus made clear to the Pharisees, you can't come up with a rule to fit every situation in life. Rules can't answer life's toughest questions.

What's your gut reaction when you consider the term "messy faith"? Is it a reality that's familiar to you? Who comes alongside you when unexpected circumstances and tough questions try to cripple you from the inside out? There is a need for followers of Jesus to wrestle with life and eternity's unknowns in light of God's Word, in community with his people, and in step with his Spirit.

When life is falling apart around us, we need a relationship with God, along with someone we can call upon, cry out to, and question. We need the assurance of love and the faith to understand that while we may not have the answers, we know the One who is in control. We can easily get caught up in doing what is right but not having the right heart. God calls people into relationship with himself *before* external life transformation takes place. And experienced disciple makers who have personally wrestled with messy faith firsthand will always err on the side of deepening interpersonal relationships over clinging to regulations.

INVITATION 3: ESTABLISH UNCONVENTIONAL COMMUNITY

My command is this: Love each other as I have loved you.
John 15:12

A good friend of mine, Kellye, hosts an annual dinner in her home at the end of every summer.[7] Most people are starting to get ready for the fall frenzy, but the desire for one more cookout, one final farewell to summer, is appealing. This is no ordinary backyard barbecue. It's an intentionally diverse assembly of friends and strangers. Kellye brings everyone together to share a meal, have communion, and tell their stories. She calls it a "Celebration of God's Goodness."

This gathering is something of an ongoing experiment, growing and changing each year. Lawyers learn from the homeless, married couples are encouraged by single parents, international guests learn about the plights of immigrants, and new believers find themselves reverse-mentoring long-term disciples. There is a great deal of laughter and tears, and the baffling array of attendees always unearths unexpected bridges of commonality. Honestly, this only happens in the family of God!

In much the same way, *Jesus established radically unconventional community among the most unlikely people.* This is the third principle of relational discipleship.

Jesus surrounded himself with a ragtag band of followers. A small number of them were called to serve in ministry with him for three years before they became his plan for catalyzing a worldwide movement. Christ deeply loved Peter, James, John, the rest of the Twelve, and Mary, Martha, and Lazarus. In assembling his team of disciples, Jesus defied contemporary cultural protocols, cutting through socio-economic barriers and bridging gaps between people of different backgrounds and upbringings. In every relationship, he kept love at the center. Jesus modeled authentic community and called his followers to do the same.

We see some of the lessons the disciples learned from living with Jesus when we examine the unconventional community of the early church in Acts 2. Less than two months after the Lord's resurrection, Peter is preaching to a crowd and three thousand people trust Christ for the forgiveness of sin and eternal salvation. These new believers are from various nations, yet they are all grafted into the family of God through faith and baptism. Acts 2:42–47 gives us a rich portrait of their life together: Christ-centered community devoted to teaching, fellowship, prayer, worship, stewardship, and serving. The church in Acts 2 is made up of poor, rich, young, old, female, and male. The breakdown of relational barriers in the early church points us back to the relational oneness we experienced with God and one another in the Garden of Eden and points us forward in anticipation of the new heaven and new Earth. The barrier-breaking, bridge-building love shown by the first disciples and the early church sets a standard for us as we seek to live in community as Christ's followers today.

discipleship = interdependence > independence

As a young pastor I remember stumbling upon this quote by Erwin McManus: "Jesus doesn't call us to *love* God and *tolerate* our neighbor."[8] At the time I was newly married, we were renting a condo, and I could not stand my downstairs neighbors. Loud music blared and cigarette smoke billowed from below, pouring into our bedroom windows. They even had the nerve to bang on the ceiling while we were playing on the floor with our newborn son. It was horrible.

But then God began speaking to my heart, starting with McManus's penetrating quote. I was convicted that I wasn't treating them with love and respect and decided to change. I began to see God was teaching me to be interdependent in my love for others, and it would mean getting to know people I might never hang out with otherwise. I knew this wasn't optional. Jesus never said, "Be nicer to people." He said, "Love each other" (John 15:12).

During that particular season of life, I was going a hundred miles an hour. Kate and I made time for my ministry, but we were not really engaged with anyone else. We were doing life alone and on our own terms, and we liked it that way! The Lord used our noisy neighbors to disrupt that life and to adjust my perspective on what it means to love. I was convicted of my selfishness and immediately started finding ways to serve and support my neighbors. This shift in my heart started to overflow into other relationships inside our church and in the surrounding community as well. And it even bore some long-term fruit. You can imagine my surprise five years later when our paths crossed again, and I discovered that one of my former neighbors had become a believer. She wanted to thank me for the Jesus-like example I had set. In moments like these, I'm grateful God uses us, even in our weaknesses.

God did not create us to be alone. We are called to be dependent on him and one another. *True discipleship is marked by interdependence over independence.* Unconventional community is about loving anyone and everyone God sends our way. In almost every other social group or community, we get to choose who we hang out with. But in the church, God chooses. Relational discipleship embraces this and brings together unlikely people, thereby healing divisions, breaking down barriers, and uniting people together in Jesus Christ.

INVITATION 4: MODEL CHRIST'S LIFE-TRANSFORMING MISSION

And teaching them to obey everything I have commanded you.
And surely I am with you always, to the very end of the age.
Matthew 28:20

Alcoholism runs deep in the roots of my family tree. In 1981, my dad made a decision that dramatically impacted the rest of his life and my own. He entered inpatient rehab as part of Alcoholics Anonymous (AA) to deal with his ongoing addiction to alcohol and drugs. My father's inner world could no longer bear the weight of his addiction. His dependency on chemical substances truly was a significant symptom, a veneer hiding the much deeper issues in his heart. My dad needed to be free of his addiction, but he first needed a revolution of mind, heart, and will to someone outside himself. He needed a new community, a group of mentors, family members, and friends who would stand by his side. AA made that possible.

By addressing a person's core values and priorities and then addressing their own responsibility for their behavior, AA has provided hope to countless desperate individuals around the globe. People like my dad are given a second chance at life. Those who enter the program are outfitted with a new internal operating system and an external support network that redefines how they view God, themselves, and the world around them.

Like becoming a sold-out disciple of Jesus, the life-transforming commitment a person makes to AA is a redemptive choice to turn away from a pathway of destruction and start heading wholeheartedly with others in the direction of life and peace.

This example leads to the fourth principle for relational discipleship: *Jesus wholeheartedly modeled God's life-transforming mission for the sake of the world.*

People were shocked when Jesus called Levi as a disciple.[9] He was a tax collector! What place do sinful tax collectors have in God's kingdom? While most people said they don't belong, Jesus taught that they're the most likely candidates for a seat at the Lord's table. He taught people that it's the sick who need eternal hope and healing, not those who are well. Jesus' approach to discipleship prioritized sinners and sought to communicate God's good news to them. Jesus offered imperfect people a renewed mind and heart and called them to turn away from the road that leads to death. John 3:16–17 clarifies Christ's role as Savior, not condemner, of the world. Jesus came to save, and the good news is there is no one who is too far from God's reach.

Every aspect of Levi's life changed forever when he responded to the call to follow Jesus. He didn't try to pretend he was something he was not. He didn't adopt a surface-level set of character traits. And he didn't take on the full responsibility to be like Jesus on his own. Becoming a disciple required some time as he learned to renounce his former way of life in full exchange for Christ's.

In Luke 14:25–33, Jesus speaks to the masses about the radical nature of discipleship. He says anyone who wants to follow him must "hate" his mother or father. Now, "hate" is a pretty strong word. Does God really expect people to disown their family in favor of Christ? Surprisingly, the answer is "yes." Followers of Jesus must come to the point that nothing else matters. They can no longer be defined by their family, by their job, by their education, by their income level. They must be defined by Jesus. The good news of the gospel presents Jesus as the substitute who pays the penalty for our sins and gives us his righteousness in return. All of this is possible as we are united with Jesus in his life, death, and resurrection by faith, and it's a gift of God's grace, not something we can earn. This is transformational through and through. As disciples, we take up our own crosses and sacrifice our lives in a way that points people back to God, to Jesus and his sacrifice for them. This is the kind of life we are called to as disciples of Christ.

discipleship = gospel > good principles

When my dad entered rehab, I joined Kids Are Special, a weekly support group for children of alcoholics.[10] The program helped me and others in similar situations unpack our pain and explore healthier ways to cope with life's various challenges and choices. Around the same time I was involved in Kids Are Special, I was attending Oak Tree Day Care and came to a point where I was deeply aware of my need for Jesus to save me. I decided to trust and follow Christ. It's no accident that my own discipleship journey parallels learning how substance abuse was impacting my life and the life of my family. I saw the need for help in my father's life and the need for a new internal operating system from God in my own life as well. I learned the importance of taking responsibility for my core values, priorities, behaviors, and relationships.

Relational discipleship is marked by the gospel and not just good principles or moral lessons. Jesus never said, "You're on your own; try harder." He said, "I am with you" (Matt. 28:20). And he did not leave us alone; he gave us the Holy Spirit to guide, direct, and empower us to follow him. As I pointed out earlier, being fully devoted to Jesus does not mean perfect performance. It's the intention of one's heart and the will to press on in the face of opposition. It's also the resolve to walk side by side with God and others regardless of resistance. Disciples and disciple makers are never satisfied with partial life transformation. Following Jesus begins with the radical good news of salvation in the gospel and it progresses as his Word and presence permeates every dimension of a person's life.

INVITATION 5: EQUIP FOR DYNAMIC DISCIPLESHIP

**My sheep listen to my voice; I know them, and they
follow me.**

John 10:27

"How can there be two Main Streets in this town, Dan? This must be an American thing."

Lawrence and I were headed to the home of a mutual friend.[11] It was dark, we were already late, and we were lost. And Lawrence was correct. There were two street signs, and they both said Main Street.

This was in the pre-smartphone days, of course. My travel companion was visiting from Zambia, Africa, so we did our best to make sense of our printed directions. We fumbled our way forward for a while before finally placing a desperate pay phone call to the person we were going to see. Our host gave us a quick handful of turn-by-turn directions, and we eventually reached our destination.

The whole thing was pretty comical, especially since Lawrence had driven me around multiple times on the other side of the world, traversing dilapidated dirt roads with no streetlights. On all of those crazy trips in the middle of nowhere, we never got lost! I was certainly humbled that night. And it wasn't the first time I've had to swallow my pride and admit I was lost. It won't be the last, I'm sure.

My experience with Lawrence reminded me how important it is to have community with God and others in order to hear the right voices along the journey of life. While walking with Jesus, we don't know every twist and turn in the road, but the Holy Spirit is there to guide our steps. We need each other too. Our faith isn't static or systematic; it's dynamic. It's unique to every believer, yet strangely similar. We need equipping to follow and walk with Christ. After all, it's an unscripted adventure with God!

Principle five of relational discipleship is this: *Jesus humbly equipped people for a lifetime of dynamic discipleship.*

The Bible is filled with examples of people who walked closely, albeit imperfectly, with God, led by his Word and his Spirit. The disciples were called by name to follow Christ, commanded to love God and others, and then commissioned to become disciple makers. Letting Jesus lead requires a readiness to listen to and learn from him. If you think you have the answers or you aren't willing to be led by someone else, you may have trouble. Being a disciple of Jesus requires humility and a willingness to follow. John 10 beautifully portrays the Lord as the Good Shepherd, the One who knows his sheep personally and puts his life on the line to protect them. And we are told the sheep know the shepherd because they recognize his voice. In listening to his voice, they follow his lead and are safe.

Romans 8:14 says: "For those who are led by the Spirit of God are the children of God." There is an element of mystery in our spiritual adoption, but we know this with certainty: being a child of God means we belong to his family. And one of the marks of a child of God is a willingness and supernatural ability to be *led*. Jesus has given his followers the Holy Spirit, an advocate who will equip and empower them.[12] They need the Spirit to lead them because Jesus didn't provide them with explicit details about every decision they will need to make. Instead, they have been given the Word of God and the Holy Spirit to guide them along the way—individually and together.

discipleship = personal > predictable

My family and I have not yet had the opportunity to experience a pre-arranged vacation, one set up by a travel agent. I hear they are amazing. You pay a little bit extra, of course, but you work with someone who knows the various options and you determine potential destinations. Based on your financial limits, you decide together what your awesome get-away adventure will entail.

Some people I know love this approach. They enjoy having a guide who can advise and recommend an itinerary for them to follow. Others I know prefer to map out their day-to-day plans on their own. Either way, no matter how much pre-planning you do, your vacation can always get derailed. It's just as important to be prepared for fun as it is for potential fallout. Charting your course has no bearing on what you may or may not encounter along the way. Every trip is personal but hardly 100 percent predictable.

Relational discipleship is marked by a similar distinction—the difference between handcrafted and mass-produced followers of Jesus. We live in a world that finds comfort in structures and systems, both of which are needed in varying degrees and contexts. We would experience chaos without objectives and plans. However, when it comes to human beings, life is more organic than organized. The paths laid out for people and the choices they make can't be fully known in advance. In light of this, it's surprising that churches and ministry leaders keep trying to find formulas to multiply disciples.

In the end, a disciple's journey is more personal than predictable. Each disciple has a unique path to walk with God while following the same leader, Jesus Christ. The spiritual gifting, personality, and passions of one disciple will not be exactly the same as another. The fruit of the Spirit will grow in both, but to differing degrees and with varied expression. Disciples need to be empowered with the knowledge and resources to stay in stride with the Lord moment by moment, not burdened with an idealistic, cleverly mapped out faith itinerary.

Jesus never said to his followers, "Stick to the program." He said, "Listen to my voice" (John 10:27). God promises to guide his children and faithfully provide for them, and often he uses common steps and approaches to accomplish his purposes. Bible studies, prayer, worship services, communion, fellowship gatherings, mission trips, and more can each play a role in a believer's growth. But living out the lessons learned from these engagements will look different from one person to the next. The church can prescribe and provide many good things, but at the end of the day, individual disciples are the ones walking hand in hand with Jesus.

Equipping people for a lifetime of dynamic discipleship means learning to navigate life with God one day at a time. We need to be flexible and willing to adapt to God's leading, and we need to multiply this trait in others. This is the way of being that Jesus called his followers to embrace. Disciples are invited to keep in step with the Lord by the light of his Word, the voice of his Son, and the presence of his Holy Spirit.[13]

The church is ultimately a family, not a building. The body of Christ should seek to be organic, although some structure will always be necessary. God's work in the world is expressed in myriad ways because he is alive and active in and through his people. Dynamic discipleship starts with the Holy Spirit living within an individual. We must recognize that each believer is on an unscripted adventure in their relationship with God, an enlivened experience that involves twists and turns, highs and lows, strengths and weaknesses, joys and sorrows. Relational discipleship recognizes the highly personal nature of faith, while honoring the reality that centuries of disciples have walked faithfully with God as followers and ambassadors of Christ.

NOW IS THE TIME TO PUT JESUS' TIMELESS EXAMPLE INTO PRACTICE

To get a new kind of disciple, we need a renewed approach to disciple making. Imagine how vibrant your church could be if it were filled with disciples and disciple makers who mirror and model Jesus' five relational discipleship invitations as a way of life. Anyone who has been disrupted by Jesus and connects with the five relational discipleship invitations can begin embedding this perspective into their life and ministry. I'll admit that these five invitations do not answer all the questions we might have. They don't tell us what to teach or how to do it. These are paradigms that are intended to get us thinking and asking questions about our methods, our goals, and our priorities in ministry.

> Jesus not only spent time instructing, training and informing; he spent much time forming a community.
>
> **Keith Anderson & Randy Reese**[14]

Kid-influencers who have been disrupted by Jesus have a high calling. Becoming a vibrant community of disciple makers is essential to long-range effectiveness. Kids and families need kid-influencers to rise above the status quo in children's ministry. Therefore, the next five chapters expand on each invitation with practical applications for children's ministry settings.

QUESTIONS FOR REFLECTION & DISCUSSION

1. What is unusual about Jesus placing a child in the middle of the disciples' conflict over who is greatest? How does this scene impact you as a disciple?

2. Describe how Jesus has disrupted you personally in the following areas:

   • When were you first convicted by Jesus' call to "follow me"?

   • What is most challenging to you about Jesus' example?

   • How have you experienced Jesus' consistent presence in your walk with God?

   • What clear invitation has Jesus put before you recently?

3. Why is it important for disciple makers to be disrupted by Jesus before taking responsibility to disciple others?

4. In what way(s) has your relationship with Christ been an unscripted adventure?

5. How do you deal with messy faith, including unanswered questions, difficult truths, tough relationships, and tragic life experiences?

6. What is the most unconventional community you have personally experienced?

7. How would you describe the life-transforming mission of Jesus? What is one area of your life you did not expect to change when you decided to trust and follow him as a disciple?

8. What is dynamic discipleship? Why is it hard for people to walk in step with Jesus on a daily basis?

9. In your church, which of the five invitations is most evident and why? Which of the five invitations is clearly missing, and what do you think it would take to introduce and cultivate it successfully?

10. How would you and/or your church benefit from embedding the five relational discipleship invitations into its ministries?

Five Life-Giving Invitations for Relational Children's Ministry

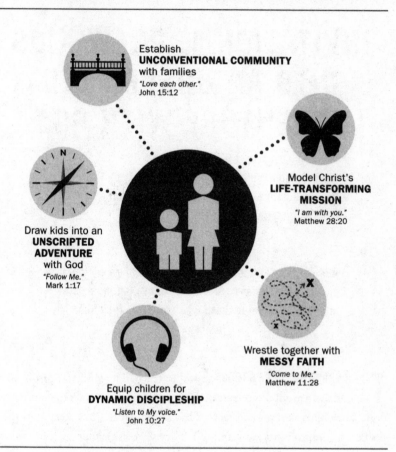

Establish **UNCONVENTIONAL COMMUNITY** with families
"Love each other."
John 15:12

Model Christ's **LIFE-TRANSFORMING MISSION**
"I am with you."
Matthew 28:20

Draw kids into an **UNSCRIPTED ADVENTURE** with God
"Follow Me."
Mark 1:17

Wrestle together with **MESSY FAITH**
"Come to Me."
Matthew 11:28

Equip children for **DYNAMIC DISCIPLESHIP**
"Listen to My voice."
John 10:27

CHAPTER 5

INVITATION 1: DRAW KIDS INTO AN UNSCRIPTED ADVENTURE WITH GOD

Children and adults are pilgrims together on the
life-walk with God working in and through the flow of
normal, changing lives and relationships.
Catherine Stonehouse[1]

And without faith it is impossible to please God, because
anyone who comes to him must believe that he exists
and that he rewards those who earnestly seek him.
Hebrews 11:6

THIRD GRADE BOYS ARE A TOUGH crowd to reach. They fidget, squirm, zone out, and run around incessantly. They interrupt. They talk to their neighbors. They blurt out random facts. They collect "stuff" and keep it in their pockets for impromptu show and tell. They stare out windows. They ask to get a drink of water. They ask to get another drink of water. They talk about superheroes. They think they *are* superheroes. You think they're not paying attention, but they are. I know; I have taught third grade Sunday school. I have coached third grade soccer. I have two sons of my own. And many moons ago, I too was in third grade.

UNKNOWN FUTURES

As a kid growing up in a home fragmented by divorce, childcare was a familiar setting to me, but church was not. So it was a shock to the system when my mom enrolled me at Oak Tree Day Care, run by a church across the street from my new school. As a third grade transfer student, the daily after school routine was still fairly predictable: line up, get counted, travel to day care, line up, get counted, hang backpack on assigned hook, color or play for a bit, do homework, line up, get counted, play outside on the playground, line up, get counted, go to snack time, line up, get counted, finish homework, color or play, get picked up by a responsible parent or guardian . . . *wash, rinse, repeat.* On the other hand, there were several differences between Oak Tree and your typical day care. The Bible stories and songs I learned. The kind yet firm way leaders spoke to and treated us. My new friends and I were given the opportunity to have fun together, but this was balanced with an emphasis on doing our schoolwork and educating us in spiritual matters. Looking back, I realize Oak Tree was more than a holding room until my mother was home. God used the leaders there to draw me into an unscripted adventure with him.

Mrs. Anderson led Sunshine Club at Oak Tree every Wednesday afternoon. For us "older kids" Sunshine Club was a treat, something special. After lining up and getting counted, my peers and I were led to a separate wing of the church, to a room that was different from the rest of the day care. I didn't know it at the time, but this area was for the weekend and midweek children's ministry. I remember Mrs. Anderson standing at the front of the room. She always had a welcoming smile on her face and a sky blue flannel graph board on an easel to her right, and her sincere care for every child was clearly evident. Her presentations were creative. Her explanations were simple. Her heart was set on eternity. Occasionally a felt cloud or a sheep would fall from the easel and we would all laugh. From time to time one of us would ask or answer a serious question. Most of the time we halfheartedly participated, knowing playground time was just around the corner.

But I do remember that regardless of which Bible story she shared, Mrs. Anderson closed every week by talking with us about following Jesus. She used several tools and techniques to grab and keep our attention. She painted a captivating picture of God's unconditional love for kids, his relentless desire to have us live with him forever in heaven, and his free offer of forgiveness through faith in his Son. She shared a compelling invitation to follow Jesus Christ and live every day in step with the Holy Spirit until the Lord's return. Sure, it was a lot for us to take in, but Mrs. Anderson broke it down into bite-sized truths for us to chew on. She centered everything on God's Word and the importance of having a relationship with Jesus and other followers of his. Her approach wasn't to teach a class; she tried to cultivate a relationship with us as children and consistently pointed us to Christ with clarity. Mrs. Anderson drew us in by sharing about her own life with God and giving us the opportunity to ask questions and share our discoveries.

A few months after I started at Oak Tree, at the end of one of our Sunshine Club meetings, my eyes locked with Mrs. Anderson's. Once again she shared about Jesus. Once again she asked if any of us would like to trust in Christ's life, death, and resurrection, to have our sins forgiven and to follow Jesus. She didn't explain in detail how life would be different from this point forward. It was simply an invitation to a loving relationship with our heavenly Father, his Son, the Holy Spirit, and other followers of Jesus Christ. Something in me knew the invitation was real. The penetrating words of the songs we sang from week to week resonated within me. The experience of being known, loved, and served by a Christ-centered community of kid-influencers had impacted me deeply, especially in light of my fractured home life. Something in me could not resist raising my hand, standing up, and praying to receive Jesus' forgiveness and respond to his life-giving words: "Follow me."

I was one of many third graders who participated in Sunshine Club. Some of us decided to trust and follow Christ; others did not. Mrs. Anderson had no idea which of us would respond to God favorably. She could have excused me from her lessons because my mom was not in favor of me learning about "God, church, and Jesus" at a Christian day care. Instead, she chose to take the Great Commission seriously and to commit herself to the business of making disciples. Mrs. Anderson modeled a meaningful life of faith, and she invited children to join the family of God. We were drawn in by the mystery, adventure, and wonder of what it meant to follow Jesus. After that day, I began gravitating toward the Bible and church. The church programs provided a safe place for me to explore truth and to learn what it meant to be a disciple. Like the first followers of Jesus, I had no idea what I was getting into, and in retrospect, I'm grateful my mom and the church community gave me space and relational support to learn and grow with God.

None of us can know the future of the children who cross our path, but the work we do has implications for all eternity. Rarely can we fully understand the circumstances in which kids come to our ministry or what they go home to. We don't fully grasp the decisions they need to make or the unique fears they face. We cannot predict the twists and turns their lives will take. In this sense, the only relationship that can speak to the unique challenges they will face is their relationship with God. But that doesn't mean we can't play a role too—an important one! As kid-influencers, we have a responsibility to get to know them, spend time with them, answer their questions, and help them respond to the invitation to follow Jesus and then learn what that means. While we would all undoubtedly agree this is our goal, unfortunately many children's ministries get tangled up in their curriculum and their checklists instead of taking the time to chart a discipleship path that really brings life change to kids and families.

FEAR FOLLOWS THE SCRIPT

Today's children's ministries are far more robust, with far more resources and tools than were available when I was a child. An entire industry has sprouted up to serve churches with cutting-edge resources so kid-influencers can teach children God's Word more effectively. There are videos and workbooks, live drama scripts and service projects, worship experiences and true-to-life storybooks. Regardless of your style or the context of your ministry, you can find something that matches your needs. But you'll still need more than good curriculum. Qualified leaders are essential to make sure things run smoothly and that you are developing relationships with the children you serve.

Typically, out-of-the-box resources won't be the cure-all you are looking for. And your leaders will need training and time to gain experience. Often, this means having a combination of both paid and unpaid children's ministry leaders, if your church can afford to do this. Your leaders are the stewards of God's truth to children, and they need to see how their work fits into a broader ministry vision within the body of Christ. Over the years, I've personally seen how easy it is to sacrifice relationships and get sidetracked by developing the right system and fine-tuning the program. But while systems and programs are necessary, they won't be the key to effectively making disciples.

Russ has served in children's ministry for many years.[2] He is a faithful follower of Christ and father to his five kids. His walk with God is genuine, refined by the fires of life's ups and downs. The small group of boys he leads from week to week is challenging to say the least. They're much more interested in wrestling with each other than with the Word of God. In the past, when Russ received the published curriculum, he would immediately start preparing. Lately he is finding himself more and more frustrated. How can he possibly get through to his guys? The materials seem to be missing the mark with this particular group. Russ feels trapped because he knows he is supposed to stick to the printed lesson, but these boys need something more. He's just not sure what to do or what to say.

After mustering the courage to share his struggles, he tells his children's pastor about the situation. Russ is told to "follow the script" because the materials were purchased by the church and all the other groups are using it. This doesn't help Russ's situation, and makes him feel he just isn't cut out to be a disciple maker for these kids. He knows something is wrong, but he doesn't want to be critical and rock the boat as a lay leader in a world of ministry professionals.

This story comes from a real situation in a ministry I was co-leading. When I heard about it, I stepped in to intervene. As a leader, I know resources are a helpful tool, and it's not always sensible to allow leaders to teach whatever they wish to teach. Leaders should be held accountable, and having a set curriculum approved by the church ensures they are teaching content that aligns with the doctrine and vision of the ministry. At the same time, this situation helped me see that when I recruit passionate, spiritually gifted people, I can't just ask them to check their ideas and passions at the door. They aren't robots to program or cogs in the ministry machine. "Read the curriculum and do what it says even if your kids are climbing the walls" is a terrible training strategy for kid-influencers. It's dishonoring and debilitating to expect leaders to ignore variables like real-life kids and the work of the Holy Spirit. Yes, it can be scary to let leaders actually lead on their own, but with some training and guidance you can find the right balance of freedom and accountability. As a disciple maker, Russ needed someone to grant him permission to build upon the approved curriculum by adjusting and adapting the material to the needs of the boys in his group.

> No formula can be written for spiritual formation, for it is a dynamic relationship and one that is highly individualized.
>
> **Dallas Willard[3]**

Balance is needed because discipleship is a faith-guided, not a formula-driven, journey. If we keep people chained to the script, we are leading in fear. Published curriculum, when used as a tool by godly disciple makers, can be very effective, but authentic relationships are the core of every children's ministry. The questions and activities provided in curriculum materials are designed to provide a template for a shared experience, not a formula for discipleship. Here is my point: *having the latest and greatest materials is not the difference maker when it comes to children's ministry.* If it were, the best resourced churches and children's ministries would be telling an entirely different tale when it comes to the lifelong discipleship trajectory of kids.

FLANNEL GRAPH STILL WORKS

Technology is great. There are things we can do today that we could not have imagined doing twenty years ago. And yet it has become commonplace; today's kids have never known a world without it. I share this because I believe technology has marginalized one of the greatest ways to tell stories of all time. As crazy as it seems, I am an advocate for using the old-fashioned flannel graph. Hear me out, and I'll explain why.

A couple of years ago I was visiting a children's ministry near San Diego, California. It was at a non-denominational church with a passion for reaching the spiritually lost. The midweek program for kids was busting the doors off the building. Children ages two to eighteen were attending from all over the region. As our host walked us from room to room, each grade level had a distinct look and feel. The toddlers were singing memorable songs, listening to Bible stories, and playing with finger puppets. The early elementary kids were playing Bible trivia games in smaller groups and putting multi-colored stickers on their adult leaders' faces for every correct answer. The late elementary boys were telling silly jokes and making funny noises to fill in any gaps during the large group Bible study, but even with all the joking around, they seemed to be engaged. After meeting in their own age groups, the middle school and high school students headed back to the children's ministry to serve the younger age levels.

All across the board I was impressed with what I saw, but the image I still carry with me, imprinted in my memory, is a full classroom of third through fifth grade girls. Their leader was standing up front attaching pictures on a large whiteboard to tell a Bible story. Everyone's eyes were locked on the teacher. She was not all that young. She wasn't wearing trendy clothes. Her language was not hip, and the story was not flashy. One of the pictures even fell to the ground during the presentation. I smiled at how "old school" the presentation method was. I was surprised when my host told me it was a weekly occurrence. Amazingly—it worked! The children were utterly captivated by the story.

Flannel graph still works? Really?!

I later learned this particular leader is well into her third decade of working with girls in this age group. And they love her. The early elementary kids can't wait to be in her group when they get older. She is a legend in the eyes of kids and families at the church and in the community. No one expects to use a touchscreen in her room, but that doesn't hinder participation. Stories abound of her commitment to Christ and how she cares for any child who comes her way. She teaches "older" songs and uses the whiteboard with pictures rather than the latest videos. My host informed me that the girls in this room *prefer* the older songs she teaches them and they *enjoy* hearing stories using pictures on the whiteboard. And it's not just the church kids, either. The children are totally comfortable inviting and bringing friends. Like Mrs. Anderson, this faithful woman has cultivated a reputation built on solid relationships and loving care for children. Her methods may be old-fashioned and out-of-date by today's standards, but the power of her teaching lies not in the medium she uses. It lies instead in the relational investments she has made in the children's lives. She is a living testimonial to the relational power of longevity and authenticity in ministry.

During that visit I felt like I had stepped back in time to my childhood. I remembered how moved I was, not by Mrs. Anderson's outdated presentations, but by her authenticity. And I saw that the same was true of the kids in this ministry. My point is not that you should go out and buy a flannel graph for next Sunday. *The method is secondary to the messenger and the message.* As noted by Christian educators and acclaimed author Walter Wangerin, faith formation in children isn't primarily determined by our abilities or tactics:

> In this case, method follows motive. *How* you tell stories will depend upon *why* you tell stories, and if your personal reasons are right, you will surely tell stories effectively. . . . [If] it is of the Lord that you are speaking, and if you love the Lord your God with all your heart, with all your strength, with all your mind, well, your delivery will have authority and power, though your method will be different from everyone else's method.[4]

In other words, your own engagement with the material will have a far more lasting impact than the material itself. Has your life been changed by what you teach? Children want to know the things that really matter to you, not just stories you read from an approved curriculum.

While God's truth is at the center, what holds the method and message together is the messenger—the very real person in the middle of it all. Modeling Christlike character plays a very significant role in the methodology of discipleship. Being personally known, loved, and served by a godly leader on a common faith-guided journey makes all the difference. And when this leader is part of a larger faith family—a church community—the impact on kids and parents further increases.

FIVE TECHNIQUES FOR DRAWING KIDS INTO AN UNSCRIPTED ADVENTURE WITH GOD

The compass of Christ's character is attractive and inspiring. It draws people in, and trust begins to form as they take initial steps to follow him, one at a time. The early church in Acts 2 had no master blueprint for disciple making, but that didn't stop them from integrating the discipleship journeys of newly converted children, parents, and others into the family of God. They undoubtedly tried several structured and unstructured approaches to growing disciples and probably had to adapt what they did for different ages and cultural backgrounds. It was all unscripted.

Catherine Stonehouse, professor and author of *Joining Children in the Spiritual Journey*, writes: "To be a good parent or Sunday school teacher of children, we do not need to be people who have arrived; God simply calls us to be on the way, seeking, finding, and rejoicing in what we find."[5] As adults we tend to fall into the trap of *telling* versus *relating* when we are with children. Relating is more than just telling a child some facts. It involves *talking, exploring, sharing, responding*, and *celebrating* the adventure of life with God and discipleship in the way of Jesus. Let's unpack what each of these looks like in more detail.

TECHNIQUE 1: TALK OPENLY WITH KIDS ABOUT PERSONAL "LIFE WITH GOD" STORIES

Have you ever crossed a river? How about a river that miraculously walled up in such a way that an entire nation could cross from one side to the other on dry ground? Such was Joshua's experience soon after Moses' death (see Joshua 3–4). God had promised the people of Israel safe passage to the Promised Land. As they stood on the swollen banks of the Jordan River with the Ark of the Covenant, they probably wondered what would happen next. Imagine their surprise when they got to experience *Red Sea Crossing: The Sequel* (minus the pursuit by pharaoh's army, of course!). Following their courageous crossing, Joshua was instructed to commission the building of an altar in honor of God's presence, protection, and provision. He selected one person from each of Israel's twelve tribes, had them gather one stone each from the supernaturally dry river bed, and made a monument to stand in lasting memory of the crossing. God specifically told Joshua to do this, knowing children would curiously ask their parents and community of faith, "What do these stones mean?" In other words, Joshua was instructed by the Lord to set up a springboard for telling a story about God. It was a lesson in children's ministry!

> Many kids don't know when and how their parents started following Christ. Most kids love hearing about when their parents met, when they fell in love, and what their wedding day was like. Why don't we do the same with our faith story?
>
> **Kara Powell & Chap Clark**[6]

God did this because he wanted to teach Joshua an important lesson. Children of all ages love stories. The settings and characters draw them in. The words and pictures captivate their minds and hearts. And as the storyline builds, so does their imagination. They identify with what is happening. They may not understand all the implications due to their age, intellect, or maturity level, but they still enjoy it. They interact with stories in a deeply intimate way. The illustrations get the information into their system, and over the years these stories serve as relational building blocks for their world-view and lives.

The Bible is vital to knowing God deeply, and it's filled to overflowing with true stories, so it makes sense that children's ministries leverage Scripture stories as the starting point for curriculum. Starting with Creation in Genesis and ending with the final return of Christ in Revelation, most children's ministry curriculums try to systematically move through the pages of God's Word from one story to the next. Yet sometimes the stories are disconnected from one another and children lack a clear understanding of the bigger storyline of the Bible—how it all fits together. Children's spiritual formation thought leaders, David Csinos and Ivy Beckwith, duly note, "Too often children's ministry offers young people different age-appropriate episodes of God's story without helping them make sense of it as a coherent whole."[7] So while it's important to highlight individual stories, we also need to help children understand the Bible is the cohesive story of God and his ongoing relationship with his people. Your role as a fellow disciple and kid-influencer is to guide kids to connect the dots. Take time to highlight biographies of those who walked with God and include individuals who turned toward or away from the Lord along the way. Children can and should hear about "life with God" directly from the pages of Scripture.

But not *only* from the pages of Scripture.

This is where many children's ministries fall short in the work of discipling children. Reading Bible stories to kids takes skill, but it's easier and safer than sharing with them openly from the heart. Don't lean on scripted storytelling and neglect sharing what real life with God looks like today. Children need trusted people to not just share stories from the Bible, but to share how the story of God is continuing today through the church and through disciples of Jesus today. Help them see that the story is not over, that it continues as God is working today, and that their lives are a continuation of the work God began thousands of years ago and is continuing until the day Jesus returns. Come alongside them so they can draw connections to the worlds and worldviews they encounter every day.

> When and where do we see God? In the Bible, God is often revealed in the ordinary routine of daily life.
>
> **Keith Anderson & Randy Reese**[8]

The difference between giving kids information about God and talking with them about daily life with him is significant. We must also encourage adults to open up about their decision to trust Christ for salvation. I find this is rarely done in the context of children's ministry (or at home for that matter). Bringing personal questions and discoveries about God to the table at a child's level is part of living out childlike faith. The opportunity to interact with someone who presently evidences the kind of life with God that is described in his Word speaks volumes to the heart of a child.

Children's ministries empower leaders who relate to God to share their relationship with kids by giving them permission to go off script. According to Stonehouse and her academic peers Scottie May, Beth Posterski, and Linda Cannell, "Lesson plans should be used more like a roadmap. A starting point is provided as well as the desired destination, but the teacher has options as to which route to take to reach the destination."[910] When the teacher-child relationship is envisioned as two disciples traveling on the same journey with Christ together, it resembles spiritual formation more than a classroom education.[10]

Relational children's ministries know it's possible to lean into prewritten materials in such a way that it nurtures real relationships. Kid-influencers will need training in this, to learn how to exercise discretion and be candid about their own relationships with Christ in age-appropriate ways. Sharing a hypothetical example about choices and consequences pales in comparison to a leader opening up about a time God personally guided or convicted them. Your kids will want to know, "Is life with God possible *outside* the pages of Scripture?" and "If so, what does it look like?"

Children have stories and unanswered questions to share as well.

Sometimes all you need to do is provide space for them to talk about those experiences. Kid-influencers, including children's ministry leaders, parents, extended family, coaches, and teachers, can all draw kids into an unscripted adventure with God by talking openly about their own unscripted stories as followers of Jesus.

TECHNIQUE 2: GIVE KIDS OPPORTUNITIES TO EXPLORE FAITHFUL GOD FOLLOWERS IN THE BIBLE

Online resources like BibleGateway.com and YouVersion.com have done a tremendous job of reminding people to get into God's Word daily. Research reveals that 84 percent of people still prefer to read the Bible in print rather than digitally or via listening to an audio recording, although the commitment to mining Scripture more than once a week is losing ground.[11] Most readers start out strong in Genesis, but only 61 percent make it all the way through to Revelation.[12] The tendency of most is to skip around from one familiar passage to the next. This means many pages in the Bible remain untouched, and with them, many of the stories of Scripture remain unread, undiscovered.

Admittedly, it's not always easy to connect the Bible directly to life. For example, without some understanding of the cultural background, the census in the book of Numbers feels disconnected from real life and is easily dismissed as irrelevant. The chronology leading up to Christ in Matthew 1 may have a few interesting characters, but it's easy to glance over. How can disciples disciple others when their ability to read and understand the Bible is limited to summaries and sidebars on the provided curriculum? If you want your kid-influencers and teachers to be more effective at discipling kids, you need to help them get familiar with more of the Bible. Obviously, you won't be able to do this all at once. But with some work, you can begin mining the lesser-known stories of the Bible for precious gems to pass along to your leaders and the children in your ministry. Let me give you an example.

Hilkiah was the Jewish high priest during the reign of the eight-year-old boy king, Josiah. Hilkiah goes on record as the one who rediscovered the Book of the Law and brought it to the attention of the king. The domino effect of his discovery resulted in the restoration of the Temple, and it reminded God's people of his law and promises. This led to a fresh commitment by them to obey and worship the Lord alone. It was a huge reformation led by a very young ruler and a turning point in the history of the Hebrew people, one that caused them to explore the depths of their hearts in light of God's truth. In the end, it deepened their relationship with the Lord and each other for a much greater purpose.

Now, imagine helping kids navigate this story in 2 Kings 22–23 as they explore the faithful God followers in this section of Scripture and find out these truths for themselves. Do your kids like the idea of being kings and queens? Would they have fun making paper crowns? Would they enjoy drawing pictures of what they would do to make the world a better place if they were in charge? Can they tell the difference between someone in authority who makes good decisions over evil ones? Are there parallel stories of kids impacting their world in significant ways today? Get creative. Pull a team together and study a passage of Scripture as a group, then brainstorm ideas for teaching it to kids. Children of all ages need opportunities to dive in and dig around in the pages of the Bible. Kid-influencers will make greater headway in discipleship when they band together and involve kids in this process.

Hilkiah and Josiah represent a godly intergenerational relationship within the faith community. Both were faithful God followers; both serve as relatable Bible biographies for people young and old today. What they uncovered and applied in their own lives overflowed into the faith community in a powerful way. Disciple makers who actively seek out this and other stories in God's Word will inevitably experience the same. Learning directly from the varied lives of people in the Bible opens up the door to a biblical worldview, character change, wise decision making, and loving people sacrificially.

Will this take work? Of course! Giving kids opportunities to explore faithful God followers in the Bible means you'll need to do some study yourself. Remember: lasting, lifelong transformation takes both head and heart work, but the process of mutual discovery, sharing what you learn and hearing what the kids learn, is what makes this an organic and dynamic process. Adults and children can and should learn side by side. Relational children's ministries help leaders and children make connections between the characters in the Bible and the character of Christ *together*. Often this simply entails asking good questions. When did the people get it right? When did they get it wrong? How do you describe someone who walks closely with God? How did their actions affect them and the people around them? These formational questions require more than simply assessing factual memory and recall. Obviously, each story will be different and the approach you use might need to be adjusted for different age groups, but the principle remains the same: explore and keep exploring and explore some more . . . and explore together.

TECHNIQUE 3: ENCOURAGE CHILDREN TO SHARE WHAT THEY ARE DISCOVERING ABOUT GOD

The story of Noah and his family is fascinating to kids. How did all those animals fit on the boat? Was the ark really that big? What did the lions eat? Who let the mosquitoes on board? What did Noah do with all the piles of poop? Why was God so mad at people? Did the earth have to be flooded? How did God close the door? Was Noah's family worried the rain would not stop? How did Noah know his dove would find its way back? Are today's rainbows really from God? There are so many unanswered questions in the minds of children. And yes, some questions are more directly related to God than others. Yet all of them are part of the puzzle they're putting together about who God is and what he has done.

Patiently giving kids space to encounter God is hard work. It's more efficient to quiz kids about lists of answers than to listen to their questions and thoughts as they process a story. We might be tempted to think that because they can answer the questions, they understand the answers they give. The perception of positive progress grants us immediate gratification. Sadly, many children's ministry programs move at an adult's pace when it comes to content and community. We typically focus on two immediate questions: Do kids remember what was covered? And are they getting along, sitting quietly, and paying attention?

But discipleship is far more than memorizing facts and paying attention to the teacher. In fact, when these two questions drive the conversation, a child's capacity to engage with God is actually diminished.

Why do I raise this? Because we need to grasp the fact that discipleship isn't isolated to a classroom environment where children learn facts. Deep comprehension and character formation in the way of Christ is complex. It requires a level of engagement with the heart, and hearing from the hearts of children is time-consuming work, often messy and unpredictable.

Connecting the Bible to life doesn't happen immediately. This can be frustrating to children's ministry leaders and parents as they try to keep to a schedule. So is there another way for children to discover truth about God?

What kids need is unhurried time to think. They need time to talk through the truths about God in Scripture. They need sacred space to unpack God's Word and consider their relationship with him. What does this look like? Well, it starts by building space into programming for leaders and children to develop relationships. Certainly, it involves looking at the stories and people in the Bible. It involves piecing together the attributes of God in light of his activity in the world at large. It involves thinking about the worlds they're closest to, *their* inner and outer worlds. How is God showing up in their thoughts and relationships? Where is God present in their home, school, neighborhood, and church? This kind of reflection doesn't happen in the context of fast-paced family life. *Children's ministries must slow down to cultivate sacred space.* Space to allow the Holy Spirit to speak to them and be with them as their hearts respond directly to God.

Can this happen? Yes! But we need to plan for it.

Carve out some guided time and dedicated space for leaders to share with kids about their lives and their own walks with Jesus. Make room for the kids to ask questions. Give them a chance to reflect. You may not see changes happen immediately, but over time, this kind of space cultivates wonder. The Lord's nature and presence becomes real to them, not simply because of what they read, but because Christ is in the room through the presence of the Holy Spirit. I'm not trying to be mystical here, but we need to recognize that discipleship is not just something we do by our efforts alone. It's a work of God's Spirit. Truth be told, the same Holy Spirit that works in adults is working in kids too. Relational children's ministry seeks to foster a rhythm of intentional reflection and response. For every disciple, of any age, the truth in Scripture about Christ from God is what empowers transformation.

So how do we know if this is happening with our kids? The most timeless way to find out what kids are discovering about God is to ask them, then listen to what they share through words and actions, and provide them with opportunities for various forms of creative expression.

TECHNIQUE 4: INVITE KIDS TO RESPOND TO CHRIST FOR SALVATION BY RECEIVING GOD'S FREE GIFT OF GRACE

The feeding of the five thousand is one of three miracles found in all four gospels. Most people know that a young boy donated five loaves and two fish to make this happen, something we learn from the Gospel of John. Jesus had a track record for elevating the marginalized, the poor, and the imprisoned, as well as women and children. Because Andrew saw potential in what one child could offer Christ, thousands were fed, and there were even leftovers at the end of the mass meal. Those present recognized Jesus as the promised Messiah because of this incredible experience. In turn, it provides us with a beautiful picture of an invitation for anyone to respond to Christ. You can check out John 6:1–14 for yourself to see what I mean.

Once again, we witness Jesus asking his disciples to do the impossible. He knew they could not feed all the people gathered through their own efforts. Yet that didn't stop him from giving them the responsibility. It was an invitation to learn something new about themselves and about God, to engage in an unscripted adventure with the Lord. Christ gave them the opportunity to exercise their faith in him and to receive his grace as they took him at his word. The task was impossible, of course: feed five thousand people with a child's lunch. But as they took Jesus at his word, they experienced the miraculous power of God at work. Everyone in the crowd benefited, both with the immediate blessing of food and the eternal blessing of revelation of God. All free of charge!

Now, fast-forward to Christ on the cross. On the cross, our Lord sacrificed himself for the sins of the entire world. John 3:16–17 provides the reason why: "For God so loved the world that he gave his one and only Son, that whoever believes in him shall not perish but have eternal life. For God did not send his Son into the world to condemn the world, but to save the world through him." This singular act changed everything, altering the trajectory of human history for those who choose to believe it. The life, death, and resurrection of Christ culminate as God's ultimate gift to his creation.[13]

Why do I share these two stories? Because in sharing about the loaves and the fish, we need to point children (and adults) to the greater gift that Jesus provides for us. Every story in the Bible is, in some way, an opportunity to showcase the wonderful love of God through the gift of his Son, Jesus. Through Old Testament stories and the miracles of Jesus in the gospels, we need to look beyond the moral of the lesson itself to the bigger picture of the Savior who came to save us from our sin. Every story provides an opportunity to respond to Jesus' compelling invitation to follow him as forgiver and leader, as Savior and Lord. The gospel is the message that drives all discipleship.

Relational children's ministries are committed to continually sharing the gospel of Jesus Christ with clarity and urgency in a relevant way. This means we need to be clear about what it means to trust and follow Jesus, and we need to look for creative ways to communicate this meaningfully with words and actions to kids and families. Some stories will show the destructive power of human sin and the failure of God's people, pointing us to our need for a savior. Others will highlight the love of God in meeting our needs, pointing us to the amazing and undeserved grace that God shows us in Jesus. Use the Bible to showcase the work of God, and then connect it to your life and the life of the children in your ministry. Each church and team of kid-influencers will need to determine its own distinct approach based on biblical perspectives, doctrinal convictions, and ministry practices. But regardless of the setting, an invitational posture that is both purposeful and pressure-free will be the difference maker in discipleship.

TECHNIQUE 5: FIND CREATIVE WAYS TO CELEBRATE MILESTONES WHILE WALKING WITH GOD

One of the highlights of any discipleship ministry is baptism. My home church is privileged to have a small body of water on its property. We celebrate baptism indoors throughout the year, but each June the entire church heads out to the lake for one incredible Sunday afternoon. Families and friends gather on the lawn with folding chairs, picnic blankets, and coolers full of food and beverage to cheer for and celebrate with individuals who have decided to publicly declare faith in Christ. It's a beautiful external display of internal transformation by the Holy Spirit. The family of God gathers in full view of a watching world to say, "Jesus Christ is worthy to be followed and worshipped. He alone is Savior and Lord."

My oldest son Avery decided to be baptized in the church lake when he was twelve years old. I was in the room the day he was born. I sobbed as he squeezed my fingers when he got his first immunization shots. I sat on the edge of my seat waiting to see if his children's ministry check-in number would come up on the screen the first time he was in the nursery. I proudly participated in his baby dedication in the presence of family and friends. I sat across from him when he ate his first whole cheeseburger from McDonald's. I took him to his first day of preschool and kindergarten (and every first day of school up through high school). I sat on the floor with him when he decided to trust and follow Christ in second grade. I remember the satisfied look on his face when I presented him with his first pocketknife at father-son camp after third grade. I was in the canoe when he caught his first largemouth bass. And I walked into the water with him when he asked me to baptize him in sixth grade. Every one of these "firsts" represents a transition between life chapters, milestones along Avery's journey of life and faith that I have been privileged to experience.

First steps are memorable. They mark transitions in life, times we can look back to and remember as significant steps toward growth. I could go on and on about all the discipleship "firsts" I have witnessed in each of my sons' lives as well as those of extended family and friends. Thirty-plus years as a Christ-follower and over fifteen years in pastoral ministry add up quickly.

Being with people as they take the step of baptism is wonderful, but baptism is not the only milestone to be celebrated while walking with God. Rites of passage present themselves across the spectrum of child and faith development. Birthdays and anniversaries are optimal times for celebrating significant moments. The church calendar, particularly Advent and Lent, positions holidays in a new light for kids and families. Serving opportunities and leadership roles equip disciples in ways that recognize age, spiritual gifting, skill level, and maturity. Within the family of God, there are so many opportunities to find creative ways to celebrate milestones while walking with him. I love that discipleship first steps are one part of a series that demonstrates movement with and toward God. And I love that each church, children's ministry, and family has the opportunity to figure out what will work best in its unique setting. Relational children's ministry, wherever it is found, is committed to bringing meaning to the significant steps along a child's spiritual journey.[14]

NOW IS THE TIME TO INVITE KIDS INTO A FAITH JOURNEY AS FOLLOWERS OF JESUS

> **People were also bringing babies and small children to Jesus for him to place his hands on them. When the disciples saw this, they rebuked them. But Jesus called the children to him and said, "Let the little children come to me, and do not hinder them, for the kingdom of God belongs to such as these. Truly I tell you, anyone who will not receive the kingdom of God like a little child will never enter it."**
>
> *Luke 18:15–17*

Jesus was inherently invitational. His person and presence drew in people of all ages and backgrounds. When Christ found Himself surrounded by children, he welcomed them with open arms. The way I see it, he established relational children's ministry once and for all. And when the disciples objected, Jesus challenged them to recalibrate their perspective, making it clear that their thinking was not aligned with the kingdom of God. Jesus had harsh words for anyone who would lead children astray, and he called out childlike faith as a model for people of all ages. The disciples didn't always understand, but Jesus was showing them how to follow him in humility and dependence, not pride, and how to invite and lead others to do the same.

> . . . Those who believed were expected to follow him [Jesus]. One did not have to know very much to take the first step, but he had to be willing to learn; that is, to become his disciple.
>
> **Robert E. Coleman[15]**

Discipleship requires long-term development. It takes time to intentionally pursue relationships with children and their families. Disciple making therefore happens cumulatively, over days, months, and years. And it's more than just meetings and big events; it happens moment by moment. Responding to Jesus when he says "follow me" is both a one-time *and* an ongoing decision. Children decide to trust Christ as their Savior and Lord, and as godly character transformation takes place, the results impact other people as well.

Mindful kid-influencers quickly recognize they're on the same faith-guided discipleship adventure as the children they serve. As they reflect on their own life experiences, they realize that their discipleship process is not formula-driven. Teaching the children through living life with God—that is itself the curriculum. As with anything, we utilize resources—Bible studies, videos, books, sermons—to support and enhance all of this. But the real learning happens in those moments of stress when we depend on God to provide. We grow when a child asks a question and we turn them toward Jesus, not packaged answers or rote responses. And growth happens in kids as they respond to the invitation to apply the gospel directly to their life situation. As kid-influencers engage with kids through talking, exploring, sharing, responding, and celebrating, disciple makers join with God in creating a divine discipleship curriculum.

QUESTIONS FOR REFLECTION & DISCUSSION

1. Who is a kid-influencer you deeply respect, and why? How has God uniquely gifted them to come alongside children as a disciple maker?

2. As you consider your own discipleship journey with Christ, what aspect is most notably "unscripted"?

3. How do you typically respond to unpredictable scenarios personally? In relationships? In ministry?

4. Why do you think it's hard for people to admit that discipleship is more about faith than formulas? What role, if any, do steps and stages play in faith formation?

5. What holds parents, teachers, leaders, and coaches back from letting go of "the script" to know, love, and serve kids?

6. Is there a tool or technique that is not perceived as "cool" but you know captures the minds and hearts of children? Explain.

7. Of the five techniques (talking, exploring, sharing, responding, celebrating), which one are you most comfortable engaging in, and why? Which one is a stretch for your personality or experience? What is a step you can take to grow in this area?

8. What is a natural way God has given you to draw kids into an unscripted adventure with him?

9. How have you grown in emulating a "follow me" approach to discipleship in the way of Jesus?

CHAPTER 6

INVITATION 2: WRESTLE WITH MESSY FAITH TOGETHER

The greatest gift you can give your children is to let them see you struggle and wrestle with how to live a lifetime of trust in God.

Kara Powell[1]

Just as a nursing mother cares for her children, so we cared for you. Because we loved you so much, we were delighted to share with you not only the gospel of God but our lives as well.

1 Thessalonians 2:7b-8

©7Michael/www.istock.com

IN MY FAMILY, we don't overplan our vacations. We might schedule a few activities or somewhere to go, but we don't fill in the details. There is a reason why we do it this way. Though we sometimes entertain the idea of treating our sons to a dream getaway, we prefer to keep things down to earth (well, except for that one time we went to Disneyland). We like day trips and road trips, soaking in everything around us. We like to explore, to find our way to nearby parks and places to swim. We check out local festivals, farmers' markets, museums, and movie theaters. I suppose there will come a day when we save up and live it up, but for now we prefer to keep it simple, to spend our vacations resting and replenishing our bodies and souls.

In the same way we bring our suitcases (filled with the same old clothes) on these trips, we bring our daily lives—our character, personality, interests, and relationships—with us wherever we go. Being together is what matters most. We enjoy just being ourselves around one another. Through thick and thin, Kate, Avery, Aaron, and I are committed to deepening our roots with God and one another in these ordinary, everyday moments of life.

During one of our family vacations about ten years ago, I dragged my family into the woods for a mid-morning hike. We were visiting family in northern California and it was my turn to pick a day trip destination. The giant Sequoias are world renowned for their magnificent height and resilience, often reaching 200–300 feet into the sky. That is the equivalent of a 20-story building! For over 2,000 years, a towering forest of redwood trees has lined this portion of the Pacific Northwest. The size of the trees is difficult to describe, so I really wanted my family to experience these natural giants face to face. Everyone else was disappointed that we were skipping the beach, so I promised ice cream for lunch. Sometimes you just have to do whatever it takes to give your family life-changing experiences and growth opportunities.

As we made our way through the winding roads of the Santa Cruz Mountains, stomachs started getting queasy, boredom set in, and everyone began growing impatient. The only person who seemed excited about the visit to the forest was me. When we arrived in the parking lot, everyone jumped out as if we had resurfaced from a submarine after months at sea. I confess I almost lost it when my oldest called me aside and asked, "Can we go to the beach now?" By God's grace, I kept my cool and after one last stop at the restrooms, the water fountain, the nature center, the gift shop, the water fountain, and the restrooms again, we were on our way down the trail into the forest. Sharing life together can be surprisingly unexpected and predictable all at the same time.

We finally arrived at a place called the Grove at Henry Cowell Redwoods State Park and I felt vindicated in my desire to show my family the forest. To put it simply, my family was in awe. They stood there, dumbfounded. None of them could believe what we were seeing: sequoia trunks in excess of six feet in diameter! As we gazed upward into the sky, we imagined what it would be like to climb all the way to the top. We were surprised that something so tall would not just topple over in the wind. We wondered how God had made these giants so strong. What was it that made these particular trees stand out from the rest, with their amazing height and enormous trunks?

We explored the forest that day: walking, talking, climbing, and learning every step of the way. Did you know that the growth rate of redwoods actually increases over time? Or that they live for hundreds of years, withstanding the natural impact of erosion, earthquakes, storms, and even direct strikes by lightning? On our expedition, we stood inside a hollow, flame-charred redwood trunk and discovered that the external bark is impervious to fire.

While there was much to be seen above the ground, what lies below the forest floor was particularly interesting. Redwood forests are made up of individual trees, but they are all interconnected with one another. The trees have a surprisingly shallow root system for support, yet they are able to find additional strength in their numbers, sprouting close to one another and leveraging the root systems of their neighbors. Redwoods grow in groves, families of trees, holding each other up as their roots become inseparably intertwined.

What did my family and I conclude that day? We were impressed that the mighty redwood has withstood the test of time for a reason. Like us, redwoods are created to thrive through thick and thin *together*.

After reflecting on this amazing truth, we celebrated with ice cream for lunch, as promised.

GROWTH IS MESSY

The imagery of redwood trees is a beautiful parallel to our spiritual life in community together. I've learned redwood forests are naturally disorganized. What I mean is, it's nearly impossible to map out their root systems. The growth rings in their massive trunks reveal record seasons of flourishing development and stunting malnourishment, periods of rain and drought, and even scarring by axe blade and flame. While each season of their lives is uncharted and unseen, there is still an inherent purpose and order to how their sustainable growth takes place. Redwoods depend on the surrounding trees for their nourishment and strength. They cooperate with the sun and soil, the water and nutrients, to become who God created them to be. Their durability is a gift from God, but it depends upon them relying on the other trees to survive the difficult and challenging seasons. Weathering unscheduled wind, fire, rain, snow, and drought, redwood trees band together to successfully make it through times of stress.

I can relate to this. As I shared earlier, my childhood family life was far from perfect. Like many kids, I stumbled through awkward circumstances and made foolish choices. The adults in my life made mistakes along the way too. By God's grace, they owned up to their failings and surrounded me with sincere truth and love. Looking back, I can see I was never alone in my journey of faith. Closely rooted together with my biological and spiritual family and friends, I learned to walk with God in community. Even my unbelieving relatives gave me space to wrestle with what it means to walk with God. The Lord ensured loving people embraced me and showed me how to follow Jesus in everyday settings. There was a natural ebb and flow between my home and church life. Both worlds were imperfect, but God's perfect love was evident everywhere. I was mindful of the different environments, but as a child I made no distinction between them as separate relational spheres.

> If your child's sense of destiny is centered in himself and dependent on his own efforts and giftedness, then things out of his control can demolish it. But if his sense of destiny is centered in God's calling and dependent on God's sovereignty, then even very difficult things outside his control can strengthen it.
>
> **Larry Fowler[2]**

Discipleship is about becoming in every way like Jesus, and to do this we must belong to the *family* of God. Disciple making doesn't happen as a result of isolated individuals having quiet times by themselves. It's the process of reproduction and transformation that happens as our lives intersect with the lives of others following God. The formation of God-honoring attitudes, convictions, practices, and relationships takes place privately, but it is also public and frequently haphazard. When you throw kids into the mix, it gets even messier. But this does not mean *all* purpose and order are absent from the process. Where our human families fall short and seem to be a mess of mistakes and failures, the larger body of Christ comes together in unity as the family of God. We find our connection in Jesus, who brings us together with all of our mess and uses this process to teach us, disciple us, and help us to grow to be more like him.

Relational children's ministry takes its cue from Jesus' words to his faithful community of followers in this passage:

Remain in me, as I also remain in you. No branch can bear fruit by itself; it must remain in the vine. Neither can you bear fruit unless you remain in me. I am the vine; you are the branches. If you remain in me and I in you, you will bear much fruit; apart from me you can do nothing. (John 15:4–5)

God's favor cannot be earned, and genuine growth cannot be fabricated. Transformation happens supernaturally, deep inside us, before it works its way out into the world as fruit borne by the work of God's Spirit. Often, we are tempted to look for immediate fruit, but Jesus reminds us that abiding in relationship with God and his people is the essential first step to growth. *True discipleship in Christ is transparent but not always immediately obvious.* We must not rush the process, as much more is happening deep inside than we can readily see. The Holy Spirit is at work everywhere, and children need adults in their lives who see this and provide grace and direction for them as they walk with God daily.

> Children's ministry is less about providing children with absolute answers and more about helping them live faithfully with questions and doubts that arise on the journey of discipleship.
>
> **David M. Csinos & Ivy Beckwith**[3]

ADOPTED BY SPIRITUAL GIANTS

When I ask my mom what she misses most about living on the West Coast, she almost always says to me "the mountains and Mama Claire." I'm not surprised by her answer. Claire was the woman God placed in charge of the daycare center where I first decided to trust and follow Christ. Claire patiently loved my mother through her emotional pain, her long-standing anger at God and people, and the intellectual barriers that kept her from trusting in Jesus for eternal life. Claire was the one who fought for the startup children's ministry at the church to stay open when others tried to close it. For my mother, Claire was more than an afterschool program superintendent. Claire and her husband Chuck became spiritual grandparents to our family. These two godly people demonstrated the love of Christ as disciples of Jesus and as disciple makers on his behalf by adopting my mom and me into their family and introducing us to the church community.[4]

Claire always parked her car in the same spot outside the church building, so I could always tell when she was at the Oak Tree office. As strange as it might sound, this was a sign of stability for me as a child. On the weekends, life was a shuffle from one activity to the next, but five afternoons a week I knew exactly where to be and when. Claire made sure the ministry to the kids was staffed well. She modeled the character traits and actions she expected of her leaders. Her consistent presence was as important as the caring community environment she created.

> Children try to understand not only what is happening to them, but why; and in doing that, they call upon the religious life they have experienced, the spiritual values they have received, as well as other sources of potential explanation.
>
> **Robert Coles[5]**

After my dad started rehab for alcoholism and eventually remarried, my mom and I moved to a new town, and I switched schools. We experienced a significant amount of family upheaval on all fronts. I felt caught in the middle, and in many ways I was. It was increasingly difficult for me to be myself wherever I went. The people in charge, rules to follow, expectations to live up to, markers of success; all of it was constantly changing. For the most part I was able to keep my head above water by using humor and compliance to fit in. But when I started struggling in school, I felt like I was losing control of my life. I started cheating, lying, and manipulating to make the grade. I coped by stuffing my emotions and keeping secrets. I began shoplifting, and fortunately I was caught (and forgiven). The Lord placed people in my life who spoke into my situation and cared for my soul. Chuck and Claire were two of the most important, and I will never forget how God used them in that tough season.

What was our relationship with them like? We informally shared meals, in homes and restaurants. We exchanged gifts at birthdays and holidays. We headed to the park or the beach for the day. We played board games and watched silly movies together. I remember singing with them at church services and cleaning up together after potlucks in the fellowship hall. We regularly prayed together. Many times my mom and I found refuge in Chuck and Claire's living room, where we talked through the highs and lows of family life and following Jesus. They were always just a phone call away and within reach when we needed their broad shoulders for support. We felt as much like their child and grandchild as if they were our biological family.

> Parents and ministry leaders can so easily succumb to manipulating kids into good behavior and forgetting what really fosters faith: a relationship with God.
>
> **Michelle Anthony[6]**

Why do I share this? Because children of all ages need an extended community that welcomes and embraces them. Biological families can meet many of these needs, but the blessing of the church is that God provides things that are lacking in our families through the diversity of the body of Christ. We find sacred spaces to meet with God in the company of others.

Exodus 33:7–11 beautifully depicts the face-to-face friendship between the Lord and Moses as experienced in the Tent of Meeting. I love that the passage ends with mention of Joshua, as a child, remaining behind after Moses left. Moses was a spiritual father to Joshua. He adopted him and brought him into his own "messy faith" experience of being with God in a sacred space.

Likewise, Chuck and Claire created sacred space for my mother and me to meet with God at church, in their home, and anywhere we were blessed to share life together. Chuck and Claire sacrificed themselves, investing time, energy, and resources like any loving family member would to positively impact our lives. There was never a question that was off limits. I could be real and raise messy faith issues with them, knowing they would listen and give me thoughtful responses.

Several years ago Chuck went home to be with the Lord. In preparation for writing this book, I made a stop at the church to see if Claire was still at the day care. There was her car, parked in the same spot, as it had been for the past thirty-one years. School was out for summer, but there was much preparation to be done as the day care ended one season and got ready for the next. It turned out to be the week of Claire's retirement. I told her about this book, including some of the stories I share here, and she reminisced with me. She reminded me how much we had endured early on and what a joy it was for her to be a part of our discipleship adventure. As always, she spoke words of strength and courage into me for the road ahead. What a remarkable legacy this woman of God has left behind.

MAKING ROOM FOR RELATIONAL ROOTS

This type of legacy is what God desires for every kid-influencer and children's ministry leader. In this information era where we are told content is king, it turns out relationship still trumps all. That's not to say creeds, doctrines, and statements of faith aren't necessary or important. They are absolutely necessary! Yet Holy Spirit-guided learning centered in Christ always happens in relationship, both with God and others. The context of community is what leads to deeply rooted life-change that goes beyond memorized facts. Even our expression of worship is relational, as is Scripture reading and reflection, prayer, evangelism, giving, serving, and fellowship. Children, in close company with peers and adults, must encounter multifaceted dimensions and applications of faith for it to take root and bear fruit. We must wrestle with and work out our faith together.

Theologian and educator John Westerhoff rightly reminds disciple makers: "No one can determine another's faith and no one can give another faith, but we can be faithful and share our life and our faith with one another."[7] Jesus' approach to discipleship paved a way for relational roots by modeling a "come to me" relationship over an "obey me because you have to" scenario. Loving obedience is a natural response to being in loving relationship with Christ. To effectively work with children, Catherine Stonehouse reminds us: "Children are born with readiness for faith but need an environment of mutual love, care, and interaction for the faith potential to become reality."[8] Kids need to experience unconditional love and acceptance. Children are in the process of identity formation, and providing a safe, supportive, and sacred space where adults foster unmerited belonging is crucial.

This process of formation happens simultaneously in the lives of adults and children, often beneath the surface. Children will show up in one relational sphere but carry with them baggage from multiple settings. Kid-influencers do not know for sure what is happening inside the minds and hearts of children, but the power of relationship creates bonds that begin to open up the world within. How does this happen? How can you help this happen in your own life and ministry? By tapping into the power contained in three relational roots: presence, humility, and empathy.

THE POWER OF PRESENCE, HUMILITY, AND EMPATHY

One morning a week I take my teenage son Aaron out for breakfast before school. I know Aaron cherishes his scheduled time with me because he tells me so nearly every week. We have been doing this for years. Most days he sets his alarm, bounces out of bed, gets ready, and waits on the couch near the front door until it's time to leave. Okay, he actually only did this once. What usually happens is much less linear, but the outcome is the same.

My older son Avery prefers to sleep in, so now that he is in high school we get together at a different time during the week. Since I already get up early to take him to school, I'm glad he is cool with this alternate arrangement.

In our family, breakfasts with dad are about one-on-one, face-to-face time. There is no hidden agenda, and there are no off-limit topics. No pressure to perform. No promise of solutions. Just time together talking about whatever comes up. We discuss friends, money, faith, school, video games, family, music, dating, sports, work, and whatever else falls under the general category of life. We spend time together (presence), we stand before God and each other with equal footing (humility), and we learn to experience a life with him by understanding each other's perspective (empathy).

Lately Aaron has started asking big questions about his life with God. He articulates it this way: "Is having a relationship with God real? Is following Christ worth it?" These two driving questions surfaced in him after several years of wrestling with various circumstances in his life. This isn't the first time Aaron has told me he wants a deep relationship with God like the one he sees in his parents and his youth pastor. Something inside my son is longing to know his Creator. It has taken us years to have the kind of relationship where he is willing to open up about these questions and struggles with me. For several weeks now, we have spent time reading and reflecting on the book of 1 John. I was amazed when Aaron texted me his detailed notes and questions after reading it on his own first. His engagement with God's Word shows me he is serious about this. Aaron is really thinking about his relationship with God and not just giving me the pat answers he thinks I want to hear.

> We see faith in fresh ways when we invite children to process their experiences with us, and we experience grace as God ministers to us through them.
>
> **Scottie May**[9]

As we study and apply God's Word together, I'll admit I'm a bit scared. What if I don't know the answers to his questions? What if I get frustrated and turn him off? How will these breakfasts impact his lifelong faith trajectory? Am I qualified to disciple my own son? Am I doing it right? It's amazing how many questions run through my mind as I sit across from him. But we just take it one verse and one question at a time. Most of the time I follow up his questions with another question, or I let him answer his own questions first. Sometimes we make progress and sometimes we go off on tangents or talk in circles, yet I am prayerful and confident that all movement is ultimately heading us in the direction of Christ. To help me battle some of my fears, I regularly utilize three sincere expressions in my relationship with Aaron. I offer these to you as tools for children's ministry, tools that will empower you to nurture community with kids, parents, and leaders.

The relational roots of *presence*, *humility*, and *empathy* grow strong when kid-influencers leverage the power of three simple phrases:

"I'm here."

"I don't know."

"We're in this together."

THE POWER OF PRESENCE: "I'M HERE."

One of the greatest gifts I received from Chuck and Claire, and one I am trying to pass along to my own kids and others, is the gift of being fully present. Being fully present doesn't mean you make everything you do about the child. It's not making them the center of attention 24/7. It simply means being fully engaged with and *accessible* to children (or anyone, for that matter). My sons can tell when my mind is wandering or locked on other pressing matters. It's obvious when I'm using my cell phone instead of paying attention to what or who is right in front of me. And while there are times when we need to focus on certain tasks, we also need to give children our full attention when they need it, especially when we have signed up or volunteered to give it!

Part of what drew people to Jesus when he said, "Come to me," was the fact that he was fully present with them. You knew that when he asked you a question or spoke with you, he wasn't distracted by something else. You could tell by the tone of his voice, by the way he spoke, that you were the focus of his attention. I love how Mary recognized her risen Savior in the garden simply because he called her by name (John 20:15–16). Learning to say "I'm here" and truly mean it is a powerful relational root in discipleship.

According to Chap Clark, "We are a culture that has forgotten how to be together. We have lost the ability to spend unstructured down time."[10] We are so accustomed to having every aspect of our lives scheduled that we can have difficulty letting go of our plans and responsibilities in order to allow life to unfold naturally. There are times when you might need to scrap your plans and focus on what God is doing at that moment through a child's life. Disciple making is both formal and informal in nature.

Catherine Stonehouse hits the mark when she says, "Foundations of faith are being laid through everyday interactions of children and adults."[11] Much of what is passed on from one generation to the next is not always planned. Beliefs and behaviors can be adopted simply as a result of experience rather than what gets properly seeded in the soul. Children begin to open up and thrive when they are in relational environments where peers and adults communicate: "I'm here," and "It's okay to be yourself." A sense of true belonging is strengthened when physical and emotional safety is upheld. This plays out anywhere children are involved: children's ministries, extracurricular sports, family counseling, and peer support groups, just to name a few.

Relational children's ministries do whatever it takes to nurture the power of presence between kid-influencers and kids. They work hard to keep child-to-leader ratios low, shooting far below maximum capacity. They press to have consistent teachers and leaders so that children can grow in trusting the spiritual models and mentors in their lives. Contrast this with public education. Most school classrooms are too largely scaled for the kind of one-on-one interactions needed between adults and children, or even children and their peers. It can be difficult for children to feel a close relationship with a teacher, especially if that person changes frequently. Since most parents are removed from the equation in public education, the church community carries a significant opportunity to invest in well-rounded faith formation that helps children look at their lives across multiple relational worlds and worldviews.

The work of disciple making happens as two or more disciples spend significant amounts of quality time in close proximity. Children are best served when it's evident to them that multiple kid-influencers are committed to being a positive presence in their daily lives. This requires regular eye contact for maximum heart-to-heart impact. It gives them a sense of security and stability. It helps them make sense of the many worlds and worldviews that surround them. They gain a tangible sense of God's presence. Relational children's ministries leverage the power of presence by designing programs and community with this intention. And kid-influencers become lifelong disciple makers when they step up to be fully present.

THE POWER OF HUMILITY: "I DON'T KNOW."

Have you ever been asked a question about your faith or your beliefs, and you didn't know the answer? Or you weren't sure what to say? People tend to freeze up when it comes to talking about matters of faith. What would you say to your neighbor if he asked you what Jesus taught about divorce and remarriage? You might not know what to say. Or even if you have an idea, you might worry that it will be rejected. Honestly, if you aren't sure of your answer or how to communicate it best, you can often just simply say to the person: "I don't know." There is nothing wrong with admitting this. I can't tell you how many times I have watched kid-influencers sit paralyzed in fear because the provided curriculum didn't include answers to the real questions coming from kids' mouths. "I don't know," is an admission that you don't have every answer, and it can be a humbling experience.

Here are some questions that are difficult to answer, and which might require further study or thought before giving an answer. In other words, you can say "I don't know" if a child asks you one of these: *Why is God so angry in the Old Testament? Who did Cain marry? How did Jesus heal the lepers? Is it possible to believe in both creation and evolution? If we walk around the school and blow trumpets, will the walls fall in? Why doesn't God answer all my prayers? What's the point of going to church? How do I stop being so angry with my mom? Is Satan real? Do I have a guardian angel? Does everyone go to heaven? If not, why?*

I know it's tempting to answer questions with quick answers or to redirect the conversation. Catherine Stonehouse reminds us why we need to be intentional in our responses instead: "Over time, our responsiveness to common questions prepares the way for children to trust us with troubling questions."[12] If you didn't catch this, reread it. Let Stonehouse's statement sink in. When you and I are able to look a child in the eye, call them by name, and dignify their sincere questions with truth, not speculative or trite answers, humility shines through and helps unlock the door of their heart. Create a "Come to me" community by saying "I don't know." This communicates to kids, "It's okay to ask tough questions."

> Never give a child an answer of which you are unsure. If the child raises a question with which you are still struggling, be honest.
>
> **Catherine Stonehouse**[13]

God invites us to be present, not perfect, in each other's lives. James 5:16 says we are to confess our sins and pray with one another. Now, I'm not suggesting kid-influencers lead groups of kids through a slideshow of all their secret sins or host a mass confession before diving into a Bible story together. I simply want to point out that Christian community is based on honest acknowledgment of our flaws and failures. We are united together by our common need for the grace God provides in Jesus. This means as adults, we cannot perpetuate a façade of perfection with the children we minister to. Kids know when people are being real or fake. They need to hear that everyone makes mistakes and to see how a follower of Christ responds to failure and sin.

It's incredibly powerful when children see adults humbly admitting they have made mistakes, showing kids their own need for the gospel of grace.

Humility is a sign of maturity. Kid-influencers can have a lasting impact discipling kids by just saying "I don't know" when they don't know the answer. Instead of presenting ourselves as models of perfection with all the answers, we demonstrate our common need for the gospel by walking with children in a way that is honest and real. Children have questions, and their hurts either hang on their sleeves or get stuffed away. Any wounds that are hidden deep in their hearts need a safe place and a safe person in order to come out into the light.

At the heart of relational children's ministry is a commitment to a community of truth and grace. Kids long for someone to come alongside them, to see the world they see, to walk side by side with them, to wrestle with their deepest questions, to hear their fears and frustrations, and to show them how to be with God every step of the way. Finding people who are willing to grow as adult disciples in the presence of kids is one key to success. Most children's ministry leaders have been trained in a model where their primary job is to teach kids the Bible. But that vision, as I hope you are seeing, falls short of what is needed to disciple kids into devoted followers of Christ. Relational discipleship in children's ministry means we must all walk humbly with God. As we come to know, love, and serve Christ together, "I don't know" becomes easier to admit even if it's still hard to say.

THE POWER OF EMPATHY: "WE'RE IN THIS TOGETHER."

I tend to get sympathy and empathy mixed up. Both words have to do with relationships and emotions, but they speak to differing levels of compassion. Sympathy is when you have compassion for someone, but you don't necessarily feel their feelings as your own. If someone you know has experienced loss, you may feel a sense of regret or sadness for them, but you don't experience the loss with them. Showing sympathy for someone is a sign that we care for them and we acknowledge that what they're going through is difficult or challenging. Sympathy is a broader term that indicates a general sense of agreement with a person in their experience.

Empathy refers to a deeper level of compassion. It involves stepping into what another person is going through and experiencing their feelings and emotions, identifying with them at a deeper heart level. It's putting yourself in the shoes of another or identifying with their experience because you have been there yourself. For example, when I lead teams overseas, I'm able to predict the kinds of thoughts and emotions of first-time international travelers because I myself was once a first-time international traveler. When luggage gets lost or sickness sets in, I can honestly say, "I feel your pain." While my perspective may not be exactly the same, I can empathize with their experience of culture shock and feel the same frustration and depression they feel being away from home.

Have you ever thought (as I know many kids do), "How can Jesus relate to me?" "Was he ever tempted to eat too much ice cream?" "Did Jesus ever want to cheat on a test at school?" "He never drove a car; does he realize what it's like out there?" The Bible tells us that all throughout his life, Jesus faced temptation. The opportunity to turn his back on God and the people he came to save and serve was around every corner. In Luke 4:1–13, we read that Jesus was tempted for forty days during his time in the wilderness. And while it's true there are modern scenarios Jesus never faced, the nature of the temptations he faced were universal appeals to the desire of the heart: pride, greed, lust, rage, etc. Hebrews 4:15 tells us Jesus experienced temptation *in every way* we do without falling into sin: "For we do not have a high priest who is unable to empathize with our weaknesses, but we have one who has been tempted in every way, just as we are—yet he did not sin." Christ remained free of sin even though he had opportunities to pursue disobedience to God. Why do I bring this up? Because kid-influencers who understand their own struggles with sin and the reality of life in this broken world can share their experiences and *empathize* with the children they disciple.

Statistically speaking, I know I wasn't the only kid to experience the life-disrupting realities of divorce and remarriage. I wasn't the only one to have parents, grandparents, aunts, and uncles who struggled with alcohol and drug abuse. I'm not the only follower of Christ who, as an adult, has a robust story of transformation to share with the generations of believers who surround me. When I speak to children, I try to leverage the power of empathy by talking about my painful past and how God has brought healing and grace into my life today. It's a gift to look into the tear-stained eyes of a child as an adult and enter into their pain (whether you have experienced the same struggles or not), and honestly say, "We're in this together. I'm not going anywhere." And it's a gift to pull together a cluster of children who can open up and honestly share their struggles and challenges and joys together.

The truth about faith is that it's messy for people of all ages, infant through adult. Relational children's ministry finds ways to help kids, parents, and church leaders discover "It's okay to lean on each other"—through personal pain, relational dysfunction, physical trauma, emotional hurts, sinful choices, and the effects of other people's shortcomings. We need to recover the power of intergenerational ministry that deploys empathy in relationships. We demonstrate true empathy when our presence and humility converge before a child who is inquiring, hurting, wondering, hoping, fumbling, celebrating, sharing, or doubting. Kid-influencers who are adept at empathy can increase disciple making in a community of faith.

Wrestling with messy faith isn't easy, but it's always worth the struggle. One of the most powerful ways I encountered presence, humility, and empathy as a child was when Claire would walk with me to the phone in the hallway at church on Sunday mornings. I desperately wanted my dad to experience what my mom and I had found through a relationship with Jesus. There were many different feelings and motivations in my desire to reach out to him. I wondered what eternity would be like for him apart from Christ. From time to time I would muster the courage to call my father and invite him to church. Claire and other adults in the ministry stood with me, loving me through my disappointment and discouragement. There were no easy answers, and I wasn't looking for someone to offer me any. I just needed someone to be with me, to be honest about the way things were and to walk with me in my sadness. I am grateful to have a strong relationship with my dad today, and I respect the spiritual journey he is still on. I'm grateful other adults in my life helped me navigate those difficult emotions with the relational roots of presence, humility, and empathy. I was blessed to be in a "Come to me" community of faith where regular eye contact led to heart-to-heart impact. The discipleship trajectory of my life was forever changed by that experience.

With some work, the same can be true for you and your children's ministry. You and the leaders who serve with you can find ways to discuss what's really going on in the lives of kids and families being served. Offer training for your volunteers to give them opportunities to practice using the three phrases with each other. Examine your current curriculum to determine if there's margin built in for real dialogue or if too much is already packed in. When you start making space for eyes and hearts to lock, you will see the relationships between children and families and leaders in a whole new light.

NOW IS THE TIME TO BE HONEST ABOUT THE NATURE OF SPIRITUAL GROWTH

Life with God isn't linear, and it's not a journey we should travel alone. Being willing to pursue a personal relationship with God is commendable. Choosing to invest in the lives of children along the way is remarkable.

> The spiritual life of the child is forming at a deep level. Healthy personality development prepares children for openness to God, whereas developmental dysfunction creates barriers to a life of trusting, growing faith. To not be concerned about spiritual formation during childhood is to ignore the very foundations of the spiritual life.
>
> **Catherine Stonehouse**[14]

I seriously doubt you would be this far along in this book if you didn't believe in the importance of personally following Christ and of relational children's ministry. As we've seen, there is a myth that creating a system of rules and regulations will align a person's discipleship trajectory toward God. This, of course, does not work. Discipleship is more than memorized facts or following a programmed process. It's a matter of heart transformation. To address the messy and unpredictable questions and motives of the heart, we must make room to wrestle, to be flexible, to change our plans and perspective when needed.

Christ calls out to each of us, bidding us, "Come to me." We must clear the way for relational roots to take hold in whatever context we find ourselves, with whatever curriculum or program we offer, and with whomever the Lord places in our communities. Kid-influencers can become lifelong disciple makers by practicing presence, humility, and empathy. Like faith in Christ and life with God, tackling this in relational children's ministries will be messy but totally worth it.

QUESTIONS FOR REFLECTION & DISCUSSION

1. Describe the messiest experience you have ever had. Did you feel the same or differently after what happened?

2. What metaphor would you use to describe spiritual growth in relationship with God and others? Explain.

3. In what way(s) is discipleship more about relationship than regulations?

4. What is one significant way the Lord used the body of Christ to help and heal you?

5. Who is someone you consider to be a "spiritual giant" in your life and why?

6. How does it feel to realize you have a seen and unseen discipleship impact on children, families, and peers? Explain.

7. What is the difference between beliefs and behaviors versus attitudes and convictions?

8. Describe someone in your life who demonstrates the power of presence, humility, or empathy.

9. Which is hardest for you to say in the presence of kids? Which one is the Lord leading you to grow in this year and why?
   "I don't know."
   "I'm here."
   "We're in this together."

10. How have you learned personally that spiritual growth is messy, not linear?

11. What can you do to carve out space for kids and parents you know to wrestle with the true nature of faith together?

CHAPTER 7

INVITATION 3: BUILD UNCONVENTIONAL COMMUNITY WITH FAMILIES

It takes a whole village to raise a child.
African Proverb

"Who are my mother and my brothers?" he asked. Then
he looked at those seated in a circle around him and
said, "Here are my mother and my brothers! Whoever
does God's will is my brother and sister and mother."
Mark 3:33–35

©CoffmanCMU/www.istock.com

IN 1960, P. D. EASTMAN penned a classic children's book: *Are You My Mother?*
The plot is quite simple. Baby bird falls out of nest. Baby bird goes on a
quest. Baby bird discovers finding home is hard. Baby bird gets reunited
with mom.

While this beloved tale is far from epic, it speaks the heart language of
family and eternity. It's a story of creation, fall, and redemption. And in
this, it touches upon the grand narrative laid out in God's Word that gives
us insight into our history and God's relationship with his creation. We read
of God's desire to be in intimate community with the people he creates. We
read of our tragic fall into sin and rebellion against our Creator. We see how
our sin and the resulting separation from God and one another breaks the
bonds of community at the deepest level. Like that tiny baby bird, all men,
women, and children find themselves fallen from the nest, far from home,
and longing for a place of safety, where all is right in the world.

Spiritually lost people have this longing in their heart, whether they recognize it as such or not. They search and search, asking, *Is this my real home?* They ask and ask: *Are you my perfect parent? Can you give me what I need?* People at every age and stage of life go to great lengths, even destructive ones, to fill their soul's deepest desires. As disciples of Jesus, we know the answer they seek is found only in relationship with Christ and our adoption into the family of God.

> For a person to be truly discipled and growing in their faith, they need more than one person discipling them.
>
> **Francis Chan[1]**

The church has a profound opportunity to engage children and adults like no one else. Its role in offering guidance and direction as they are on this spiritual quest is unparalleled. But the opportunity involves more than providing an answer to a question. In an era when families are frenzied and fractured, the body of Christ offers unconventional community modeled on the relational principles and teachings of Jesus and his disciples. Cultivating this type of community will not be easy; it will take courage and creativity. It will require humility and an honest look at the way things *are* and the way things *could* be. Kids and parents will need lots of help on the journey home to their heavenly Father. It requires encouragement and redirection to understand how a relationship with Jesus recalibrates our relationships with one another as well. The family of God is the primary context for a disciple-making revolution. It's where it all begins.

ARE YOU MY BROTHER?

I met Steve when I was in third grade.[2] He was a high school student serving at Oak Tree. My earliest memory of Steve was in the wing of the church where we played floor hockey when my homework was done. Steve was intense. He was fast. He was competitive. But he was also kind. As I shared earlier, I was an only child with a tough situation at home and at school. My family was falling apart and so were my grades. I started sneaking around, testing the limits to see what I could get away with. I started lying to my parents and my teachers. I lied a lot. I took stuff that was not mine, and I took credit for things I did not do. My deception in this difficult season of life helped me feel loved, in a strange sort of way. It numbed the emotional pain I felt about the loss of my family, and it was an unconscious cry for help.

As an adult, I now realize I was on a family finding mission without knowing it. I was asking, *Are you my mother? Are you my father? Are you my sister? Are you my brother?* Something drew me to Steve. Or rather, *someone* drew me to Steve. Psalm 68:5 says: "A father to the fatherless, a defender of widows, is God in his holy dwelling." This psalm tells us that God is a gracious and merciful heavenly Father who pays close attention to kids in need like me. I was technically not an orphan since both my parents, while separated by divorce, were still in the picture. I had loving relatives around me. But God also provided the "extended spiritual family" I needed to grow in my relationship with Jesus and God's people.

As a disciple of Jesus and a children's ministry leader, Steve was intentional about being a kid-influencer and lifelong disciple maker. He was almost always at church when I was there, and I watched the way he interacted with the other kids, his peers, and adults. During the week he was at the day care. On the weekends he was at the services, Sunday school, and Awana Club. His smile lit up every room (and it still does).

Steve's energy made the boring stuff fun and the fun stuff even better. I loved when he would pick me to be his one and only floor hockey teammate. We'd play, just the two of us against all the other boys, and Steve was my all-star goalie. I felt like we could take over the world. When I was in fourth grade, after seeing my self-made pinewood derby entry the year before, he helped me reimagine and shape a new racecar from scratch (I won third place in design!). Both from the sidelines and by his side, I saw Steve love and lead well for many years. He modeled character that helped me better understand God and what it meant to be a man. I looked up to Steve. I watched his every move. I wanted to be like him (or at least beat him just once in floor hockey).[3]

As I grew older, Steve mentored me in a Paul-Timothy sort of way.[4] He became a spiritual brother and eventually a father figure who guided me in my faith journey. Long before the days when a full FBI background check was needed to work with kids at church, Steve talked with my mom and asked if he could take me out of school during lunch to talk and discuss God's Word together. As a sixth grader, I was honored to have this time with Steve. During the week we would each do a chapter of the same Bible study guide, including discussion questions and Scripture memorization. While I didn't always like the homework part, hanging with a young man who believed in me and was willing to find creative ways to build into me was inviting. These mentoring meetings left a deep impression on my life. And they meant a lot to my mom, a new believer at the time, as well.

It might surprise you to hear this, but Steve never pushed a religious agenda on me. He let me and my mother proceed at our own pace relationally and spiritually. We were provided with a safe place to learn, heal, and grow. And we were given a godly example to consider. Love was the church's primary tactic, the starting point for an inclusive, grace-filled ministry. In very tangible ways, Steve cooperated with God to care for us, to reach into the heart of our home by building unconventional community with my family. In line with James 1:27 and Romans 12:15, the Lord led this particular congregation to love on orphans and widows, to do so through seasons of joy and sorrow, rejoicing and mourning.

When kid-influencers step beyond the confines of church programs, it can make a lasting difference in the lives of children and families. Steve's approach was simple but significant. It was personal and gutsy. Taking a risk as a disciple maker to reach out to kids and families beyond the established programs and meetings isn't always easy. In fact, there is a growing divide between the church and the family that is increasing each year. Church leaders and parents seem to be at odds even if they desire the best for the same kids. Effective children's ministry leaders need to consider how they can become bridge builders and reverse this pattern.

THE GROWING CHASM

Families across the demographic spectrum are in need like never before. A lot gets blamed on over-committed schedules and misaligned priorities, but double- and triple-booked calendars are just surface-level symptoms of deeper issues at home. Stressors come from all sides. Education issues raise red flags for parents regarding their kids' futures. Job insecurity weighs on the minds of even the most faithful employees. Healthcare concerns escalate matters for families. Inundation by technology, cell phones, social media, video gaming, and targeted marketing is overwhelming. Divorce and remarriage rates continue to skyrocket, along with the accompanying relational complexities. From financial struggles to finding solutions for aging parents, today's parents and their children are finding life is hard to navigate alone.

My wife recently completed her graduate degree in education and began teaching kindergarten in an under-resourced community. Kate and her colleagues struggle with these changes in the family on a daily basis. The children in her school come from diverse cultural, socio-economic, and religious backgrounds. Most speak one language but not necessarily the same one as the rest of their classmates or teachers. Some parents are highly interested in their children's academic engagement and progress; others couldn't care less. Some families are intact; others are fractured. There is inconsistent attendance. Kids don't complete their homework. The children have dramatically different perspectives on faith, moral values, and relationships.

What is true for my wife as a teacher is equally true for those of us who lead in the church. To reach the hearts of children, we must reach into their homes. But how? While the church doors remain wide open, doors to homes are shut tight. And given all that is available for children today, the idea of scheduling more, doing more, spending more, and giving more is often overwhelming. Long gone are the days when a cadre of extended relatives live down the street or at least in a neighboring town. The majority of moms and dads find it difficult to make ends meet on one income. Parents are more isolated than ever while demands and expectations have only increased.

Still, most parents love their children and want what is physically, emotionally, and spiritually best for their kids; they just don't know how to provide it. So what keeps the church and the home apart? It's helpful to look at church attendance trends by families as one window into the problem. After all, if parents and kids are not around, it's hard for children's ministry to make a difference in discipleship. And the trend lines are telling.

Families Appear to Be
Leaving the Building

The number of Americans who "seldom" or "never" attend church has risen from 25 percent to 29 percent between 2003 and 2013.[5]

Overall church attendance has dropped from 43 percent to 36 percent between 2004 and 2014.[6]

In the minds of attenders, "regular" church attendance has changed from three or more times per month to once every four to six weeks.[7]

In short, church *affiliation* has replaced formal church *membership* in the eyes of many people today. What is affiliation? It describes those who attend church once a month or every six weeks, but not every Sunday. Attending occasionally like this typically isn't much of a problem for parents, but the relational and spiritual effects are significant for kids and difficult for churches trying to serve them. So how can the church provide meaningful faith experiences that build from week to week when many of the children are inconsistent in attending? How can homes nurture spiritual growth when parental participation in the life of the church is sporadic? How will a cross-section of discipleship relationships and intergenerational community happen in the lives of kids and parents if regular time with the family of God is on the back burner? Smart decisions in this area begin by understanding that attendance is not merely about who shows up and how often. Attendance patterns tell a story, a tale of what matters most and what is missing in a parent's or child's life.

Another indicator of the separation between the church and the family is found in how parents are viewed, how they self-identify with faith, and how the church provides support to them.[8] Often, there is a "one size fits all" approach to resourcing family discipleship. Church leaders offer help with simple recommendations: *Read these faith-building books at home. Say these prayers before meals and bedtime. Listen to more of these family-friendly*

A Fresh Look at Families:
Four Distinct Family Personas

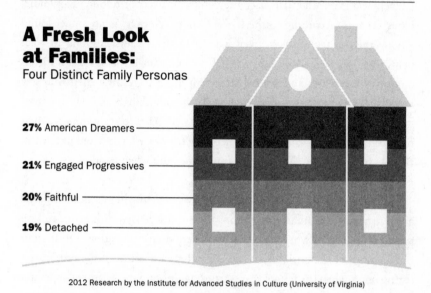

27% American Dreamers

21% Engaged Progressives

20% Faithful

19% Detached

2012 Research by the Institute for Advanced Studies in Culture (University of Virginia)

radio stations in the car. Attend these special children's ministry gatherings. Serve together at the church in these ways. All of these are good things, but prescribed solutions can feel overly constrictive or even out of touch with reality. We need to remember there is no singular formula for steering families toward spiritual vibrancy. Maybe you've said something like this before: *Because parents are the primary spiritual influencers in the home, every family should* _____ [fill in the blank]. But let me offer a word of caution here. Inadvertently, communicating this well-intended message can create guilt and subtly shame parents who aren't doing something or aren't sure how to lead their children spiritually. Compliance to a single model of parenting is not what the gospel of Jesus Christ is ultimately all about. Instead of advocating a "one size fits all" approach to parents, focus on common biblical convictions and practices that reflect godly character, helping families to see that no one individual or family or parenting model expresses faithfulness to God in exactly the same way.

Many families have already left our church buildings, disillusioned or disappointed. And yet they still need (and for the most part want) some type of spiritual, emotional, and relational support in raising their children.

The church is not the first place they go for answers or resources anymore. Consider this: according to the Barna Group, "church" is no longer found among the top ten answers given when American adults respond to what helps them grow in faith.[9] Surprised? I was too. But if this is true, it means children's ministries and church leadership need to rethink their ministry models. A good percentage of the parents in your church and in your community are standing at arm's length, wanting churches to accommodate their needs on their own terms. Many others stay further away to avoid judgment. Bridges between church and home cannot be built when hands are preoccupied with placing blame.

A couple of years ago, as my oldest son was starting high school, my wife and I attended freshman orientation. Kate and I believe strongly in full-on parent engagement when it comes to our children's education. Opting out of our parental responsibility is not an option (at least until sometime after spring break when the school year starts dragging and the weather cooperates for going to Cubs games). We want our home to be the hub for our sons' lives, and this means maintaining a partnership with schools and educators. We know we can't do this alone or we will end up waving a white flag of surrender. So we walked into the school building, connected with a handful of other parents, and took our seats. We heard the same start of the year spiel we hear every school year:

> You are the primary influencer in your child's education. It's your role and responsibility. We are here to serve and support you. We also need you to partner with us so your kid can succeed. Reading and learning together at home is really important. Talk about what they are studying. Ask them questions. Share your own stories and experiences with them. Encourage them to get to know their teachers. Challenge them to try new things and make new friends. Help them build their character so they make a lasting difference in this world. Your time investment and fund-raising support is vital in your relationship with us as well. Volunteering with the other parents and supporting your student's teachers will ensure that these years become some of the best years of your family's life.

Sound familiar? If you have children of your own, you are likely acquainted with this message. If you are a kid-influencer or children's ministry leader, it probably resonates with you too. So why do I bring this up, since we all agree it is an important message? Well, as I sat in the auditorium listening to this speech and the accompanying laundry list of frustrations surrounding disengaged parents, I realized I had actually heard this message at least *four times a year*, twice for each son, for over a decade. In fact, as a pastor I had given a variation of this talk to parents to begin every ministry season for the last ten years! With a few tweaks and the addition of a select passage from the first part of Deuteronomy 6, many churches are saying the same thing as our schools. *And while the message is true, it's not always helpful.* Faith communities and educational institutions keep pushing the responsibility on parents with marginally successful results. And parents feel overwhelmed and lost. Conventional approaches aren't working. Is there a better way? Are there other options?

In my experience, a great question to ask yourself first, and then your church and children's ministry leadership, is, "How much finger pointing is going on between our church and homes these days?" Imagine standing at the edge of the Grand Canyon. Off in the distance, way on the other side of the chasm, stand parents. What are they saying? Are they pointing fingers at the church demanding more or asking to partner? Now, from your side, what message is the church sending? Is it demanding more from parents or asking to partner? Both sides need each other to be the best kid-influencers they can be. Get ideas down on paper that reflect what you desire to communicate and provide to kids and families. Get with parents and hear directly from them. Work together to reach across the great divide for the sake of the children you're both seeking to serve.

We need bridge building to replace finger pointing if lifelong discipleship is going to happen in churches and homes. Unconventional community is a key factor. To break the impasse and help families today, I believe kid-influencers will need to forge new approaches to reaching, relating to, and resourcing this current generation of families.

BUILDING DISCIPLESHIP BRIDGES BETWEEN CHURCH AND HOME

In 2002, Dr. Will Miller and Dr. Glenn Sparks coined the term "refrigerator rights" to describe how our relationships with family and close friends ought to operate.[10] When a host says "make yourself at home," it generally means something different to a first-time dinner guest than to a lifelong friend. New acquaintances remove their overcoats, possibly their shoes too if it is customary, and then take a seat to sip a beverage over casual conversation. It's cordial at best and may turn into something more meaningful with time. At the opposite end of the spectrum, overly familiar companions barge through the front door, toss their coats on the sofa, head straight to the kitchen, reheat leftovers from the fridge, take a nap in the guest room, and borrow the car on their way out the back door! It's a lot more like college students coming home for the weekend. Miller and Sparks argue that the absence of intimate relationships, familial-like ties that allow others to see us just as we are, is detrimental to emotional health. Humans were not created by God to live in isolation from him or one another (Gen. 2:18). A family unit fundamentally needs to experience interdependent community at home and in the world. Churches would do well to begin fostering "refrigerator rights" relationships with parents and kids.

A relational children's ministry needs to have a vision for ministry that reaches beyond the boundaries of the church building. Regular service times and scheduled programs are helpful, but today's families need support from surrogate mothers, fathers, sisters, brothers, grandparents, aunts, uncles, and cousins in the family of God throughout the week in a variety of different ways. Let me be clear: biological family matters immensely. But both our biological and spiritual family connections directly impact the faith foundations of the home. The pattern of life and promises declared in Deuteronomy 6 were given to *parents* and to *all of God's people*. Families will succeed in rearing children who follow Jesus when they receive the right *care, coaching*, and *challenges* they need. The church has an amazing opportunity to equip and train parents in disciple making. There are three bridges into the home to realize this vision.

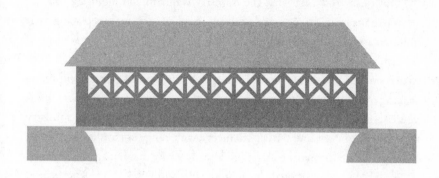

BRIDGE 1: THE CARE BRIDGE
ONGOING ENCOURAGEMENT

I love covered bridges, but they are harder and harder to find these days. For one thing, they're costly to build and maintain. Yet we are drawn to the iconic imagery of these historic wooden structures. Besides the beauty of their construction, covered bridges are practical as well. Like all bridges, they afford access between one side and another, but they also have the benefit of keeping travelers shaded and dry during inclement weather. They shield people from life's passing storms. They provide sojourners with shelter, safety, and security. So when I think about how the church can reach out to families, I naturally think of building bridges—covered bridges that provide shelter, safety, and security to care for real needs.

When I visit children's ministries, I look for "help wanted" signs. I do this for a couple of reasons. First, I am curious if the ministry views its leaders as merely volunteers who fill a need or as spiritually gifted servants. Beyond that, I wonder if the ministry is aware of how these appeals are perceived by newcomers. Letting people know there is a need for additional help can sometimes communicate the wrong message. Some signs mistakenly shout out that the ministry is overwhelmed and potentially not safe: "Welcome! We're so glad you're here! We love serving families. We don't have enough help, but your child is safe with us." Or they communicate a sense of guilt: "Thank you for dropping off your child! We will gladly serve him for the next ninety minutes. We're not keeping track, but technically you owe us ninety minutes a week. So please sign up to serve at least once a month!"

Obviously, this isn't what the ministry wants to communicate. But it's what parents hear. Moms and dads want to make sure they are placing their children in safe environments surrounded by loving people. In seasons of hardship, this need is even greater. The co-op punch card is already full for many parents, so feeling coerced into serving is the last thing a spiritually seeking or emotionally struggling parent needs. Exercise discernment when you communicate your need for volunteers. Let them know your ministry offers shelter, safety, and security to meet a wide range of families and needs, but don't add to the many frustrations already felt by these struggling parents.

To build unconventional community with families, kid-influencers need to build a care bridge that communicates ongoing encouragement. Parents are easily discouraged. They regularly get down on themselves for not knowing if they are rearing their kids well. Regular reports from teachers, coaches, family members, and other parents indicating their children are far from perfect compound this. Sometimes it's difficult to distinguish between poor parenting and a child's poor personal choices. Add to this the complexities of financial strain, dysfunctional relationships, and emotional pain. The church family is called to be a beacon of hope to the families of this world. Consider what would happen if kid-influencers chose not to build care bridges of ongoing encouragement in one way or another.

Fellowship Housing is a Christian non-profit ministry in my area that serves single moms and their children who are facing the harsh reality of homelessness.[11] Case managers walk alongside the women in a two-year program that provides transitional housing and a structured path to independence. The program is intense. It addresses financial, professional, relational, emotional, and spiritual matters. It requires a high level of commitment from the moms and from the ministry staff and volunteers. It truly builds unconventional community between moms who need ongoing grace, truth, love, and accountability in healthy relationships.

One of the things I love about Fellowship Housing is that it networks with outside partners to provide families with what they need. No ministry or church can do it all alone. Fellowship Housing is great at housing homeless women and children, social casework, financial coaching, community building, and so on. But when it comes to spiritual nourishment, they connect to local churches that are building care bridges to kids and families, and they lead moms there.

Fellowship Housing relies on churches that offer midweek discipleship classes, Awana programs, food pantries, pro-bono legal counsel, special needs ministries, recovery groups, grief support, and divorce/marriage ministries. As part of their two-year program, the moms and kids participate in the life of a local church. They attend services and classes to worship God, learn his Word, and grow in relationship with Christ and others. Their kids get to be part of engaging children's ministries on both weekends and weekdays that center on evangelism, discipleship, Bible teaching, Scripture memory, and serving. Bridges of ongoing encouragement built by churches help these moms and kids make it through one day at a time while still shouldering the load that comes with everyday life.

Imagine what would happen if churches didn't recognize the need to build care bridges. Diverse care ministries would not exist. Ongoing encouragement would become hard to find. Moms and dads and children would not get the relational, emotional, financial, and spiritual support they need as they come to know, love, and serve Jesus Christ. Not every church or children's ministry is called to address every struggle families face today, but every kid-influencer can work to build bridges of ongoing encouragement in some way.

GALATIANS 6:10

Therefore, as we have opportunity, let us do good to all people, especially to those who belong to the family of believers.

Galatians 6:10

Galatians 6:10 is a foundational verse to consider as you are building a bridge of ongoing encouragement to families. "As we have opportunity . . . let us do good . . ." Relational children's ministries plan and develop opportunities to strategically serve families. They do good so that families come to love God, his Word, and his people. It may be that your church and children's ministry is poised to address serious issues facing families in your community, such as homelessness, poverty, unemployment, addictions, divorce, and special needs. What existing ministries in your area could you join forces with? On the other hand, until God gives the green light in areas like these, you can step up your level of ongoing encouragement toward kids and families. Through "no strings attached" parent nights, family friendly events, extracurricular mentoring, sports leagues, milestone celebrations, neighborhood gatherings, and needs-based outreach, you can build care bridges of ongoing encouragement that eventually lead to unconventional community with families.

Here are two care bridge builders you might consider implementing sooner rather than later.

Mom/Dadfest: Hallmark ensures Mother's Day and Father's Day cycle around every year. Make these weekends memorable by celebrating moms and dads in special ways. If you do, parents will look forward to it annually. Set up special stations for moms and dads to take pictures with their kids. Provide moms with a "parenting survival kit" that has an encouraging verse, a piece of chocolate, the phone number of their child's leader at church, and a coupon for two free hours of childcare. Remind dads they've got this "dad thing" down (even if they don't believe you!). Hand out lots of free bacon, give them a coin or card inscribed with a fatherhood verse to carry around, buy them a Frisbee with the name of your church or children's ministry on it, and give them a map that highlights the best local parks to play with their kids . . . and then give them more bacon.

"The Doctor Is In" Booth: Remember Lucy from Charles Schulz's beloved *Peanuts* cartoons? She had a booth offering psychiatric help for 5 cents per visit. No one took her up on the offer because she clearly wasn't an expert. In your church and children's ministry, the opposite is true. Parents and kids look to you as experts in one way or another, but most kid-influencers shrug it off and never put up a booth. Create an island, information booth, or hotline for moms and dads. Let them know you're not a doctor (unless you are) and give them access to get the parenting encouragement they need. This could be a physical location at your church or you could find ways to meet up for coffee in a local café or playground. Take time to listen, and then listen some more. Don't just give out advice. Just love on moms and dads until their hearts are open to counsel and coaching. Free high-fives, handshakes, and hugs go a long way in building unconventional community with kids and families. And if you can get 5 cents per visit, bonus!

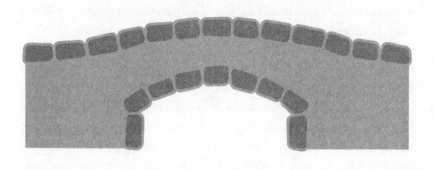

BRIDGE 2: THE COACHING BRIDGE
TIMELY EQUIPPING

There is a classic scene in the tale of *Robin Hood* that illustrates another way churches can build bridges to families. It takes place at a treacherous river. Robin, looking for ways to reach the other side, notices a slender footbridge and begins to cross, but he comes up against a significant obstacle. He comes face to face with a big man named Little John. The two discuss each other's fate and then decide to duel for the right to cross from one bank to the other. In a battle of ability and wit, Robin and Little John joust and jest until they're both in the river floating downstream. Through this encounter the men become comrades in friendship and in the fight against the Sheriff of Nottingham.

The parallels are far from perfect, but this story paints another picture of what churches need to do to reach the home. Roving bridges, like the one Robin Hood tries to cross, are generally built from wood planks or stones. They serve an immediate need like crossing over a creek, walking through a muddy field, navigating forest terrain, or passing over a short gap in the pavement. Roving bridges provide an instant solution to get from point A to point B on the way to the next destination. When a bridge is only wide enough for one person to cross, an encounter is inevitable when two people heading opposite directions meet on the bridge. Going separate ways or pushing the other into the river is an option, but that certainly doesn't build community. I love that Robin Hood and Little John clashed at first, but they came to a point of setting aside their differences for the common good. This is the imagery we need in lifelong discipleship and family ministry. Church and home must forge alliances to establish unconventional community.

To succeed, parents need someone to come alongside them and offer help and direction. This is where the church can serve by offering *coaching*. Parents may initially see the church as an enemy, but with the right approach, a church can find a common cause with the parents in the neighborhood and the community around them. Parents want help, and they need to be equipped in the right way at the right time. The family of God can have a huge impact on the faith trajectory of kids and parents by building a coaching bridge between the church and home.

Years ago I was working with a new family at our church. A single dad came to me because he did not know where else to turn. His marriage had ended several years earlier, and he was having a hard time finding work. His sons were struggling in school. He did not know how to address the mounting challenges ahead. He needed care, but he also needed timely equipping through coaching. We connected him with people he could talk to, who could offer guidance and direction specific to his situation. He also chose to participate in financial counseling, and we provided some support for him in his job search. He joined a group of parents for Bible study and encouragement, and his sons got plugged into relationships with peers and leaders in the children's ministry. Whenever he faced a challenge or struggle as a full-time dad, he now had a parenting toolbox to draw from and phone numbers of trusted friends he could call in a pinch. The church did not solve this father's problems, but we found a way to coach him while providing care for his family. I still get occasional updates from him, and I'm humbled by how God continues to work in his life and the lives of his sons.

DEUTERONOMY 11:18–21

> **Fix these words of mine in your hearts and minds; tie them as symbols on your hands and bind them on your foreheads. Teach them to your children, talking about them when you sit at home and when you walk along the road, when you lie down and when you get up. Write them on the doorframes of your houses and on your gates, so**

that your days and the days of your children may be many
in the land the Lᴏʀᴅ swore to give your ancestors, as many
as the days that the heavens are above the earth.
Deuteronomy 11:18–21

The book of Deuteronomy is the retelling of the law originally given to Moses by God in the book of Exodus. In this passage from Deuteronomy 11, we get a retelling of the "cornerstone" family ministry passage in Deuteronomy 6. This repetition underscores the importance of walking with God day by day, one step at a time, as a family. Moses wants the people to understand that the precepts and promises of the Lord are to be passed on from generation to generation. The purpose of the coaching bridge we are looking at is to effectively resource parents so they can disciple themselves and their children. Churches must rethink their approach to discipleship and recognize that disciple making is something that happens both inside and outside the home. It includes church programs as well as the time parents spend with their children throughout the week. Relational children's ministries should empower families with innovative resources to help them grow as spiritual leaders. Ideally, this *begins in the home,* but it shouldn't end there. And if it can't begin at home, relational children's ministries can play a role in helping it happen.

You might think otherwise, but parents actually have a hard time knowing what to say when it comes to spiritual matters. They feel ill-equipped to discuss what the Bible is about. The idea of praying at mealtimes is intimidating. For many moms and dads, the notion of trying to pull the family together for the purpose of discipleship is just plain scary. They've never done it. It's never been modeled. They don't know where to begin. That's where you, your church, and your children's ministry can step in to bridge the gap.

Some friends of mine are launching a new resource for families called SproutBox (check out www.sproutboxkids.com). They realize parents need coaching when it comes to biblical literacy and engagement with God's Word in the home. Through this monthly subscription service, families receive a highly creative, solidly biblical, incredibly intentional experience. It uses the latest augmented reality technologies to tell a Bible story. The digital app provides interactivity and a super-cool factor, but this isn't the purpose of the resource. The goal is to equip parents so they can immerse their family in God's Word through storytelling, discussion, activities, crafts, and more. My friends are developing this product because they see a gap when it comes to coaching parents in discipleship. They are disrupting the status quo because the gospel and God's Word matter more than entertaining kids and pacifying parents.

Why do I bother bringing up SproutBox? It's because we need even more innovation when it comes to providing parents with timely equipping for discipleship. Churches and children's ministries create great ideas all the time, and word needs to get out. I know a kid-influencer who leads a small group of parents while their children are participating in midweek children's ministry. They read through parenting books together, do Bible studies, talk about family strengths and struggles, and give each other tips to try out at home. There are MOPS ministries for mothers of preschoolers all over the country that bring biblical principles to life during these foundational parenting years. Another children's ministry pastor I know invites parents to participate in specific evangelism weekends and events. Moms and dads hear the same gospel presentation as their child. They receive a discussion guide and time to talk with their child one-on-one about the A-B-Cs of salvation: *Admit* to God that I'm a sinner, *Believe* Christ died and rose again, and *Choose* to know, love, and serve the Lord forever. Giving parents real-time experience talking about spiritual matters is one of the best ways to reproduce disciple making in homes.

There are many creative ways to build up and build into parents as disciples and disciple makers. You can offer classes or training seminars that cover crucial parenting topics. You can resource parents with sermons and Bible studies, utilizing various media including CDs, MP3s, podcasts, and streaming videos. You could SMS "parenting tip texts" to provide timely encouragement and accountability to parents who want short reminders throughout the week. In addition, you can leverage the power of the church community by organizing reading groups and hosting parent and family retreats. Consider teaching classes on saving for college and financial stewardship or movie nights followed by discussions on biblical worldviews. Organize serving projects in local neighborhoods. Provide helps for parents through Scripture memory motivators . . . the ideas are endless. The key is to provide timely tips and tools that coach parents by equipping them in their discipleship journey as a family.

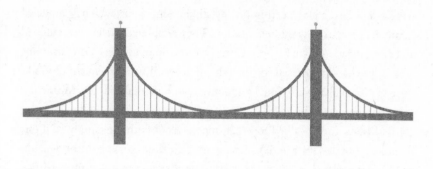

BRIDGE 3: THE CHALLENGE BRIDGE
LOVING ENGAGEMENT

The Golden Gate Bridge in San Francisco, California is one of the most recognizable suspension bridges in the world. It opened in 1937, and until 1964 it had the longest main span between towers in the world. This engineering feat connects a mile-wide, three-mile-long channel between San Francisco Bay and the Pacific Ocean. Innovative in its design and construction, the bridge deployed state-of-the-art moveable safety netting to heighten safeguards for hundreds of steelworkers. The Golden Gate Bridge stands as a symbol of strength and service. It is able to withstand the eroding effects of saltwater spray, dense fog, periodic earthquakes, and the constant automotive and pedestrian traffic it transports.

This historic bridge carries special meaning for me. I lived in the Bay Area before moving to the northwest suburbs of Chicago as a teenager, so my familial and faith roots are there. I love bringing my wife and kids home to see the sights, to reconnect with family and friends. It gives them a window into what life was like for me as a child. Whenever possible, I make my way to Santa Cruz Beach and the San Francisco Bay to be reminded of God's goodness to me and my family over so many seasons.

A few years ago, I walked from one side of the bridge to the other side and back again with my lifelong friend Joshua.[12] We met in third grade, and over the years he became like a brother to me. We lived just a few blocks from each other, went to the same school, played Little League in the same town, and ran with the same circle of friends. His parents were faithful Christ followers with an incredibly grace-filled backstory. They took me under their wing when I was just starting on my discipleship journey. They modeled family in a way that was foreign to me. They celebrated each other, laughed and cried together. The Bible and church came up in conversation naturally. They served and sacrificed for the sake of others. I was a recipient of God's unconditional love every time I set foot in their remarkable home. More than three decades later, this is still true.

As Joshua and I walked together, memories of faith, his family, and our friendship flooded my mind. It was not my first time crossing the bridge, but on this particular day—as we took in the bridge one step at a time—I saw something new. My eyes were opened to the significance of long-term support for families. Today's parents need community that has Christ at the center and has staying power—community that sticks together for the long haul.

Parents and kids alike are looking for love that lasts. Cultural shifts have increased the mobility of moms and dads. This has led to a swell of relational breakdowns. Unexpected tragedies and ailments raise serious issues for families. Societal stressors impact emotional stability and create rifts in relationships. Divorce debilitates family systems. Substance abuse destroys healthy homes. Financial pressures lead to misaligned priorities. Failure upon failure undermines hope for the future. Sin is embedded in the fabric of family life, and the effects of sin carry over from generation to generation. And, to the surprise of most church and children's ministry leaders, these concerns hit home in the family of God as much as they exist in the surrounding world.

What is needed? Loving engagement over the long haul, a bridge that is solid and secure and will stand the test of time. Families need kid-influencers who will demonstrate the character of Christ and the principles of lifelong discipleship through thick and thin.

Churches that establish a challenge bridge like this need to think about how to stay committed long term, beyond weekly programs and special events. The challenge bridge builds upon the coaching bridge by emphasizing the need for equipping and training parents to be disciples and disciple makers in the home. It also recognizes how people change over time, through the many ups and downs of life. Care and coaching is great in the short term, but as trust is formed over time, a healthy amount of challenge is needed as well.

Moms and dads need accountability so they can take spiritual responsibility for themselves and their children. They need someone to encourage them in the hard work they're already committed to living out. They need gracious, truthful reminders of what matters most. If some parents aren't there yet, kids and their families will benefit from a larger church family where they see kid-influencers modeling loving engagement in the way of Christ through different seasons and with all kinds of families.

In my own experience, I've found loving engagement is delivered best *through* the church family, but not necessarily *at* the church building. This is why the church must see itself as a partner, not the sole solution. Churches partner with parents well by providing care and coaching, but also by challenging them to be the primary spiritual influencers in their children's lives and sticking with them over the long haul.

ROMANS 12:15

Rejoice with those who rejoice; mourn with those who mourn.
Romans 12:15

The purpose of this third challenge bridge is to support families through the unexpected seasons of life and parenting so they can have long-term consistency. Parents rise to the challenge by serving other families at home or at the church through their prayers, by sharing resources, and by being involved in day-to-day needs as they come up. When a family member is sick or there is a sudden loss, families in the church are there to provide comfort and assistance. When a child or parent is making bad decisions that are hurting others in the family, trusted friends from the church can step in and speak truth.

You can apply several of the bridge-building ideas in this chapter to establish a challenge bridge in your own context. There's one ministry I'd like to highlight because the need is so great and this model can be multiplied in a variety of ways. *Jill's House* (visit www.jillshouse.org) is a ministry originally founded by the pastoral leadership at McLean Bible Church in Virginia. They are committed to serving families who deal with the effects of intellectual disabilities daily. Whether it's autism, Down syndrome, or a host of other diagnoses, disabilities affect everyone in a family, not just the special needs individual. Providing one-on-one partners for special needs children is a critical need in children's ministry. However, it's easy to overlook that moms, dads, and siblings all need support too. *Jill's House* finds ways to give affected families a "rhythm of respite" by creating safe, consistent, planned times "off" from daily responsibilities and challenges. Just one weekend away can make a huge difference. Imagine the impact of one weekend per month! You don't need to adopt the *Jill's House* model in your children's ministry to make a difference for special needs families. Just raise the question: what is God calling us to do in our church and community to build a long-term bridge of loving engagement? We need more minds and hearts wrapped around matters like these so all kids can be known, loved, and served in the way of Christ.

Personally, I am grateful for those the Lord used over the years to speak into my family's life, to invite us to step up as fully devoted followers of Christ. Steve and others at the church encouraged my family to stick with things like reading and reflecting on Scripture, being regularly involved in the church community, and using our spiritual gifts to serve others. They were by our side when things got painful at home. Through the years, I have personally been blessed to see the body of Christ lovingly engage parents amidst deaths of family members, infertility, special needs situations, emotional issues, divorce, remarriage, chronic illness, employment transitions, and unexpected tragedies. Romans 12:15 stands at the heart of what it means to love in the way of Jesus, to enter into the presence and pain of others. Unconventional community requires a "love one another" perspective that permeates every encounter.

NOW IS THE TIME TO BECOME BRIDGE BUILDERS TO FAMILIES

Jesus was a radically relational bridge builder, and as we build bridges we build upon the work he has already done through his life, death, and resurrection. The cross is the ultimate bridge, overcoming the gap between a holy God and his sinful people. Christ is the bridge who reconnects us to God, closing the loop on the story of humanity and eternity. He graciously invites us to cross that bridge through faith in him, his words, and his work on our behalf.

God's people in Deuteronomy 6 and the early church in Acts stand in parallel as examples of true biblical community. Young and old, male and female, rich and poor, friends and foreigners, all living in unity under the greatness and goodness of one heavenly Father. Biological family matters greatly, but it is our spiritual family that endures forever. Bridge-building churches and children's ministry leaders need to provide a spiritual family that endures longer than a mid-week program. This requires an invitational relational ministry focus, one that invests in children and their families over the years, through the ups and downs of life.

Today's families need help. They need to be surrounded by Christ-centered community. Neither families nor the church can reproduce lifelong disciples on their own. The world is changing and discipleship bridges between church and home are critical for both sides to reach their God-given potential. There are no quick fixes, because becoming an unconventional community that radically exemplifies "love one another" in every way requires purposefulness, perspective, and planning. It also demands patience and persistence. But over time, the seeds you plant will bear fruit. Kid-influencers who commit to building discipleship bridges that bring care, coaching, and challenges to families will see children grow into mature disciples of Jesus.

QUESTIONS FOR REFLECTION & DISCUSSION

1. Where are some good and not so good places kids go searching for relationships, and why?

2. Who has God placed in your life as unexpected spiritual family? What have they provided that your biological family could not?

3. What are some reasons the gap between church and home are increasing in your context? Can anything be done to address what you are experiencing? Explain.

4. What unconventional community stories are you aware of in your children's ministry?

5. What hurdles must be overcome for kids and families to shift away from independence in favor of interdependence within the body of Christ?

6. For lifelong discipleship to take place in homes, what do you believe needs to happen first?

7. Of the three bridges (care, coaching, challenge), which one does your ministry succeed at most naturally? Which one needs the most attention right now, and why?

8. What resources do you have inside your ministry to help families? What are some outside resources that you trust and recommend?

9. What will happen in the lives of kids and parents if bridge-building between the church and home takes place?

CHAPTER 8

INVITATION 4: MODEL CHRIST'S LIFE-TRANSFORMING MISSION

You teach a little by what you say. You teach most by what you are.

Henrietta Mears[1]

The righteous lead blameless lives; blessed are their children after them.

Proverbs 20:7

©CathyKeifer/www.istock.com

EVERYONE KNOWS water is central to life. Without it, people eventually die. Communities who want to survive plant themselves, like trees, by streams of water. We need water for drinking, cleaning, bathing, and cooking. Water can be harnessed to generate power and to grow crops. It can be used for transportation and recreation. When it's freely available, water is a gateway to a good life, and the absence of water often leads to death and the destruction of communities. Is it any wonder Jesus used water to illustrate his offer of eternal life to the woman at the well, or that he spoke of the Holy Spirit as a stream of living water, a gift he would give abundantly?[2]

Relational children's ministry is about giving children and families access to water—to the spiritual water of life. We do this by modeling the way of Christ in all its fullness. This means kid-influencers must themselves be transformed from the inside out to be effective disciple-makers. No child should be discipled by someone who is uncommitted to his or her own discipleship journey. If a person has not received the life-transforming gift of eternal life, of God's living water, this gift cannot overflow from them into the lives of others. They need not be perfect, but they must be drawing regularly from the spring of living water, from the grace of God made available to them by the gospel and the power of the Holy Spirit.

It's not impossible, though it's certainly more challenging, to guide people where you have never been before. We have help, thankfully. But as we discussed in previous chapters, curriculum is merely a road map. Our relationship with God and with others is the road we travel. This is one reason children's ministries struggle to find people who are truly equipped and able to effectively equip others. Many have read the map, but only a few have journeyed the road themselves. Only leaders who are personally growing in relationship with God and mindful of their role as lifelong disciple-makers will be able to interact with kids at a heart-to-heart level.

As with parent-child relationships, the Holy Spirit is able to fill in character and experience gaps in disciple-making relationships. So there is hope for all of us! Still, the best way to make a positive impression on another person's heart is by mirroring a mold that has been cast in your own life. We disciple others out of the unique ways God's Word and God's Spirit have shaped our lives. That's why every disciple maker needs personal experience in what it means to be radically shaped by Christ. Every kid-influencer who experiences the crucible of change will have opportunity to replicate this in other people's lives. This will require the setting of new disciple-making molds to conform fully to Christ's total life-transforming mission.

BREAKING THE MOLD

The beauty of Monarch butterflies has captivated me since my childhood. Within an hour's drive from my home, I could catch the annual migration of these incredible specimens. It was a highlight each fall when our school would take a field trip to Natural Bridges State Park to see the massive clusters of Monarchs hanging from an aromatic forest of eucalyptus trees. Having transformed through a short life cycle from eggs to caterpillars to chrysalides to butterflies, they were now fully on display for all to see. Even when I was a child, the mystery of such total life change grabbed my attention.

After we moved from California to the Midwest, God placed my mother and me in yet another vibrant church family. We knew we needed to be surrounded by godly people who could be with us as we stumbled and soared.

The community we found was not without problems and faults, but that's the nature of family. People aren't perfect; they make mistakes. But we work through them and grow together. This church provided another wonderful environment for me to spread my wings and grow as a follower of Jesus, both privately and publicly. Kid-influencers continued to equip and encourage me to practice personal and corporate spiritual disciplines. They came alongside me in the process of discovering and stewarding my God-given gifts and talents. One person in particular stepped into my life at that time and broke the mold of disciple makers: my youth pastor, Bob.[3]

The church had a growing relational focus on the children's ministry, but Bob rose above the status quo in his work with tweens and teens. It was obvious that Christ's life-transforming mission had radically changed his life, and he freely modeled his faith for the kids in his sphere of influence. Bob guided us with integrity and a consistent, serious-minded approach to discipleship. He regularly opened his heart and his home to us. Bob didn't treat us as second-class disciples; he clearly believed children of all ages are called and commanded to be like Christ in every area of life. He raised the bar for us, and we responded to the challenge. His disciple-making resolve came through as he spoke about the biblical mandates given to us by Jesus: "Go and make disciples of all nations" (Matt. 28:18–20), "You will be my witnesses" (Acts 1:8), and "Whoever claims to live in him must live as Jesus did" (1 John 2:6). Bob taught us that all disciples, including kids, are empowered by the Father, commissioned by the Son, and sent by the Holy Spirit. He clearly believed Christ's life-transforming mission was not something God reserved for adults.

Jesus told his followers in John 20:21, "Peace be with you! As the Father has sent me, I am sending you." Bob took this example seriously. He helped us think through what this looked like in our lives, how we could engage in ministry as disciples of Jesus. He repeated Jesus' invitation and let us know, "You're not alone. I am with you" (Matt. 28:20), then showed us what gospel ministry looked like.

The gospel is the power of God for the beginning, middle, and end of salvation. It is not merely what we need to proclaim to unbelievers; the gospel also needs to permeate our entire Christian experience.

James Wilhoit[4]

Bob taught us that the gospel of God's grace in Jesus should challenge us each day. It was more than a one-time message to save us from sin; the gospel has the power of God to transform our minds, hearts, and actions so we can live as faithful followers of Jesus. Bob recruited other adult leaders who became a community of guides on our unscripted adventures of life with God. Each person brought different strengths and skills to the ministry table, but all of them were committed to helping us come to know, love, and serve Christ. We learned from God's Word together, and Bob helped us to shape a biblical worldview in light of changing relational and cultural realities around us. We learned about personal devotions, the purpose of corporate worship and prayer, and how to care for the poor. We learned the natural rhythms of discipleship, how to be a consistent disciple of Jesus at home, at church, at school, on sports teams, and in our work.

This season in my life was fueled by a commitment to serving in the body of Christ. I stepped up to serve in children's ministry, led Bible studies with my peers at church and school, and planned outreach events. I sang my heart out in the music ministries and participated in sports leagues as a relational bridge to those outside the church (although most seasons I was better friends with the bench than the ball). I served on short-term missions teams every chance I was given. Bob and the other kid-influencers in my life set the expectations of discipleship by helping me understand what Jesus had done to save me from my sins. In light of God's grace, how could I not respond to God in loving obedience? I became a participating member of the church and eventually part of the student ministry leadership team. The Lord built upon the faith foundations established in my early childhood, and I have never looked back.

A number of years ago, as I was entering a new, full-time season of children's and family ministry, I reconnected with Bob. He had followed God's call to mission by pursuing a teaching degree. He now taught science at an inner-city public school. I recalled the days when Bob came alongside me as a teacher, as a mentor, and as a friend. He provided a safe haven of support marked by the love of Christ, and his sacrifice changed my own discipleship trajectory. During our conversation, I was surprised to hear him speak somewhat critically of the intensity of his ministry activity during those years. "I would have done a lot of things differently," he said. Again, he broke the mold and modeled for me the humble attitude of a life-long learner by his words and thoughtful insights.

Recently we reconnected again. Bob shared with me about another significant assignment he has accepted from God. He is being led to launch apologetic ministries on college campuses, a mission that aligns with his passion, gifting, and experience. God continues to break the disciple-making mold through Bob's life as he pours himself into others for the sake of Christ.

ALL THINGS NEW

You may be wondering why I've spent time talking about the ministry of Bob. After all, this is a book about children's ministry, not youth ministry. I recognize that there are important differences between the two age groups. The life stages of younger children are vastly different from those of early and late adolescents. Tweens and teens can step up to the discipleship plate in more visible ways. They can engage more deeply with the greater faith community in what they do and how they contribute. But I share the example of Bob with you to illustrate how disciple making with kids extends into disciple making in every phase of growth. Children become teens; teens become adults. The process of spiritual maturity spans a lifetime.

Like the monarch butterfly's, our transformation is a process with each stage of growth preparing us for the next stage. It's a total transformation of character from the inside out, a process that lasts a lifetime. Relational children's ministry recognizes this and strategically considers how to effectively prepare kids for their adolescent years. One of the most important things we can do for children during their younger years is to teach them that discipleship is more than classes and events—it is a lifestyle of learning, growth, and walking faithfully with Jesus.

God's Word contains many truths, but they all point to a single timeless message: Christ died for our sins and was raised to life that we can have new life with God through the gift of the Holy Spirit.[5] The life, death, and resurrection of Jesus declare the central truth that complete forgiveness and eternal life with God only come through faith and a relationship with his Son, Jesus. This free gift can't be earned; it's granted solely by God's grace through faith.[6] Though churches may have doctrinal differences, we are united in our belief that God's grace extends to all who believe and ultimately place their trust in Christ alone.[7]

The Bible says that saving faith is a "childlike" response to God and his Word. As Jesus said to his disciples, we must become like little children to enter the kingdom of God. This means every follower of Christ must exchange their self-sustaining, self-gratifying desires for the heart of God. We approach God in true humility, like dependent children. We know we need help, we need to grow, and we need to change.[8] Regardless of age, gender, ethnicity, accomplishments, socioeconomic status, or strength of will, there is equal footing before God at the base of the cross of Christ.

> God meets children in the same way God meets adults—through the mystery of the Holy Spirit's work, through relationships among the people of God, through the revelation of God's will and purpose in Christ and the Scriptures.
> **Scottie May**[9]

In a relational children's ministry, we embrace the mission of Christ and model it. We encourage children to embrace and model it as well. What is true for adults is true for kids!

"Therefore, if anyone is in Christ, the new creation has come: The old has gone, the new is here! All this is from God, who reconciled us to himself through Christ and gave us the ministry of reconciliation" (2 Cor. 5:17–18).

Everyone who follows Christ is included in this. Children are entrusted with the same ministry of reconciliation as adults. And this ministry, the mission of Christ, is about more than telling nice, moral stories. Christ came "to seek and to save the lost" (Luke 19:10), and he "did not come to be served, but to serve, and to give his life as a ransom for many" (Mark 10:45). His mission was intentional and sacrificial—he sought out those who were in need of God's grace and he gave of himself on behalf of those in need. His mission was a total transaction: his life for ours. He voluntarily laid down his life in obedience to the Father in order to save us, his beloved people. And he was raised in power by grace, demonstrating he is the true Lord and King of all.[10] Jesus Christ's life-transforming mission brings true reconciliation between God and people, and now he gives us a mission as well—to spread the news of what he has done to all people. It doesn't matter how old or young you are. Each of us is called to bring this message of reconciliation to the world.

EMBODY THE HEART OF THE GOSPEL

How do we do this? How do you bring a message of reconciliation to the world? Well, you do it one child, one parent, one leader at a time. Making disciples is about more than learning to play nice with others or being good for goodness' sake. It's about following and learning from Jesus how to live life as if he were living it through us. This involves God changing us from the inside out, at the level of our desires, motives, and affections. A divine life exchange leads to character change.[11] Disciple making is as much about what happens inside as what is demonstrated on the outside.

> The compassionate works of Jesus attracted people to Him, but they did not explain the reason for his presence in the world. If he had lived among us only as a doer of good deeds, doubtless he would have been regarded as the most selfless example of love who ever lived, yet still we would die in our sins without eternal life. His redemptive mission was not clear until he articulated the Gospel.
>
> **Robert Coleman[12]**

Becoming like Christ is our goal. It's possible, but it always starts in the heart. If kid-influencers understand this, they are better able to serve in their role as disciple makers. They know the goal is not to get kids to behave correctly—to keep them quiet and standing in a line. The goal is character growth and life change. As adults, kid-influencers must be mindful of the state of their own hearts and sensitive to the hearts of the children they are discipling. Proverbs 4:23 says, "Above all else, guard your heart, for everything you do flows from it." And Jesus, talking about earthly treasures, says, "For where your treasure is, there your heart will be also" (Matt. 6:19–21). The heart is the epicenter of life, inseparably connecting our inner and outer worlds. It includes our emotions, but it is more than just how we feel. The heart is the seat of our desires. It determines our choices and thoughts, and it defines who we are. That's why true change begins in the heart. Who we are on the outside is an overflow of what is on the inside. As Jesus said, "Out of the overflow of the heart, the mouth speaks" (Luke 6:45).

Christlike character is formed privately, before God uses it publicly. It's who you are when no one is looking. There is no formula that will make up for character deficiencies. Commenting on the role of the teacher in the classroom, Professor James Wilhoit reminds us, "The teacher's spiritual maturity is not a private matter, because it affects one's students."[13] I find that this principle is equally true in leadership, with pastors, parents, coaches, and kid-influencers. Who we are, our character and our spiritual maturity, will be what we pass along to those we influence. Colossians 3:12–14 says we are called to "put on" the character of Christ, but there is the constant danger of putting on a show of maturity. This only makes matters worse. If you are not speaking or influencing out of the reservoir of God's life in you, what you say will not have the power to transform others. I often watch how children check out by withdrawing or redirecting when kid-influencers lack the genuine fruit of the Spirit.[14]

As I said earlier, there is no magic formula for growing in the Spirit. Spending extended, reflective time in John 15 is a great place to begin. This passage reminds us that we bear fruit as we abide in Christ. The more we identify with Christ and see ourselves united to him—in his desires, his mission, his heart for people, and his love for the Father—the more fruit our lives will bear. This passage reminds us of the delicate balance between life-transformation and loving obedience. When kid-influencers learn to remain in Christ privately, the Lord nourishes the garden of the human heart. By God's grace, we cooperate with God as the spiritual seeds he has planted grow to produce lasting fruit.

Whether you take time alone or with a few children's ministry colleagues, I strongly recommend spending time getting familiar with John 15:1–17. Jesus brings several issues to the forefront regarding the quality of our relationships as disciples and the results of our labor in the Lord. It's hard to believe that all of our activity in children's ministry, if done apart from close unbroken connection with God, is fruitless. Christ doesn't sugarcoat the way things work in God's kingdom. In John 15:5 he says, "I am the vine; you are the branches. If you remain in me and I in you, you will bear much fruit; apart from me you can do *nothing*" (emphasis added). It would serve us and our teams well to prayerfully consider what this means. Nothing grows without cooperating with the giver of life. Seeds need soil, water, sun, nutrients, and time to blossom. The results are up to God, but that doesn't mean we are off the hook when it comes to cultivating the ground and caring for what's beneath the surface or beginning to sprout. The principles in John 15 can be used for discussion and application personally and with the leaders you serve.

CULTIVATING YOUR CHARACTER GARDEN: FIVE TRAITS OF EFFECTIVE KID-INFLUENCERS

Kate and I knew the birth of our sons would change our lives, but we had no idea what that would look like (or what we were doing, really). I know some couples will get a dog or a pet to learn what it takes to care for someone else, but we decided to buy some flowers for the back patio of our tiny rented townhome instead. We thought: "If we can keep plants alive, we'll do fine as parents." So my pregnant wife and I headed to the garden section of our local hardware store, picked out some window boxes, and grabbed a flat of petunias and a bag of potting soil. Then, we proudly paid for our little experiment and headed home. Having a couple rows of pretty flowers on the porch was lovely. It brought life into our home. We took this new task very seriously, with a heightened sense of responsibility, and we were quite impressed with our horticultural expertise. For the first couple of weeks we were thrilled to be doing this. Then, without warning, our garden dried up and died.

We panicked, thinking, *We can't even remember to water a handful of flowers. How are we ever going to care for a child?* Thankfully, we recovered from the trauma, went on to have our children, and to this day they have not yet suffered the same problem as our flowers.

In the sixteen years since that time, Kate and I have learned there are some differences between gardening and parenting. Plants don't say anything. There is no alarm or warning light that tells you they need something. But kids have God-given noisemakers to remind parents when there is a problem. What parenting and gardening do have in common is that both plants and children need ongoing care and nurture. Just as a garden must be cultivated, watered, fertilized, and cared for, wise parents will nurture the hearts of their children through life-on-life relationships with them. This process of tending to the heart of a child is key to developing godly character in them and in us.

> We are formed spiritually through the ongoing mystery of the Holy Spirit as God brings to completion the good work begun in a believer's life. Paradoxically, there is nothing we can do to cause growth. Growth is a gift given as we learn to attend to the presence of God in our lives.
>
> **Keith Anderson & Randy Reese**[15]

Character formation happens as people interact and what is deep inside starts to surface. In children's ministry, it's easy for disciple makers to become visibly impatient over small things children do, snapping at children in moments of frustration. We all make mistakes, and frustration is common, but we need to pay attention to our own hearts as well. Is our gut reaction a one-time occurrence, or is it common? Is something deeper going on inside us? As leaders and kid-influencers, we need to take the first step and work through the things that lie below the surface in our own hearts in order to effectively disciple the children we serve.

Christ's work in our lives is pervasive, encompassing every part of us. Like working in a garden, kid-influencers may need to spend time doing some weeding and digging around with God's Spirit in the spiritual soil of their heart. The heart needs to be watered and fed regularly with God's Word and prayer, and given opportunities to grow in obedience by serving faithfully on behalf of God's Son. Over the years, I've identified five character traits that are necessary for every kid-influencer to actively cultivate in the garden of their heart if they want to effectively model Christ's life-transforming mission. The five traits are borne of God's Spirit: humility, integrity, holiness, faithfulness, and perseverance. Let's look at each of these in turn.

HUMILITY: WHERE ARE SEEDS OF PRIDE GROWING IN MY LIFE?

> **Do nothing out of selfish ambition or vain conceit. Rather, in humility value others above yourselves, not looking to your own interests but each of you to the interests of the others.**
> *Philippians 2:3–4*

I don't always know *why* people sign up to serve in children's ministry, but I am always impressed that they do. Like parenting, working with kids is often messy, sticky, loud, tiring, and generally thankless. While adults may say they value the next generation, working with kids is not often highly esteemed. Children's ministries are seen as a form of Christian childcare, or they are relegated to backrooms and windowless basements. In some churches, the resources are extremely limited and the expectations are high. I know firsthand that serving kids and families is hard, humbling work.

You might expect serving children would naturally result in the growth of humility, but as with anything we do, it is still possible for seeds of pride to creep in. Are leaders serving out of guilt or obligation, or do they really love being with kids? Do leaders view themselves as "above" the children, or do they value them as disciples of Jesus at a different stage of the same journey? Is a spirit of self-righteousness surfacing, or are leaders confident in their calling and the ministry's place as part of the body of Christ? It can be discouraging to discover that pride and selfishness have taken root in your ministry, and even in your own heart.

The antidote to pride is the cross of Jesus Christ. His life, death, and resurrection were all marked by humility. Jesus set an example in Philippians 2 that is both admirable and challenging. In our world, submission is viewed as weakness. The idea of serving other people's needs seems absurd and weak. Imagine what your life would be like if you spent an entire week, or even a day or an hour, thinking about others first. That's the high goal God has set for us as followers of Christ.

My prayer is that every children's ministry leader, paid or volunteer, would be fundamentally committed to this exhortation from Philippians 2:14: "Do everything without grumbling or arguing." When we grow frustrated and are tempted to complain, we need only look at Christ, who emptied himself of all privilege, power, and position to become a poor human being and sacrificially suffer death for the sake of the world. We want to cultivate in our hearts the same spirit of humility that led Jesus to wash his disciples' feet. Like Jesus, relational disciple makers stand up to lead by first kneeling down.[16]

Take an honest look at your heart. Has pride moved in? Is a sense of entitlement growing? Do you feel you deserve more thanks, a pat on the back, or recognition from others? Are there jobs that need to be done around the ministry that you think are below your status? Does it frustrate you that your children's ministry isn't as big, well-funded, cool, or talked about as much as the church down the street? Is there another leader at the church who seems to be more successful than you? The seeds of pride result in a heart that is self-focused, thinking only of having its own needs met. May God grant us humble hearts that recognize God's mercy and freely extend that mercy to the children we serve!

The more we receive from God, the more we have to pour into the lives of others. Kid-influencers cultivate the trait of humility in their lives by cooperating with the Holy Spirit and intentionally choosing to put the needs of others before their own. They reflect on the cross and meditate on the undeserved gift of God's mercy toward them and the great love they have been shown. They are transparent with other believers, sober-mindedly using spiritual gifts and serving without seeking to be noticed. In this environment, Christlike humility can bud and blossom.

Turning kid-influencers into lifelong disciple makers requires a strong commitment to rooting out pride at all costs. If you find it showing up in your own life, pull the root. If it starts growing in the church or children's ministry leaders around you, call it out. You don't want the seeds to spread in such a way that they multiply into the kids and families you serve. A simple way to address pride is to ask if it's present. Get your team together, ask if the ministry is marked by pride and if so, how. Write down what you see, discuss it, and make changes as necessary. Pride, if it's widespread, won't disappear overnight. On the other hand, if it's widespread, you probably won't do the exercise as a team anyway. I pray you choose the former.

INTEGRITY: WHO AM I WHEN NO ONE IS LOOKING?

Whoever walks in integrity walks securely, but whoever takes crooked paths will be found out.
Proverbs 10:9

The New Testament is mostly a collection of letters. The epistles were written by the apostles, sent from one family of believers to another, and adhered to as a way of life. Lifelong discipleship depended on the teachings of Christ making their way from one church to the next and being lived out fully. Peter and Paul knew they could not be everywhere all the time. They needed to multiply their leadership into others through their examples, teachings, and writings.

So what do letters have to do with the character seed of integrity? In Philippians 2:12, Paul writes: "Therefore, my dear friends, as you have always obeyed—not only in my presence, but now much more in my absence—continue to work out your salvation with fear and trembling." Paul recognized as a spiritual leader that when the cat's away, the mice will play! It's a silly saying, but you get the point. People do all kinds of things when no one is watching. Pranks at school happen behind the teacher's back. Office employees clock back in a little later from lunch when the boss is out of town. Paul specifically called out the Corinthian believers so this wouldn't happen. They needed to know the character bar was still high even though Paul wasn't around to keep tabs on them. Integrity is a matter of the heart, not what's measured when someone who matters is watching. Truth be told, God sees it all . . . all of the time.

Dr. Henry Cloud describes integrity as being the combination of two aspects of character: ethics and essence.[17] On one level, character is evidenced by garden-variety traits like truth telling and being on time. It is a sincere commitment to making moral choices and generally doing right versus wrong things, actions that demonstrate that he or she can be trusted. This aspect speaks to our effectiveness—are we generally trustworthy and responsible? There is another aspect of integrity that can only be found further below the surface. It's part of a person's make-up, like the chassis of a car or a hull of a ship. This reflects the inner heart of a person, if they are consistent and whole-hearted, acting out of their convictions and deep beliefs.

Cloud defines integrity this way: "When we are talking about integrity, we are talking about being a whole person, an integrated person, with all of our different parts working well and delivering the functions that they were designed to deliver. It is about wholeness and effectiveness as people. It truly is 'running on all cylinders.'"[18]

People are trustworthy because their external behaviors reflect the true disposition of their hearts. How we engage in activity (doing) and how we engage with others (relating) must work well together for character (being) to stay afloat. How does this relate to disciple making, especially among children? Children pay close attention to what adults say and what they do, and they are quick to spot inconsistencies. Our words and actions should match who we are, and if we say we are disciples of Jesus, we must walk in that calling with integrity both when people are watching and when they're not. Our integrity is shaped and maintained when we continuously walk in "a manner worthy of the gospel of Christ," even when no one is looking over our shoulder.[19]

Not long ago I was invited to speak at a regional gathering of children's ministry leaders in California. Heidi is one of the finest kid-influencers, lifelong disciple makers, and children's ministry leaders I know.[20] Her ministry is remarkable, as are the people she surrounds herself with. Heidi is known for taking every precaution to elevate safety for the kids, families, and leaders connected to the ministry she leads. Heidi also maintains an impeccable personal and professional work ethic. She knows the stakes are high in God's kingdom, and she doesn't want anyone throwing stones at her life or her leadership. Heidi is fully committed to serving the Lord whether other people are watching or not.

While I was in town to speak, Heidi invited me to join her family for frozen yogurt after the event. How could I refuse? She wanted to spend time talking through what went well, what didn't go well, what stories attendees shared about their leadership challenges, what could be improved for the next year, and so on. It was fun to connect, troubleshoot, and plan for the future as fellow disciple makers and children's ministry leaders. I was already impressed by Heidi's integrity, but then something even more incredible happened.

As I headed to my car, I asked if she and her husband were heading home for a nap to recoup before the madness of Sunday children's ministry hit. They said no and something about needing to make a stop on the way. Remembering that several extra lunchboxes were in her car from the big event, I asked a follow-up question. They quietly told me they'd be passing the food out in an impoverished part of town. Apparently it's a regular practice for their family, but they don't make a big deal about it. I was floored. Tired from speaking and leading and relating all day, Heidi didn't bat an eye at the thought of serving others in need. It was a picture of integrity. I was grateful to get a glimpse at the person Heidi (and her family) is when no one is watching.

> The reality is that the way in which a leader conducts his personal life does, in fact, have a profound impact on his ability to exercise effective public leadership.
>
> Samuel. D. Rima[21]

You have a choice when it comes to cultivating integrity. The seed is already planted, but its successful growth requires you to cooperate with God's Spirit. Who are you when no one is looking? Can you be trusted to do what you say? More so, can you be trusted to be the same person in every area of life regardless of who is paying attention? Children and children's ministries need leaders who are wholeheartedly committed to integrity as a way of life. Integrity is a character quality you can talk to trusted family and friends about. They'll tell you the truth if you're open to it. And if they're really on your side, they'll walk with you as you step forward to grow in this key dimension of total life transformation.

HOLINESS: WHAT DO MY ACTIONS REVEAL ABOUT MY HEART?

Don't let anyone look down on you because you are young, but set an example for the believers in speech, in conduct, in love, in faith and in purity.
1 Timothy 4:12

I painted the above words from Paul to Timothy on the wall of the first church where I worked. They were a daily reminder to all of us involved in the ministry, a challenge to kids, leaders, parents, guests, elders, pastors, the janitor, and even contract laborers (yes, we needed minor repairs from time to time). Kids and leaders actually started holding each other accountable, holding up the challenge of this verse to one another. Often, those who are young do not realize the potential power of their faithful example. And those who are older tend to overlook "reverse mentoring" opportunities because of traditional paradigms.[22]

"Speech, conduct, love, faith, and purity" cover a lot of ground, but the word "purity" stands out to me in particular here. The core idea is that the people of God are called to be set apart as holy, and wholly God's, from the rest of the world. Purity and holiness go hand in hand. Like a computer operating system upgrade, new followers of Jesus should live and love differently. Their compass is set to a different north, and their actions are determined by different motives. Leviticus 19–20 lays out God's desire and rationale for his people to be holy. And Jesus reiterates this in Matthew 5:48: "Be perfect, therefore, as your heavenly Father is perfect." In 1 Peter 1:14–16, the scattered church is exhorted to holiness as God's obedient children. Purity is about more than just our sexual ethics; it is a call to a life of holiness, living set apart from sin and dedicated to the call and the mission of God.

Although it may not be discussed much in some churches, kid-influencers must take their personal purity very seriously. Why? Because what we see, hear, and do affects the heart, and when we draw from our hearts to serve others, we do this consciously *and* unconsciously.

What we do in our private lives will directly affect our ministry to children and its effectiveness. I'm reminded of the classic children's ministry song, "Be Careful, Little Eyes, What You See." If you are like me, you are now singing it in your head (and trying to figure out how to make it stop!). But think about that song. How many things have you seen, heard, or done that you wish you could un-see, un-hear, or undo? Thankfully, our ability to stand before God is not based on our past sins, on anything we have done or will do. It is based on what Christ has done for us. But while our acceptance from God is sure, we still feel the effects of sin in our lives. Disciple makers are never flawless, but we must guard our hearts, minds, and thoughts and ask God to purify our motives and desires so we do not fall prey to temptation.

The timeless teaching of Philippians 4:8 is helpful here: "Finally, brothers and sisters, whatever is true, whatever is noble, whatever is right, whatever is pure, whatever is lovely, whatever is admirable—if anything is excellent or praiseworthy—think about such things." I will often ask myself, and those serving in ministry, "What do I think, say, or do that misrepresents Christ?" It's a great question to put on a volunteer or employment application, if you're bold enough to follow it up in a face-to-face interview. This question inevitably uncovers impurities in my life. Finding unholy attributes is not the difficult part. It's the next step that is the hardest. Are we committed to eradicating all impurities, any sinful patterns that are exposed? Anything I knowingly hide or am unwilling to address head-on will be a snare to my growth and ministry as a disciple of Jesus. The pursuit of holiness requires a strong commitment to walking in the light with others, confessing sin, and cultivating joy and desire in the Lord.[23] The Word of God is uniquely able to cut cleanly through the surface of our lives and get at what is really going on in a human heart.[24]

You're likely familiar with the "iceberg" principle. It gets used in leadership circles all the time to talk about what's above and below the waterline. Icebergs are really big, but the tip that breaches the water's surface is relatively small. Knowing this helps the sinking of the Titanic make more sense. The massive ocean liner was taken down by what was below, not what could be barely seen off in the distance. Character works the same way.

We might be able to see glimpses of holiness in the words, actions, relationships, and successes that are visible. Conversely, we might see the lack of holiness as well. But that's not the whole story or the full picture of who we are. What's going on in our hearts lies below the waterline. Our desires, motives, secrets, hidden agendas, and more live lives of their own at the base of our character iceberg. We need to be mindful of what's obvious and not so obvious if we long for traits like humility, integrity, and holiness to thrive. It's important that we look in the mirror and allow other people to be a mirror for us. They will love us in the right direction as we seek to follow Christ. Total life transformation must take place through and through, not in part.

So, how's your heart doing these days? If you're serious about cultivating holiness, it's probably time to get it checked out.

FAITHFULNESS: WHO AM I BECOMING?

**Whatever you do, work at it with all your heart,
as working for the Lord, not for human masters.**
Colossians 3:23

Rose began serving in children's ministry in the early '80s. Ten years later, her husband Ed joined her. When Ed and Rose's daughter began school, the two of them began serving weekly with children in kindergarten and first grade. For over seventeen years, this amazing couple invested their lives in kids and families in their church. Taking into account holiday weekends, vacations, and occasionally calling in sick, that is well over 800 weeks of volunteering![25] On the far other end of the spectrum, if statistics about children's ministry leaders are accurate, you'll be tempted to turn in your resignation letter before you finish reading this book.

When they started out, Ed and Rose had no idea how long they would be serving in children's ministry. Today, the number of lives they have impacted directly and indirectly for God's glory can't begin to be counted. Many kids come back to see them when they hit the junior high, high school, and college years, and several stick around to serve in the ministry with them. Yet while Ed and Rose demonstrate tireless dedication week in and week out, there is more than a hard work ethic motivating them. Their loyalty to Christ and his church inspires me. They are faithful, dependable, and responsible. What lies at the root of all this? How do they faithfully, dependably, and responsibly serve for such a long time? They have cultivated something we all need: discipline.

Much has been made of the connection between the words "disciple" and "discipline." Perhaps, when you first think of discipline, you think of a child sitting in the time-out chair or being sent to the hallway for a talk. But discipline is broader in definition and purpose. It's the fertilizer for growing character qualities like faithfulness, dependability, and responsibility. These things must be evidenced and witnessed over time. You don't develop a reputation of being faithful or dependable by doing something right once. You must follow through on core commitments, time after time. This is about more than simply showing up on time when scheduled (although that is a good start). It's about developing habits in your life, settled practices that give your words and actions power.

To become responsible in any area of life, you need discipline. Responsible teachers study and prepare faithfully. Responsible athletes train regularly. Responsible parents reflect and readjust frequently. A disciple is a life-long learner. Discipline is about developing practices that will aid and enable learning and growth. It's no secret that attitudes of the heart are formed through repetitive actions. If you want to grow in love, choose to love others, even when you don't feel like it. The same is true for all fruit of the spirit: joy, peace, patience, kindness, and so forth.[26] Of course, lasting fruit is not a matter of sheer willpower. It requires us to meditate on God's Word and cooperate with the Holy Spirit in spiritual disciplines that create new habits and destroy old patterns of thinking and behavior.

So what kinds of disciplines are needed to become like Jesus? Historically, practices like reading and meditating on Scripture, the practice of prayer, spending time in solitude, confession of sin, private and corporate worship, fellowship with other believers, financial giving, and serving have played a key role in nurturing spiritual growth.[27] Every disciple and every kid-influencer should be learning to practice these disciplines and taking active steps to grow closer to Jesus. The truth is that all disciples are kid-influencers; some are just more naturally gifted, passionate, mindful, and equipped. Intentional disciples are those dedicated to self-discipline as Paul describes in 1 Corinthians 9:24–27. They read and study the same Bible, pray to the same Almighty God, fully participate in the same spiritual family (the church), and live out the same gospel of Jesus Christ privately and publicly. They are just intentional about it. No one said it would be easy. Cultivating a character of dependability and responsibility takes effort, but it is invaluable heart work.

Kid-influencers in your ministry, you included, can become more faithful with effort. The more consistent you are about making a plan and sticking to it, the better. Spontaneity and flexibility are important, especially as God's Spirit leads, but keeping commitments matters too. So set up your program and run it. Schedule your people and hold them accountable. Map out the calendar and follow through with excellence. Maintain the same level of faithfulness personally as you do publicly. Invite team members to talk about where self-discipline is on track and where it's lacking. Give them opportunities to partner together so their strengths can flourish and their weaknesses can be supported. Regular meetings for encouragement, brainstorming, prayer, and accountability can cultivate faithfulness. You'll be tempted to cancel these huddles as soon as people stop showing up regularly. Resist it! Lovingly course-correct and challenge your team to be disciplined together. Lifelong discipleship depends on it.

PERSEVERANCE: HOW DO I ENDURE WHEN THE GOING GETS TOUGH?

> **Let us not become weary in doing good, for at the proper time we will reap a harvest if we do not give up.**
> **Galatians 6:9**

Kim brings her best self to serve in children's ministry as a leader week in and week out. Why? Her life is ordered around a handful of Christ-centered priorities, and she follows through with her core commitments. She is known for her consistency on multiple levels. Kim's relationship with God is primary, then her family and friends, followed by her work and ministry in the world. She is the first to admit when these concentric circles of care become disordered, misaligned, or overwhelming. Kim looks to the Bible and biblical community for guidance and support. Her prayers are bold. Her relationships run deep. She joyfully and sacrificially serves Christ within her areas of passion and giftedness. And she makes herself available to mentor and be mentored as a follower of Jesus.

When kids, parents, and leaders interact with Kim, they leave encouraged. They feel listened to and loved. They know children's ministry is not the sum of Kim's life, but when she is with them she is fully present. Her kid-influence flows from her priorities, and she doesn't quit when things are difficult. She is committed to staying the course over the long haul.

Research in child development regularly highlights the importance of being reliable in your interactions with children. What does reliability refer to? It means you are a person of principle, of unwavering character. You're consistent, dependable, and steadfast. These are individuals who take inventory of their relationships and the way they live their lives. They evaluate themselves against their goals and their calling and refuse to give up midcourse, even in the midst of struggle and difficulty. They are committed to this work because they recognize the eternal stakes in their work with children and families.

There are two passages that are particularly helpful to me in thinking about consistency in children's ministry: 1 Timothy 4:16 and 2 Timothy 2:15. First Timothy 4:16 says, "Watch your life and doctrine closely. Persevere in them, because if you do, you will save both yourself and your hearers." This verse alludes to the role prophets played in the Old Testament. God's word to his messengers was that if they faithfully communicated his truth, over time people would be saved. If they did not, their blood would be on their heads. There is a call to persevere, to stick to the mission and not give up, with the promise of salvation at the end. Consistency matters. Walk the walk and talk the talk. It will speak volumes to kids and parents who are in need of the gospel of Jesus Christ.

Second Timothy 2:15 says, "Do your best to present yourself to God as one approved, a worker who does not need to be ashamed and who correctly handles the word of truth." I first learned this verse in third grade in Awana.[28] This verse was a helpful reminder that perseverance is critical in reading Scripture and serving the Lord. Endurance requires boldness and tenacity. We must read the Bible with integrity and intentionality, not picking and choosing verses like fortune cookie quotes. Some sections of Scripture are difficult to grasp, especially those that grip us deep inside. The Word of God needs to read through me even as I read through it—it needs to be internalized and applied to our lives and bring conviction to our hearts. To become like Jesus, disciples must spend consistent effort seeking to know, love, and serve Christ through God's Word and service to him.

Over time, our lives become transparent to others. How are you cultivating the garden of your heart? Are you seeing the seeds of the Word of God grow and bear the fruit of humility, integrity, holiness, faithfulness, and perseverance?

NOW IS THE TIME TO LEAD KIDS TO INTEGRATE THE GOSPEL INTO THEIR WHOLE LIVES

Whatever happens, conduct yourselves in a manner worthy of the gospel of Christ. Then, whether I come and see you or only hear about you in my absence, I will know that you stand firm in the one Spirit, striving together as one for the faith of the gospel.
Philippians 1:27

How do you reach the heart of a child? By reaching the hearts of kid-influencers and turning them into disciples who make disciples. What matters most in your ministry? Are you developing your kid-influencers and ministry leaders into disciples and teaching them to make disciples of the children in your ministry? Or are you simply running a program and going through the motions? What you value will determine your results, or as Jesus said, where your treasure is, there will your heart be also. Those leading the charge will set the focus of ministry activity. If evangelism is important to a leader, it will show up on the calendar and in what she does and says. The same is true for Bible study, prayer, Scripture memory, worship, supporting mission projects, sports, serving the poor, caring for orphans and widows, and so on. Relational children's ministry cannot thrive as an add-on environment or experience. It has pace-setting potential for the whole congregation as a launching pad for discipleship and lifelong disciple making.

QUESTIONS FOR DISCUSSION & REFLECTION

1. In what way(s) has a relationship with Jesus revolutionized your way of living? In what area(s) have your thoughts and actions changed most dramatically?

2. Who do you admire for breaking the mold by being fully devoted to Christ as his disciple, and why?

3. How can you and your church leadership increasingly highlight the fullness of discipleship transformation in the lives of children?

4. "When it comes to discipleship, Christlike character is formed privately before God uses it publicly." Do you agree or disagree with this statement? Explain.

5. Which of the five character traits of effective kid-influencers is God's Spirit prompting you to personally focus on in this season of discipleship and ministry?

   Humility: Where are seeds of pride growing in my life?
   Integrity: Who am I when no one is looking?
   Holiness: What do my actions reveal about my heart?
   Faithfulness: Who am I becoming?
   Perseverance: How do I endure when the going gets tough?

6. How would you define the gospel of Jesus Christ? How do people share this in word, deed, and attitude?

7. Would you say your current model of children's ministry is centered on embodying the gospel or promoting good principles? Explain.

8. What is one change you could implement that would ensure kids and kid-influencers in your church live out Christ's life-transforming mission more fully?

CHAPTER 9

INVITATION 5: EQUIP CHILDREN FOR DYNAMIC DISCIPLESHIP

It's easier to build up a child than fix an adult.
Frederick Douglass[1]

I have no greater joy than to hear that my children are walking in the truth.
3 John 1:4

HAVE YOU EVER CONSIDERED the difference between running track and running cross-country? I think it's a helpful analogy for discipling kids. Too many of us who love kids and families end up creating situations where they run around a track week in and week out. The track is short, and we move them through quickly. Sometimes we add hurdles or change the length of the race or implement baton passing to heighten the challenge or bolster community. But everyone ends up following the same circuit. We find ways to mix it up, adapt lessons, change up décor, and bring in new teachers or leaders, whatever it takes to keep things fresh for kids. Yet after all those years spent running in circles, when the kids "graduate" from the track, they discover they are not prepared to run off road. They have never learned to run the distance, to run cross-country.

Cross-country running follows a course, but the course changes. There are other runners running at different paces. Runners adapt as the seasons change, modifying the course and facing hills and varying elements. Running through a field or forest is different from running around a track. Each step presents unique challenges and unforeseen obstacles. The coaches are still present, but their voices quickly fade into the distance as the race continues.

Both track and cross-country have defined destinations. You know when you've successfully finished the race, but life is less like the track and more like the cross-country path: unpredictable and subject to change. As followers of Jesus, most of our running is off-road, off the beaten path. We follow the road less travelled, not the familiar track.

GOING OFF ROAD

Children's ministries all over the country have created fantastic settings for kids to learn about God's Word. But most of this learning happens apart from the noise of everyday life. And while most of these programs and classes emphasize the importance of applying the Bible to life—"Don't just take it in, take it home!"—we need to be honest. This doesn't always happen. Kids enjoy the program or the meeting and take the handout, but most of the week is spent in another world where the things they learn on Sundays are disconnected from their day-to-day lives. Let me be upfront and remind us again, once and for all: there are no silver bullet solutions. There is no magic formula we all need to follow to ensure lasting change is happening with kids beyond the walls of church ministry. And the ideas that do exist aren't easy to implement. Follow up with kids and families? Great idea! But how do you do so in a systematic, meaningful way? And what about parents who aren't interested? Most children's ministries stick to what works: telling Bible stories, linking Scripture to everyday scenarios, asking relevant comprehension and personal life questions in small groups, and then challenging children to head home and make a difference.

Unfortunately, this model perpetuates the cycle of disconnecting church from "the real world," where kids live each day—the context where their multiple worlds and worldviews collide.

Relational discipleship recognizes that the journey of following Christ is different for each person. And relational children's ministry is about helping kid-influencers shift from a predictable to a personalized approach to disciple making. The goal isn't to run the track; it's to run cross-country. Running with the Lord in the company of others is a deeply personal and community-oriented experience. It is not tied to the school year or the church calendar.

The goal of relational children's ministry is to disrupt the discipleship trajectory most kids in the church are on today. Why? Because it isn't making disciples who make disciples. This means we need to radically uproot the system. If your discipleship is currently more like a hamster wheel of activity, and you measure effectiveness by how many turns you run on the wheel, you have a problem. Running the wheel is not the goal. Our effectiveness isn't measured by a particular curriculum or calendar schedule. It's measured by spiritual growth; by children learning, one stage at a time, what it means to passionately love and follow Christ.

WHO'S GUIDING YOU?

The ministry of Awana was a significant part of my children's ministry experience between third and eighth grades. At Awana we were encouraged to invite non-Christian friends weekly, share with our parents what we discovered and memorized in God's Word, and step up to serve inside and outside the church. But Awana was about more than the content we learned. Every kid spent face-to-face time with a leader who cared for them. Today there are children in over 100 countries around the world being impacted by their involvement in Awana each week. I am grateful to be one child of millions whose disciple-making trajectory was changed forever because of this worldwide ministry's heart for making disciples.

David was one of my favorite children's ministry leaders.[2] He was a high school student who served in Awana, but he was also a student attending the program for his age level. There was something powerful about knowing we were on the same discipleship journey. I knew David was further along, but we were heading toward the same goal. He invited friends. I did too. He explored God's Word. So did I. He shared what he was learning with his parents. I did as well. We both served inside and outside the church. And we each had leaders who would look us in the eyes each week to remind us how much we mattered to God and to them.

I looked up to David (and not just because he was really tall). I wanted to be like David. His athleticism, sensitivity, patience, and strength were inspiring. His passion for the Bible and devotion to the church community motivated me. And even more than being a volunteer leader with kids, David modeled what it meant to be a guide. He was living out his own unscripted adventure with God in relationship with the Lord and others, and he wrestled with messy faith and modeled Christ's life-transforming mission. He guided people as God's Spirit guided him along. Disciple making seemed to be part of his DNA.

When I was in fifth grade, David came knocking at my door. Awana was offering a week away for kids who completed a certain number of lessons, including Bible reading, Scripture memorization, serving, and several other activities. It was a great incentive, but keeping up with the workload was not easy. Knowing my family situation and what it would take for me to earn a scholarship to summer camp, David worked out a deal with my mom to make it happen. Each week he would come by our apartment before or after his job as a lifeguard so we could study the Bible together. The Awana program season was over, but the deadline to complete the assignments was not up yet, so I knew he was going beyond the call of duty. I have no idea how many hours we spent together, but in the end, with his help, I earned a scholarship to camp.

> Let the Bible fill the memory, rule the heart and guide the feet.
>
> **Henrietta Mears[3]**

David didn't teach from a podium. There were no dramas or skits. No slideshows or overhead projectors. It was just the two of us, our Bibles, and the Holy Spirit. But the Lord used David and other guides like him to impact my life by experiencing what it was like to encounter the truth of God's Word together and prayerfully engage in response to the Holy Spirit's leading. Sometimes we followed a curriculum, but other times our interaction was more informal.

What did I learn? That being a disciple wasn't about a class or a curriculum or jumping through hoops. It was about relationship and allowing God's Spirit to use his Word to dynamically guide my discipleship journey.

LEARN TO TRUST WHAT'S TRUE

Not long ago I was traveling with Nancy, a longtime friend and ministry colleague.[4] It was raining and we were in an unfamiliar town, heading to a new location for the first time. We were visiting a local children's ministry that was trying out a new curriculum we had helped develop. I had just finished typing in the church's address on my phone's GPS when Nancy said to me: "Dan, I'm so grateful that you are taking care of all the navigation. Thanks." I appreciated the encouragement and mentioned how much easier travel was these days, thanks to technology. With twenty minutes to arrive at our destination, we left the parking lot and did whatever the soothing voice on the dashboard told us to do next.

You can probably guess where this story is going.

After traveling on the same road for quite some time, Nancy and I noticed fewer and fewer streetlights. The road narrowed considerably. Eventually the voice on the dashboard told us we had arrived. All we could see was a tree-covered hillside on the right and a guardrail keeping us from driving into a river on the left. Up and down the road we went looking for the entrance to the church. Now we were nervous and feared we might arrive late. Nancy graciously nudged me to call our host for help. As I hung up the phone, I said to Nancy, "Apparently there's a bridge on the other side of town with the same name as the road the church is on. We are by that bridge."

We entered the new address into the GPS and again listened for the soothing—and now slightly annoying—voice to give us instructions. This led to another wild goose chase and twenty-five additional unnecessary minutes on winding roads along and across and back up the river. In the dark, in the rain, we gradually returned to civilization and made our way to the church. We had planned to be early and finally arrived over an hour late. After laughing off our mistake with the children's ministry team (and learning that we were not the first victims of GPS malpractice), Nancy and I drove back to the hotel. It took us all of four minutes.

What did we learn from our adventure with our GPS? Nancy and I both knew something was off target long before being told we were, in fact, lost. We both knew deep down that we should trust our intuition, not the voice on the dashboard. Yet we kept going. *Had we paid closer attention to what we knew to be true, we would have trusted and followed the right voice.*

Jesus, the Good Shepherd, once said, "My sheep listen to my voice; I know them, and they follow me" (John 10:27). God's Word is full of his Spirit and teeming with life.[5] The relationship we have with Christ lays the foundation for us to respond and take risks as he leads. Scripture becomes the GPS we rely upon for direction and discernment, and while we may lose direction along the way, it will happen less often as we learn to listen to the right voice. Disciples of all ages need to walk in step with the Holy Spirit.[6]

> We don't need to invent moments of God experience for people; we need to help each other see and listen and know.
>
> **Keith Anderson & Randy Reese**[7]

In 1 Samuel 3:1–10, we read the story of Samuel and Eli. This passage reminds me of when my kids were very young and they would innocently wake me up during the night to ask me if it was morning yet. I'm encouraged to see Eli, in his old age and grogginess, needing three chances to figure out that it was the Lord who was waking up Samuel. I think it's also important to note Samuel's disposition toward God. In verse 7 it says, "Now Samuel did not yet know the Lord: The word of the Lord had not yet been revealed to him." In other words, this was a learning experience for the boy, a way of teaching him to recognize the voice of the Lord. In verse 10 the story reaches an apex when Samuel responds to God saying, "Speak, for your servant is listening." Following Eli's guidance and humbly replying to the Lord, Samuel begins to learn to identify, listen to, trust, and follow the voice of the Lord.

Note how Samuel came to recognize the voice of God. It was God's Word (spoken audibly), God's Spirit (helping him to hear and understand), and God's people (through Eli). Samuel's story is unique, of course, but it should remind us that God has not changed. He still speaks today. Jesus said his disciples were "blessed" because they could hear with their hearts, not just their eyes and ears.[8] When I was a kid, two passages that spoke to me about trusting and following God's voice were Psalm 119:105 and Proverbs 3:5–6. Early on, I learned that the Bible is a guide for my discipleship journey. I also learned that trusting God and what he says in his Word, rather than my own instincts apart from him, would straighten my discipleship path. These key verses continue to guide me today, and they shape how I guide others.

> Who can say when, in a child, the dance with God begins? No one. . . . As long as there is mystery, there may be change and growth and the freedom for the dance.
>
> **Walter Wangerin Jr.**[9]

God's Word, illuminated by the Holy Spirit and clarified in the community of other disciples, creates a guiding authority for the Christian life, a discernment matrix. This matrix has guided me for decades. In relational discipleship, we need to teach children how to listen to the voice of God through Scripture and how to apply the Word to their hearts and lives with the help of other believers. Learning to identify God's voice sets kids up for a lifetime of dynamic discipleship. And to successfully help kids do this, kid-influencers need to guide them to grow with God in four areas.

FOUR GROWTH AREAS FOR DYNAMIC DISCIPLESHIP

We do not know much about Jesus' early years, particularly those when he was a child or teen. We can speculate about his childhood in light of what we know about child development and his Jewish upbringing.[10] Based on this, we can surmise that he engaged in a work apprenticeship alongside his earthly father, Joseph. We know Jesus amazed the rabbis in the temple at age twelve, but apart from this one story, we have little else to go on.[11] Yet one verse stands out as we think about the childhood years and the training of children through adolescence into adulthood:

> And Jesus grew
> in wisdom and stature,
> and in favor with God
> and man.
> *Luke 2:52*

This verse covers a lot of ground. It's a summary statement that tells us Jesus grew and matured, and that his growth was fully integrated, both internally and relationally. It dawned on me one day as I was reading Luke 2:52 that this verse provided me with a simple framework for having conversations with my sons. I shared the passage with them and suggested that our conversations fall into the three categories mentioned: wisdom, stature, and favor. My boys liked the simplicity—and the depth—of focusing on these three areas. We tried this for awhile, but after finding that words like wisdom, stature, and favor were hard to grasp, we redefined them as four key growth areas: character growth, physical growth, spiritual growth, and relational growth. Now we use these phrases to guide our conversations about the variety of different ways my boys are growing and maturing. Avery and Aaron know they can talk with me about anything. For them, being able to pinpoint where a topic fits in these four areas of growth makes it easier for them to bring up questions. And I've found after sharing this with other moms, dads, and children's ministry leaders that the concept resonates with them as well. I think it's a great way of making sure your relational children's ministry is addressing the whole person and the diverse ways in which we must grow as disciples of Jesus.

CHARACTER GROWTH: GROWING IN WISDOM

As I shared earlier, Deuteronomy 6 tells us that the family at home and the family of God are called to work in tandem to train up children in the way of the Lord. The biblical approach is an integrated discipleship model, and kid-influencers are in the perfect position to invite kids and parents to respond to the call of Jesus and be his disciples. Proverbs 4:11–12 says, "I instruct you in the way of wisdom and lead you along straight paths. When you walk, your steps will not be hampered; when you run, you will not stumble." This passage paints a picture of what it looks like for a person to hear and obey God's guidance. It emphasizes the centrality of the Word and the Holy Spirit in the development of Christlike virtues.

Kid-influencers can facilitate experiences where kids imitate God's example and walk in the way of sacrificial love like Christ.[12] The stories and lessons of the Bible must be unpacked in context through dialogue and applied to life. This means we need to talk about sin, salvation, spiritual growth, and the big picture of God's mission, not just moral lessons or stories that steer children toward a checklist of character traits and behaviors.

Children can and should be given the opportunity to uncover the character of Christ, or lack thereof, in their own hearts with the goal of becoming more like him. For kids to grow in wisdom, they need to be taught to reflect on their choices and encouraged to consider their motives, as well as the consequences their actions might have on others. This is how they grow in wisdom.

In your ministry, disciple makers can set the tone for growth in wisdom. It's important that kid-influencers equip children to attune to the truths of God's Word through consistent engagement with the Bible and prayer. As leaders model this, kids discover how to hear God directing them as well. Ideally your curriculum provides experiences rooted in Scripture coupled with space to reflect and respond in prayer. If not, find ways to build it in. It would be great if every child and children's ministry leader could get a special set of headphones to hear directly from God, but it doesn't work quite like this. However, if you take growing in wisdom seriously, you'll equip kids in ways that enable them to discern the voice of their heavenly Father in the moment.

PHYSICAL GROWTH: GROWING IN STATURE

Ages and stages are always popular topics with new parents. They want to know what to expect as their child grows, what to watch for, and what to watch out for. *When will my child sit up? When will he crawl? When should I anticipate she'll start walking? How about driving and getting a job?* There is obviously some predictability to these areas, yet every child's maturity process is still unique.

Physical growth milestones in every child's life tend to be obvious. First words spoken. First steps taken. Losing baby teeth. When pre-adolescence hits, voices start changing and bodies change shape. I will never forget the day I first noticed a five o'clock shadow on my son's upper lip, and I realized that he was becoming a young man. As children get older, the milestones come more and more quickly.

People grow, but not without struggles and challenges. Muscles get stronger when they experience healthy stress and strain. And physical growth and health affects our spiritual growth as well. Proper diet, exercise, and sleep are necessary for healthy discipleship. Kid-influencers can model physical growth and even guide children by incorporating physical aspects of life into whatever ministry they offer. Without turning your ministry into a weekly carnival of fun and games, there is some real benefit to "getting the wiggles out" before you dive into God's Word. Look for opportunities to tie physical activities to your discipleship and instruction. Jesus taught his followers to love God with all their strength, and we must not forget that training is a matter of the mind, heart, will, *and* the body.[13] Growing in stature encompasses both our physical and emotional growth.

When Israel was readying itself to take the Promised Land, God said to Joshua "be strong and courageous" four times as the people installed him as the new leader.[14] The challenges he was about to face would be many and they would be difficult, yet the payoff would be tremendous. Joshua, having learned to meet with the Lord as a child in the Tent of Meeting with Moses, was equipped to trust and follow God's Spirit and lead his people with spiritual wisdom as well as physical and emotional strength.[15] Kids and kid-influencers today need encouragement to "be strong and courageous" for the sake of Christ as well.

Relational children's ministry recognizes physical growth as a central part of dynamic discipleship. We aren't just interested in one aspect of a child; we care about the whole person. Being human means celebrating strengths and weaknesses and the shifts and changes our bodies experience over time. God created his children as individual masterpieces, and growing in stature does not happen overnight.[16]

What can you do to mark milestones along the way as kids grow and develop in your ministry? Birthdays are fun to celebrate, and children love getting mail. Ask volunteer leaders and spiritual grandparents in your ministry to send a card to every kid who celebrates another year of life. The start and end of the school year is another biggie for kids. What can you do to kick off fall and summer so parents and children know you're aware of the world outside the walls of the church? Like many parents etch notches on a wall to mark their children's physical growth, relational children's ministries maintain eye contact with kids as they mature from birth all the way to adulthood (and beyond). Enlist ideas from your leaders and put something meaningful into practice today.

SPIRITUAL GROWTH: GROWING IN GOD'S FAVOR

It is impossible to grow without proper nourishment. Jesus teaches in John 15:1–17 that he alone is the true source and sustainer of life, and nothing of value can grow apart from him. Remaining connected in unbroken relationship with Jesus Christ is essential. While we must not wrongly separate the "spiritual" from the physical, emphasizing this aspect helps us focus on how we are intentionally pursuing the means of grace God has given to us. As I've touched on earlier, these means include things like studying the Bible, spending time in prayer, reflecting on our motives, and listening to the desires of our hearts and bringing them before God. In many ways, growing in wisdom and growing spiritually are two sides of the same coin. It includes time spent serving others, experiencing the grace of God in fellowship with other Christians and in sacrificial service to our neighbors. It includes moments that "feel" spiritual and those that do not.

If I could place my finger on a single moment that captures the heart of this aspect of our Christian growth, apart from Christ's death and resurrection, it would be the moment of Jesus' baptism by John. "As soon as Jesus was baptized, he went up out of the water. At that moment heaven was opened, and he saw the Spirit of God descending like a dove and alighting on him. And a voice from heaven said, 'This is my Son, whom I love; with him I am well pleased'" (Matt. 3:16–17).

The imagery of the Trinity is so powerful here: the Son emerges from the water, the Spirit descends as a dove, and the Father speaks unmerited words of approval. Christ had yet to accomplish anything at this point in his ministry. His temptation by Satan in the wilderness had not even happened yet. And still, the Lord unashamedly calls out his Son as beloved and rightly establishes his identity in relationship to God the Father. God's glory pours out, and the Father speaks words of approval, affirmation, and love to his beloved Son.

This scene powerfully speaks to our own identity as adopted children of God. By faith, the life of Christ, including his baptism, is ours. When God speaks these words to his Son, he is speaking them to you and to me. Romans 8:15–17 reminds us that when we receive God's Spirit, we are adopted as heirs with God's Son, Jesus. When children hear and understand this message of God's unconditional love and favor, their spiritual growth skyrockets.

Guiding children in spiritual growth begins with what they believe about God. Who is God? What is he like? Once children grasp who God is, they need to understand who they are and what it means to have an identity in Christ, to be a co-heir in God's family.[17] Younger children often associate their worth before God in connection with parents and other adults, and this can be both good and bad. Our affirmation and love for children can positively communicate God's love for them, but we must also help them understand God's love and approval as something distinct from the way they are treated by parents, peers, and others. Leaders and parents who confess their own failure and need for God model this to children, and the truth of Scripture equips kids to respond to who God really is, and what he has done and will do in human history.

God is the one who will complete the life-changing work he initiated.[18] The hard work of growing in God's love means learning to rely more and more on his person and presence for power. This is not about earning the Lord's favor; rather, it is a response of loving obedience to his greatness, goodness, and grace.

God recently called my longtime friend Nat out of youth ministry to work directly with children and families by building into the leaders who know, love, and serve them.[19] He's just getting started, but the Lord laid a strong vision on his heart for the ministry focus moving forward. Three simple words encapsulate what he believes the heartbeat should be: *Awe. Wonder. Response.* This doesn't speak to specifics of how and what. It clarifies the central purpose for existing as a ministry. Nat wants to make disciples who are in awe of who God is and what he's done. He wants to inspire and build on their curiosity as they wonder about the things of God. And he wants each person to have the opportunity to respond however God leads. It's so simple and yet it captures the essence of spiritual growth.

How does your ministry cut to the heart of discipleship so everyone is on board and heading in the same direction? Can you describe the essentials of spiritual growth? I'm sure you believe there are core practices and activities that will bring honor to God and grow kids and kid-influencers in the faith. Invest the time and energy to bring focus to your efforts for the sake of disciple making.

RELATIONAL GROWTH: GROWING IN PEOPLE'S FAVOR

I know a dad at church who discovered something about his daughter recently. She's someone different wherever she goes. She's not even in junior high yet, and she's already finding ways to fit in with whomever she's with. She hangs with the choir kids at practice before school. She hangs with her classmates at the lunch table. She rides the bus home with a few friends from church. She plays soccer with girls from another school at the park. And when she's home she likes to spend time alone and acts like she doesn't have any friends at all. It's possible this girl is a social butterfly. Or maybe she's an introvert in need of downtime. Perhaps something is going on in her family that's causing her to withdraw. Is this normal? Concerning? It's hard for parents to know without probing deeper. What is clear is that it's not uncommon for kids to become like chameleons these days. To survive in a sea of multiple worlds and worldviews, many people will do whatever it takes to fit in with their surroundings. This girl really is a good kid and I'm proud of her dad for asking the hard questions about what's going on with and inside her. Healthy relational growth over a lifetime requires a strong sense of self, beginning in childhood.

Peer pressure is a cliché phrase these days, but it's still a reality. Children wonder how to make their way in the world and look to family, friends, media, and culture for answers. They explore various aspects of their personalities and try on other people's behaviors. It's not uncommon for kids to lose themselves in the process in order to be liked and feel accepted. This is not a healthy approach to relational growth or growing in people's favor. Kid-influencers need to be mindful that identify formation in young children is important so they can establish healthy ways to express intimacy, respect, and love throughout their lives.

Part of our role as kid-influencers is guiding kids to wisely choose whom they walk with closely. Proverbs 13:20 says, "Walk with the wise and become wise, for a companion of fools suffers harm." Our role is to guide kids to be mindful of how surrounding people influence them[20] and how they are an influence on others. We need to help kids understand that although there are voices all around them crying out for their attention, not all of those voices are trustworthy.

Children develop their identities and learn to trust in the presence of long-term, loving relationships. When this happens, they can express Christlike love to others as they grow and mature. Listening to them and taking their questions and concerns seriously builds this kind of relationship. We also need to help them see that they influence others and to teach them how to show compassion toward others in the world. Relational growth continues to take place as children begin to see, hear, and feel the needs of others, especially the needs only Christ can meet.

If you're looking for relational growth ideas, check out this one. Kirsten and her team developed a unique approach that gives kids choices every time they come to midweek children's ministry at church.[21] They can participate in team building, art, or drama. It's just one part of their evening together, but it's honoring for them to be able to choose something they want to do and then live with the consequence of their choice. If they switch options from week to week, they meet different friends and get led by different leaders. The activities change too. What I love most about this approach is that the art and drama experiences are others-focused. The crafts and projects teach a lesson, and often they are given to people in need at a local food pantry or nursing home. The drama time also teaches a lesson, but through kids working in teams to create real-life scenarios using improvisation techniques. It's brilliant! Relationships with peers and adults are formed. It connects to

God's Word and the world outside of church. And kids are fully engaged in the experience. What a tremendous way to build into children (and leaders) in multiple areas of growth.

> As they [children] mentally move into abstract awareness and begin to reflectively wrestle with their identity, they realize that Christianity is something they need to discover and decide to embrace on their own.
>
> **Kara Powell**[22]

So much of what it means to know, love, and serve Christ is outwardly expressed in practical, tangible acts of love toward others. When this stems from a strong foundation in relationship with God, the fruit is a gift to those in need. Growing in wisdom, stature, and favor is ultimately not based on our righteous works or moral achievements. It is the gift of God to those who come to him in dependence and rely upon his grace through Jesus Christ. We must remember it's ultimately by his Spirit that God brings hope, healing, and wholeness to a growing child.[23]

One word of caution in all of this: don't get caught up in trying to capture everything on film. I'm speaking figuratively here. We prefer to measure outcomes that can be seen, counted, and photographed, right? God, on the other hand, looks at the heart. He's concerned with his children learning to listen to his still, small voice and respond in love. Whatever measures you take, do your best to shape what's going on in the heart, not just behaviors you hope to replicate.

NOW IS THE TIME FOR KIDS TO BE GUIDED BY GOD FOR LIFE

Equipping others for dynamic discipleship is an ongoing process. Kids and kid-influencers need tools in their tool belts to hear from God and respond to him moment by moment over a lifetime. Bible reading, prayer, Scripture memory, serving, fellowship, worship, and evangelism are all essentials. I love the imagery of a divine wardrobe and way of life in Colossians 3:12–14:

Therefore, as God's chosen people, holy and dearly loved, clothe yourselves with compassion, kindness, humility, gentleness and patience. Bear with each other and forgive one another if any of you has a grievance against someone. Forgive as the Lord forgave you. And over all these virtues put on love, which binds them all together in perfect unity.

We need positive peer pressure in discipleship. We need to maximize these godly virtues in our lives, to model them with kids, parents, and leaders, and to multiply them in every disciple we make.

Michelle Anthony fittingly reminds us, "Kids benefit from the opportunities provided or from the spillover of the adults who are living in the Spirit."[24] I know a mom in our church whose daughter decided it was time to make some bagged lunches . . . but not just any bagged lunches, bagged lunches with a purpose. Jamie was ten years old at the time.[25] She knew that her mom passed several homeless people on her way to work in Chicago each day. She also knew her mom frequently stopped to talk with these people, not just passing them by and occasionally tossing them a nickel or two.

One day, Jamie decided it was time to put together some lunches for her mom to hand out. Jamie made it clear that these were special lunches. Each one included an apple, a banana, a baguette (yes, she insisted on a loaf of French bread), a note to let them know how much God loves them, and a verse from the Bible written out this way: "John 6:35 says, 'I am the bread of life. Whoever comes to me will never go hungry, and whoever believes in me will never be thirsty.'" Where did Jamie learn to do this? It was the example of Jesus in the Bible and the daily example of her mom.

There are many examples I could mention of children all over the world who are learning to know, love, and serve Christ in remarkable ways. They are growing in wisdom, stature, and in favor with God and others. Relational discipleship recognizes that disciple making is about setting the course, not all of the steps. All disciples are called to become like Christ in every way regardless of age, but how this happens is different for each person.[26] The target is clear, but the path to getting there is unscripted, messy, unconventional, life-transforming, and dynamic!

QUESTIONS FOR REFLECTION & DISCUSSION

1. In what way have you experienced yourself "running track" as a follower of Jesus and as part of the church family?

2. How do you know when your discipleship relationship with God is dynamic? What happens to you inside when it begins to feel static?

3. Would you say your children's ministry sets kids up to go "off road" as disciples? Why or why not?

4. How is discipleship prone to becoming predictable instead of remaining personalized in your church or children's ministry?

5. Describe a time when you heard from God in a special way. What did he impress upon you, and what step of faith did you take as a result?

6. What role do God's Spirit, Word, and people play in how you relate and respond to Christ day by day?

7. As you follow Jesus, how does the Bible impact your relationship with him and other people?

8. How does your children's ministry currently help kids and kid-influencers grow side-by-side:
   - In wisdom (character growth)?
   - In stature (physical growth)?
   - In God's favor (spiritual growth)?
   - In people's favor (relational growth)?

9. When you consider the nature of discipleship as dynamic, what do you desire for the kids, families, and leaders you encounter regularly?

10. Share a story of a time when a child or new believer surprised you by how they listened to and obeyed God's guidance.

PART THREE

REALIGN YOUR CHILDREN'S MINISTRY FOR A NEW TRAJECTORY

RESET

CHAPTER 10

RECOMMIT TO DISCIPLESHIP AS A WAY OF MINISTRY LIFE

There is only one way of being a disciple and that is by being devoted to Jesus.
Oswald Chambers[1]

Follow my example, as I follow the example of Christ.
1 Corinthians 11:1

©michaklootwijk/www.istock.com

SORRY, I'M GOING to have to hang up. I just entered a construction zone and I've got to find an exit quick."

I was driving to the airport, talking on the phone, and I had just realized my gas tank was almost empty. Now I was entering a construction zone. Not a good place to be. I hung up the phone and immediately started looking for an alternate route.

It's not as if I had failed to plan ahead. I left the office in plenty of time to park and get to my gate. I had simply forgotten to factor in terrible traffic and the fact that my gas tank was almost empty. Unfortunately, I could not find an exit, at least not one that would keep me headed in the right direction. The shoulders of the road were narrow. I couldn't even pull off to the side. I could feel my stress level rising.

Eventually I found an off-ramp, changed lanes, and got off the highway. I missed my flight. But I'll tell you one thing: filling up my tank never felt so good!

It's risky to run on empty. This is true for your car, but it's equally true in life. When you are burned out, drained, and feel like you have nothing left to give, it's an indicator that something needs to change. You need to stop. Rest. Refill your mind, body, and spirit. Your priorities and your pace may need to be reset. Warning lights are there for a reason. When one lights up, it signals something is in need of your attention.

"E" IS FOR EMPTY

Like many others, I survived the crisis affectionately called Y2K. Today, it seems like an overblown panic, but if you could go back to that time you would realize the calendar year changeover from 1999 to 2000 created a lot of headaches and long nights at work for many people. I remember watching online for telltale signs of global meltdown as people celebrated the New Year. At the time I could not afford a generator, but I was prepared. I had filled our family's pitcher of water and placed it in the refrigerator. We were all set! Thankfully, the world did not fall apart that night.

I remember that time for another reason: I realized my inner tank of gas had hit empty.

That was the year God had gifted Kate and me with our first child. On the outside, things were looking great. The ministries I was leading were growing spiritually and numerically. Signs of success abounded, yet on the inside I felt dry and empty. Even worse, I had no idea what to do. I was either unaware or unable to address the issues in my heart, to look into that inner world. The dashboard lights were coming on as my frustration levels increased. I could feel my patience decreasing and sense things falling apart. I could see the impact of my anger on people close to me. I knew many of my relationships were shallow. And while the church leadership seemed pleased with my performance, when I finally raised the white flag of surrender, they began to express concern for me.

As a youth pastor, I had always burned the candle at both ends. My wife and I filled our family calendar with church-building activities. Even though I was the one hired by the church, my wife, Kate, jumped in with both feet to serve in children's ministry and student ministries. For three full years, I ran junior high ministry on Wednesday nights, high school ministry on Thursday nights, college ministry on Sunday nights, weekly Sunday School for all three age groups, monthly outreach events for all three groups on Friday or Saturday nights, bi-annual retreats for all three groups, and annual intergenerational missions trips. I also made sure the church van was clean as a whistle.

During the week I was busy preparing to teach, writing small group materials, copying handouts, shopping for event supplies, meeting with volunteers and parents, and attending extracurricular events at all the different schools my students attended. I somehow found time to learn how to play the guitar and lead the worship band. I participated in the worship services on Sunday mornings and the evening service on Sunday nights. I recruited, trained, and multiplied adult and student leaders. Our apartment was always filled with people, a hub for several weekly Bible studies and multiple leadership team meetings each month. Kate and I hung out with church families and the church staff. I personally mentored several teenagers and adults. I worked at our local park district teaching soccer to get to know families in the community (and snag a little extra income). I somehow found time to squeeze in "other pastoral duties as required" and still keep up on the latest culture trends in order to stay relevant in ministry. And oh yeah, I almost forgot. I started attending graduate school part time.

Are you exhausted yet? Clearly, my pace was not sustainable. And predictably, burnout hit me like a ton of bricks. But in those days, if you had asked me point blank, I would have told you I was doing great.

> For an inner life fraught with unresolved drives will not be able to hear clearly the voice of Christ when he calls. The noise and pain of stress will be too great.
> **Gordon MacDonald[2]**

In October 2000, I attended a leadership conference and had a meltdown. I began crying uncontrollably. I was attending the conference by myself, and I came to realize my soul felt dead, like it had shriveled up. If a dried-up grape is a raisin, my soul felt like a small pebble. My relationship with God did not reflect what I was teaching and challenging others to live out. The scariest part was that no one noticed the inconsistency but me. And while I hoped someone would step in to help, no one told me to slow down. I wrote in my journal: "The rate at which I am doing ministry is working *against* what Christ wants to do in me." Sadly, I've since discovered my experience is all too common in ministry leadership.

I resigned from full-time church ministry to manage a nearby coffee shop. Shortly afterward, I attended a small group leadership retreat where I heard pastor and author Bill Hybels talk about a similar season in his own life. He shared how the speed of his life and the state of his soul were at cross purposes: "The pace at which I've been doing the work of God is destroying God's work in me."[3] He talked about the need for self-leadership that is dependent on Christ. Slowly, God used my coursework and professors at seminary to begin opening my heart to him again. My life slowed down. I began to feed on classic and current books about the contemplative life, about walking closely with Christ. These books shattered my existing paradigms of discipleship and leadership. God's Word and his people ministered to me in unexpected ways. Past and new mentors began listening for the Spirit's leading for my life. They spoke words of encouragement and wisdom to me. As I revisit my notes and reflections from this time, I'm reminded how faithful God was and still is, despite my fickleness.

This experience as a ministry leader shaped the next decade of my life and work in ministry. I had to start over by asking myself questions like, *Am I still called to ministry? What are my spiritual gifts? What are my natural strengths and weaknesses? What passion is the Lord leading me to pursue? Whom does he want me to walk alongside in this journey?* It was even more discouraging to go through wilderness periods where I knew God was near but life felt more like wandering alone in the desert.[4] Asking these questions was gut-wrenching but good at the same time. Looking back, I can see the Lord's hand in it all. He never left me on my own.

I believe every leader has or will experience a time when they find themselves empty. Personally, I learned that I desperately needed help. Before I could disciple others, I needed to be discipled by Jesus. I needed God's Spirit, through timeless spiritual practices and renewed relationships with others in the body of Christ, to restore my soul to health. The Lord changed me as a disciple, husband, father, and leader. But Jesus' approach to disciple making is not something we can switch on like a light. Instead, we need to develop disciplines and habits that consistently refill us spiritually so that our tank doesn't hit the danger zone.

HEALTH RISKS OF RUNNING ON EMPTY

Heart attacks are unpredictable, but they can often be prevented. They are frequently the result of a series of decisions, made over time, wherein we fail to properly care for our bodies. These decisions don't automatically lead to a heart attack, but they can increase our chances of succumbing to otherwise normal stresses. I have a friend who experienced this. He wasn't expecting a heart attack, and it came as a complete surprise. Now he wears a monitor to keep tabs on his heart. The technology he uses is remarkable because it alerts him in advance of life-threatening problems.

Like a physical heart attack, we can also suffer from a spiritual heart attack. Proverbs 4:23 says, "Above all else, guard your heart, for everything you do flows from it." As we saw earlier, the heart is the center of life, the core of our thoughts, emotions, decisions, and affections. It is the seat of our desires. And when we fail to guard our hearts, when we fail to tend to them, we run the risk of a spiritual heart attack. When I was running on empty in ministry, I knew I was not guarding my heart as I should have been, and the consequences were devastating. I needed spiritual healing before I could move forward in ministry.

If I had been more aware, I would have noticed the warning signs. I am not convinced I would have changed my course until it became absolutely necessary, but I have learned from my mistakes, which is not easy. More than one person has told me over the years, "If I knew I was going to live this long, I would have taken better care of myself a long time ago." Hindsight is always 20/20, right? My friend who suffered a physical heart attack is deeply aware that there were things he could have done differently to avoid the health risks. But change can be difficult, both physically and spiritually.

> Nothing conflicts with the love of Christ like service to Christ.
>
> **Henri Nouwen**[5]

Running on empty limits our leadership and our long-term ministry impact. We may genuinely long to know, love, and serve people, but if we are not tending to our hearts, we only end up harming others with our sinful attitudes and actions. Parched hearts have little to offer. If we're burned out, we simply can't pass along the spiritual nourishment people need. Our spiritual health can end up deteriorating prematurely, and disciple making across generations is hindered when leaders have nothing to draw from the well of their own resting in Jesus.

When leaders are empty, the whole faith community feels the negative effects. Leaders who run on empty tend to flee the scene when everything comes crashing down. The body of Christ suffers an amputation, rather than wearing a cast that could have brought healing given enough time. Leaders reach a breaking point and give up on ministry. Marriages end and families suffer the consequences. Sometimes people recover, and I'm thankful that recovery was my own path. But others take the escape route, like the prophet Jonah, when they face difficult ministry situations. Some never return. Leaders need to be mindful of whether they are stepping away in step with God's Spirit or bailing because they got burned (or burned out).

I remember the day Kate and I decided our weekly rhythm needed to change. We audited our commitments and discovered we did not have one day without something scheduled before or after work hours, including on weekends! As we started building margin back into our lives, we immediately noticed a difference. Several months later we audited our calendar again. We took "before" and "after" pictures because the contrast was so remarkable.

Mach 1 is great for an F-16. It is terrible for your soul and your relationships. And yet slowing down is difficult because in our culture, moving fast and keeping busy are things we value and praise. We are constantly letting people know how busy we are as a way of affirming our worth. They ask us, "How are you?" and we are quick to reply—"Busy!" A full inbox makes us think we are important, needed, and necessary. But this busy-ness simply hides the emptiness in our hearts. It leaves us living shallow lives, since friendships cannot flourish when we keep people at arm's length. In *Ordering Your Private World*, pastor and author Gordon MacDonald nails it when he writes, "The world is full of disorganized people who have lost control of their time."[6]

Maintaining a full schedule is common because in our culture, *identity* is easily tied to *activity*. We think to ourselves, *If there is no one who needs anything from me, am I really needed?* I remember wrestling with this when I was running on empty. My relational tanks were depleted, yet I kept pushing ahead, giving myself away to meet other people's never ending needs. And while I was "serving," I was really doing it all alone. The work of ministry fed my identity. Instead of finding my identity in what Jesus had done for me and resting in that, I was looking for value and worth in the things I could accomplish. I was looking to save myself rather than resting in the salvation Jesus provides in the gospel.

Running on empty also blinds us to the unique needs of children and families. When we are overly busy or empty we hastily pick programs or products to solve problems, rather than prayerfully considering what is needed. Have you ever found yourself looking through catalogs or searching online for a quick and easy solution for a talk you need to give or an activity for the kids? Or even just looking for whatever is cheapest and easiest to implement?

This also becomes a problem when we do it with our leaders. Recruiting leaders becomes more about filling slots than finding the most passionate, gifted, and qualified people. We lead out of our deficit rather than out of the overflow of God's grace and his Spirit. When we do this, we miss out on an opportunity to grow. Yes, the work might be harder for a while. We may need to make difficult decisions and even end some programs. But over the long term, a relational children's ministry must be based on the work of God's Spirit and not simply a program that meets a logistical need.

I understand the challenges. There is constant pressure to keep existing programs running smoothly. And when you are running on empty or nearly empty, this becomes your number one priority. You can talk about how discipleship and disciple making are important, but there is no long-term strategy rooted in prayer. The standards for success become noses and nickels: how many people attended and how much money was saved. Running on empty is a health risk to life-giving, relational ministry.

Reading this, you might think, "This is horrible! I would never let that happen." Do not be deceived. I talk with ministry leaders all over the world and they all admit (when they're honest) they have felt the creeping pressure to perform and have seen this sabotage their best intentions. That's why the Bible warns us to *guard* our hearts. Life-giving gospel ministry is always under attack, and we need to make radical changes in our thinking to develop and protect a relational children's ministry.

Even if you and/or your ministry are experiencing some health risks right now, I have good news. Heart attacks can be debilitating for a season, but they can lead to a renewed appreciation for life after recovery—if a person is willing to change.

READY TO RESET? THREE DISCIPLESHIP COMMITMENTS FOR RELATIONAL CHILDREN'S MINISTRY

Grab your Bible and read through Mark 1:21–38. You'll notice that what Jesus accomplished in this twenty-four-hour period is remarkable. His life was full, and yet his heart was never hurried. He remained closely connected to his heavenly Father and his disciples. Notice that he rose early to spend time alone with his Father. Personally, I dislike waking up before the sun breaches the horizon. But the Bible tells us it was a special time for Jesus: "Very early in the morning, while it was still dark, Jesus got up, left the house and went off to a solitary place, where he prayed." Christ stepped away from the demands of ministry to reset, to recalibrate his soul in relationship with the Father. The Gospel of Luke also confirms that he routinely stepped away from the hustle and bustle of everyday life to talk with God.[7] Jesus faced demands beyond those you and I will ever face, and yet his ministry always overflowed from the deep reservoir of his relationship with the Father and the Spirit, which came first.

Jesus modeled a way of life we can all follow, teaching his disciples his patterns in the midst of busy ministry. Take a close look at Mark 6:30–32:

> The apostles gathered around Jesus and reported to him all they had done and taught. Then, because so many people were coming and going that they did not even have a chance to eat, he said to them, "Come with me by yourselves to a quiet place and get some rest." So they went away by themselves in a boat to a solitary place.

Notice that after hearing all about their incredible ministry encounters and experiences, Christ calls his closest followers aside. In line with Proverbs 4:23, they get away to guard their hearts. Jesus understood the dangers of an empty heart, the temptation to find your value in the work and not in the grace of God. He knew the disciples were in need of physical and spiritual nourishment. Jesus' followers had to learn to emulate his pattern to combat spiritual fatigue. Christ was dedicated to recharging in order to be a faithful conduit of God's message and ministry, and I believe church and children's ministry leaders can make three discipleship commitments, based on the example of Jesus, that will lead to healthy relational children's ministry.

COMMITMENT 1: BE CONSISTENT IN DISCIPLESHIP COMMUNITY

By now, the importance of personal discipleship should be a clear principle. No disciple maker should be in a position to impact other people if they are not on their own discipleship journey. If you're not sold out on the principles of disciple making, don't bother challenging others to this end. Can you imagine hiring a self-proclaimed plumber who was only trained in carpentry? Would you get in a rocket with someone who owned a space suit but wasn't trained to fly to the moon? If you want to know, love, and serve Jesus, follow people who are committed to knowing, loving, and serving him.

Reading and reflecting on Scripture, prayer for forgiveness and guidance, worship as a way of life, genuine fellowship with other believers, sacrificial serving and stewardship, and evangelistic ministry each play a role in cooperating with the Holy Spirit for total life change. You're on an unscripted adventure with God, but that doesn't mean you aren't going somewhere important. Take your walk and talk seriously behind the scenes. Then set the pace publicly and invite others—kids *and* kid-influencers—onto the journey with you.

The principle here is to be fully committed to transparency, to be consistent in discipleship community. Your example has an impact on the kids and kid-influencers around you. Jesus calls his followers out of hypocrisy into humility. This requires being in right relationship with God and regular relationship with others. You cannot grow in the way of Christ on your own, so don't try to fly solo. Routinely explore answers to questions like: How am I growing as a disciple? Who am I letting into my life and growing with? Who is calling me out of my comfort zone to lead with integrity of heart and purpose? You need the body of believers if you truly want to become a lifelong disciple maker.

COMMITMENT 2: BE INTENTIONAL ABOUT WHY YOU DO WHAT YOU DO

I once met a man who was commissioned to teach English at a school in China. As he described the children at the school, I noticed something about the way he spoke. In the words he used, in his expressions and tone, his compassionate heart for the kids was obvious. This was a man who loved children. Teaching was more than a job for him. While teaching English was how he got to China, it was not why he was still there. Sure, he enjoyed teaching English, but he loved entering into relationships with the people. He loved having spiritual conversations. He told me he was not permitted to speak about Christianity in the classroom, so he had found an indirect way to spark conversations. He learned that students in China revere education and their teachers. They would take copious notes during every class period. So, from time to time he would say, "Every educated person believes in God and Jesus." Though they were surprised, the students would not say anything. They would nod in agreement. He would simply add, "If you'd like to discuss it more, I'm happy to meet with you outside class." Using these two sentences, he had seen many students and some of their parents decide to trust Christ after coming to the teacher's home to discuss Christianity.

The disciple-making mission of Jesus is ours to own. Jesus will return one day, but until he does he gives us one primary task: preach the gospel and make disciples. This mission includes meeting emotional and physical needs, and it includes preaching the eternal need for the forgiveness of sin and for salvation. To guide others to know, love, and serve Jesus Christ requires contextually knowing, loving, and serving the people God places in your natural path of life. Followers of Jesus are compelled to make every effort to overcome cultural barriers, socio-economic inequities, racial discrimination, and injustices of all kinds. Children and families need kid-influencers who are connected to the body of Christ and who will mirror and extend God's unconditional love in grace and truth.

Using "love" as an acronym, I break down the "be intentional" mission this way: Listen, Observe, Verify, and Engage (L-O-V-E). One of my favorite leadership stories in the Bible is the account of Nehemiah and the rebuilding of the wall in Jerusalem. Nehemiah is a prophet who risks his life by prayer-fully going before the king, asking to return home. He receives permission, safe passage, and supplies, explores the ruins in Jerusalem, creates a plan, gains the support of Israel's leaders, begins working on the wall with a big team, encounters opposition multiple times, and in a matter of just 52 days the wall that was down for 140 years is back up!

Nehemiah listened to God, observed what was going on around him, verified the vision of what needed to happen, and then engaged with God and others for it to become reality. L-O-V-E. Now fast-forward to the New

Testament and the early church in Acts 2. Fifty days after the resurrection of Christ, the promised Holy Spirit arrives on the scene and approximately 3,000 new believers are baptized and added to the community. Today that would be a church administrator's nightmare. Imagine what Peter was thinking before and after when he decided to stand up to give his first sermon. The disciples listened to Jesus' instructions, they paid attention by observing the situation leading up to Pentecost, the verification of what they should do came by way of prayer in community, and then when the time was right, they engaged in step with God's Spirit. L-O-V-E.

Intentionality in ministry is critical. The mission is urgent. The message is completely life-altering. You will leave a legacy for better or worse, and I pray you will be mindful of that. It's your job as a leader to be purposeful in the work the Lord has called you to do. Your relationships need to be intentional. Kids and families can be impacted in a lot of ways by church and children's ministries. But on your watch, the only ministry that really matters is the one you lead. Take the L-O-V-E acronym seriously. Work through it as a team with your children's ministry leaders. Listen, observe, verify, and engage so that what matters most will drive your vision, relationships, values, and engagements.

COMMITMENT 3: BE FULLY AVAILABLE, BUT WITH CLEAR BOUNDARIES

How do you respond when you are interrupted in the middle of something? Fortunately you do not have to report in right now, but my guess is that you are not a big fan of unexpected breaks. It can be frustrating to be "in the flow" only to get a phone call, a text, an email, a knock on the door, or a package delivery. Even when the power goes out or a fire alarm goes off, people are annoyed. Most interruptions are people-related. I once knew a librarian who never told people her name. She just had a standard name placard on her desk that read, "Interrupt Me." What a life lesson I learned by seeing that reminder.

Ministry is a 24/7 calling, but that doesn't mean you have to be on call 24/7. Children's ministries need kid-influencers who have clear boundaries *before* they can be fully available. Setting limits is hard for people who serve people because the needs are never ending. How do you know when to pull away? One indicator is when interruptions lead to explosions. If your heart rate starts skyrocketing or your temper starts getting the best of you each time you get interrupted, it's probably time to take a break. Even Jesus stepped away to pray and didn't always allow his time to be directed by the needs of everyone else.[8]

Prideful people try to be available all the time and accomplish everything, usually on their own, because deep down they're convinced they can do it smarter, faster, and better. This is not the way of discipleship and disciple making in relationship with Christ as part of the family of God.

> We will come to understand that for the most part our hurry is really based upon pride, self-importance, fear, and lack of faith, and rarely upon the production of anything of true value for anyone.
>
> **Dallas Willard[9]**

Children need you. Parents need you. Your ministry team needs you. Church leaders need you. Your family needs you. The list never ends, really. They have real names and real faces, and somehow that heightens the stakes. You are responsible for finding a way to balance being a kid-influencer who makes disciples and living as a finite human being. God created you to know, love, and serve others, but that doesn't mean you are the only one called to make this happen. There are people all over the body of Christ with similar callings, some of whom are in your church or children's ministry. You have limited time, resources, gifts, passion areas, and so on. You also have close relationships and calendar commitments to keep. Make sure you set clear boundaries so that when you are present and needed, you can be fully available to the people and tasks in front of you.

Effective discipleship requires margin for relationships to flourish between families, the children's ministry, and the church. This margin doesn't just show up. It's hard won. The battle typically starts at home before the day begins. This is where we get clarity with God about where and with whom to spend the time he's entrusted to us. There are children and families and leaders who are depending on you being fully available to them. The Lord will guide you to decide how much time that entails, but he will also give you the ability to be totally with them when you are. This is the heart of relational disciple making as Jesus modeled it.

Whether disciples believe it is true or not, Jesus meant what he said in John 15:5: "Apart from me you can do nothing." Yes, there are a lot of things we *can* do in life. What we must come to terms with is that nothing of any value can be done if it is disconnected from the vine that gives and sustains life. Abiding in relationship with God takes time, openness, vulnerability, patience, and faithfulness. The same is true of relationships with the people he invites us to serve. When relationship with God is prioritized first and foremost, then kid-influencers can be fully available to children, families, and one another in relational discipleship.

NOW IS THE TIME TO STOP RUNNING RAGGED AND PURSUE SPIRITUAL HEALTH

I wish I could say my experience hitting the proverbial wall in 2000 was the last time I experienced burnout. Periodically the Lord still calls me aside to get some extended time with just him. By sitting on the sidelines for a season, Christ reminds me who is really responsible for fruit bearing. God restores my perspective on life, ministry, and myself, and assures me of my calling.

During one particularly difficult heart-reshaping season, I read *The Making of a Leader: Recognizing the Lessons and Stages of Leadership Development* by Robert Clinton. Nancy, a former professor of mine, and now a mentor, ministry colleague, and friend, had given the book to me years earlier. When I finally cracked the book open, God used it to change and challenge me. The Holy Spirit formed in me a true north ministry leadership axiom I'll never forget:

If I lead, I will pay a price.
If I don't, others will.

There's a lot packed into these two short sentences. "If" is important. It signals that there is always an escape hatch nearby. Choosing to lead is a sacrificial choice for the leader. If you believe your calling as a kid-influencer and disciple maker is crystal clear, then you must lead. But there will always be a price. At the same time, holding back on a God-given vision is also costly. You need to sense if God is truly calling you to pay the price—you must count the cost. If you do not serve, others will step up. It may take a bit longer, but God will accomplish his purposes.

My encouragement to you is this: take a good look at your life. Examine your heart—are you leading with integrity? Examine your motives—are you leading in tune with the mission God has given you for the glory of God or for your own glory? Examine your schedule—are you setting appropriate boundaries and building in margin to spend time with the Lord? It may be time for you to hit the reset button and realign your children's ministry for a new trajectory. Turning kid-influencers into a disciple-making community is not easy, but it's totally worth it.

If you are ready to reset, the next two chapters give you two more buttons to push: (1) recalibrating your discipleship target in children's ministry, and (2) reconsidering the discipleship resources at your disposal for the journey ahead.

QUESTIONS FOR REFLECTION & DISCUSSION

1. Describe a time when you had to hit "reset" in some area of your life. Was it easy or hard? What was the outcome? Explain.

2. When was the most recent time you felt like you were "running on empty" physically, emotionally, spiritually, or relationally? How did you know your inner tank was empty?

3. Have you ever officially burned out in a role or relationship? What happened? How did you recover from the pain and drain?

4. What unhealthy ministry outcomes have you experienced because you or someone around you was running ragged in ministry?

5. What needs to happen in you personally for your children's ministry to get realigned for the sake of lifelong discipleship?

6. Which commitment do you need to work on most? Which one do you want to challenge other kid-influencers to build up in their own lives as disciples?

   • Commitment 1: Be consistent in discipleship community

   • Commitment 2: Be intentional about why you do what you do

   • Commitment 3: Be fully available, but with clear boundaries

7. Listen, Observe, Verify, Engage is a helpful model for strategic vision and direction. As a leader, what is an area of ministry God is guiding you to move forward in for the sake of lifelong discipleship with kids and families? How will L-O-V-E assist you in moving forward?

8. "If I lead, I will pay a price. If I don't, others will." As a kid-influencer, do you agree with this statement? Why or why not? How have you experienced this to be true in your own life as a disciple following Christ and leading others to do the same?

CHAPTER 11

RECALIBRATE YOUR DISCIPLESHIP TARGET IN CHILDREN'S MINISTRY

It takes as much energy to wish as it does to plan.
Eleanor Roosevelt[1]

In their hearts humans plan their course, but the Lord establishes their steps.
Proverbs 16:9

RUBIK'S CUBE is one of the most recognized, best-selling toys in the world. Originally created by a Hungarian inventor and professor of architecture in 1974, this simple brainteaser has mystified kids of all ages for over forty years.[2] I remember my first encounter with this mysterious object as a child of the 80's. If memory serves, I traded a friend some Hot Wheels cars and a pack of Hubba Bubba bubble gum for the opportunity to try my luck with this test of genius. The concept seemed simple in my mind: *Six sides; six different colors. Mix up the 3x3 cube. Twist and turn until the colors get back to where they started. How hard can it be? Bring it on.* So began my miserable relationship with this unassuming toy.

Five minutes. Ten minutes. Thirty minutes. Three days. Three weeks. I kept retreating into my room, door closed, hoping beyond hope to emerge triumphant! Day and night, Rubik stayed at the forefront of my mind. Eventually my heart could not take the roller coaster ride any longer. I felt drained and began to lose my ability to focus. "I think I did it," I would say under my breath. Then, "Oh no! Wait, how did that piece end up on the opposite side?"

Again and again I tackled the same problem. It was maddening, but I couldn't quit. My obsession finally got the best of me. I wedged the head of a flathead screwdriver in between one of the individual blocks and dismantled my nemesis into a pile. One by one I placed the twenty color-coded pieces around its six-sided core, careful to match up each face perfectly. When I eventually pushed in the last remaining block, a sense of accomplishment (and a tinge of guilt) swept over me. "Problem solved," I thought as I exhaled a sigh of relief and placed the completed cube on my trophy shelf.

Ernő Rubik, the creator of the cube, once said, "If you are curious, you'll find the puzzles around you. If you are determined, you will solve them."[3] I love finding solutions to problems. If something breaks, I fix it. When someone opens a "some assembly required" present on Christmas or birthdays, everyone turns to me. To my wife's surprise (and mine), I once installed an entire closet organizer with a golf pencil, a keychain level, a broken disposable hacksaw, and a small Swiss Army knife. If there is a puzzle, I am drawn to it. I will try one approach after another until a solution is found.

God has gifted me in areas like creativity, innovation, and leadership. And yet I've had to learn that people aren't problems to solve. *Puzzles involving people are moving targets.*

Without people or problems there is no need for ministry. Yet successfully "solving" people-related challenges requires a different set of intentions, questions, tools, and skills. Children's ministry professor and practitioner Michelle Anthony highlights the quandary kid-influencers face in discipleship: "A mentor relationship or parent relationship is subjective. We're hands-on eyewitnesses to a person's life. This is not something we can measure statistically."[4] In relational disciple-making communities, we must continually recalibrate our perspective and approach in each situation and setting. Discipleship is a process, not a destination; it's a long-term trajectory, not a finite target. Succumbing to the temptation to "solve" or "fix" people results in a faulty, often damaging, model for disciple making. Seeking out static solutions is fundamentally at odds with the vision of relational children's ministry.

Alignment is not an event; it's a process.

Michael Hyatt[5]

Today I have four Rubik's Cubes in my office. They are all different sizes. The 2x2 cube reminds me of smaller challenges. The 3x3 is for medium, 4x4 is for large, 5x5 is just insane! I have now served in all different kinds of churches and communities, in multiple denominations, from small to super-sized. And while larger ministry settings may be more complex, the critical issues remain the same. There is a center around which every side is constantly shifting. God's Word never changes, but his Church is in an ever-changing relationship with culture. Recalibrating a discipleship trajectory in children's ministry requires clarity about the unchanging core and the ability to adapt to the changing world. Rubik reminds me each day that I need an ongoing commitment to alignment.

MISALIGNMENT MAYHEM

This past Sunday, an innocent skirmish between a brother and sister ended up needing minor medical attention. Fortunately for us, their mom is a doctor. Surprisingly, the first-aid kit was right where it was supposed to be and stocked with everything from surgical gloves to sterile tweezers. I grabbed the cold compress, a Band-Aid, and a tube of antibiotic ointment and dashed back to our twos and threes room to save the day—everything was going to be okay! Mom went to the service, the young girl grabbed a tissue or two, and we were on our way . . . that is, until one of the teachers stopped me in the hall ten minutes later. Apparently the "one-time instant cold pack" had already been used "one-time," and it was therefore still at room temperature. The only thing cold we could find in our church freezer was a giant bag of frozen chicken and a few cheese Danishes. I had to make the call. Fewer germs, *I thought,* we'll go with the plastic-wrapped pastry. *From now on we'll make sure everything is stocked and ready to roll for the new year!*

This happened several years ago, and I wrote it down in my journal so I wouldn't forget. Maybe you've had similar experiences. You plan and prepare, and yet when the crisis moment comes along, you are still scrambling. This kind of ministry triage is common. *A lot* of prep work is involved in making a children's ministry run smoothly, and yet it's never quite perfect in execution.

The cheese Danish incident was silly, but it was a good reminder for me. It was easy to restock the first-aid box, yet I knew the missing compress was indicative of broader ministry problems we were facing. And there were always things we weren't aware of yet. While running out of ice packs is not a big deal, I knew there were things looming on the horizon that I couldn't see yet.

This incident reinforced my belief that taking inventory matters. During this season, my children's ministry leadership team and I talked, and we uncovered some key areas of misalignment between our vision for the kids and the overall direction the church was heading. For example, we knew we wanted every child and adult to feel loved by God, and we wanted our ministry to reflect that love. But we also knew the short transition time between our two weekend services was too rushed for meaningful interactions. The curriculum we used, while fine, was too traditional for use in our outreach-targeted ministry where many kids and parents were new to the Bible and church. Whenever we proposed changes, we were told they couldn't work or funds could not be allocated to make improvements. Our midweek ministry had potential for growth, but at the time it was nothing more than childcare to support the adult worship and Bible teaching time.

To our surprise, though, our children's ministry volunteer rosters and the total number of children participating began to soar on the weekends. We had more kids and volunteers than ever before. We wanted to build into these teams and families, but the overall ministry was stuck behind where God was working. We also uncovered a discipleship disconnect, one that desperately needed to be addressed.

What was the disconnect? I knew the deeper problem was that the church did not have a commitment to value children and ministry to children. Sure, there were programs but in a low priority way. The strange thing was that while I recognized a discipleship disconnect at church, I began to see the same thing evident in my own home. At the church and in my home, we were trying to do good work for God. But I knew we were missing out on the best because we were spinning too many plates. Misalignment was everywhere.

It took a concerted effort to help everyone recognize what C. S. Lewis stated so well: "Children are not a distraction from more important work. They are the most important work." Instead of doing more of the same, we needed to freshen our perspective on our "why" before re-launching the "how" and "what."[6] We were confident the church mission was well grounded in biblical truth. What was not clear was how children's ministry fit into that mission. Disciple making is a church-wide, intergenerational mission. So our goal was not to elevate children's ministry *above* other ministries of the church. Instead, we were looking for alignment. How could our children's ministry align with the broader mission of the church so we could all work together toward a common goal, instead of working at odds with one another?

> It is the responsibility of leaders to remain faithful in safeguarding the mission of their organizations.
>
> **Peter Greer**[7]

It wasn't easy to get the ball rolling. I had to pull together the children's ministry leadership, the senior pastor, other key ministry leaders, and families. It was obvious we were all on different playing fields. In the absence of a unifying vision, ministry prayers and plans go in myriad directions. Distrust erodes confidence and collaboration. Turf wars turn into ministry battles where no one wins. Leader and author Michael Hyatt wisely says, "While weak leaders blame their followers for a lack of alignment, strong leaders know that it is their responsibility to create it. Alignment doesn't just happen. It is *created*."[8] Leaders take ownership to move themselves and others forward.

Just like a Rubik's Cube takes focused, patient, ongoing twisting and turning to get all squares back to their starting positions, the same is true for mission alignment in ministry. To reset your discipleship trajectory, you need to clarify common ground between children's ministry and church leadership. Here's how you do it.

ONE MISSION: DEFINE YOUR DISCIPLESHIP TARGET

IKEA. This one word has changed the face of home furnishing. If you do not have a store near you, you should check out the catalog online. Tom, one of my dearest friends and mentors, once said to me: "I had to stop going to IKEA. Every time my wife and I went, I discovered hundreds of items I never knew I couldn't live without. Our retirement account just couldn't take it anymore." IKEA cuts through the noise of a competitive industry with its simple, functional approach. Its stores warehouse practical solutions for everyday life. They set up best-practice floor plans for customers to experience the products before purchasing. What Legos are to kids, IKEA is to adults (which may explain my fascination). IKEA's philosophy of providing affordable "stuff" my family needs or wants appeals to me. This global company knows the core of their business.[9]

Tom and his wife, Georgia, are faithful followers of Christ and are as close as family to us. We've spent hundreds of hours together in coffee shops and serving side by side at church. He and his wife stepped in as stand-in grandparents when Kate and I did not have family nearby. We share a common heart for discipleship ministry and disciple-making community, and I am regularly inspired by Tom's devotion to God's Word and biblical community. He and Georgia are servants of God in the purest sense of the word. I believe every generation needs every generation for the body of Christ to thrive, and Tom and Georgia model this.[10]

Over the years, Tom and I have wondered, "If businesses like IKEA can formulate a crystal clear mission and stick to 'true north,' why is it that churches often miss the mandate to 'go and make disciples'?" Many start out biblically sound and strategic, but are derailed along the way. That's why a recalibration—a new or renewed alignment—is needed.

Let's take another look at our working definition of discipleship for relational children's ministry:

> Discipleship is the lifelong transformation of someone who decides to trust Christ for salvation and become like him in every way. This happens individually in the context of community through the cultivation of God-honoring attitudes, convictions, practices, and relationships.

Your church will need to decide on its own definition. It might end up being close to this one, but every church has a unique culture and context that needs to be taken into consideration. Regardless of the specifics, every church and children's ministry needs clarity about the ultimate destination of discipleship and a plan for how to get there. You'll also need some long-term commitments to persevere together through the peaks and valleys. In Matthew 28:18–20, Christ gave his followers the ultimate goal—"make disciples"—but he didn't spell out many details. He spoke of living out the gospel story, of teaching people to obey his teachings, and of baptizing them, bringing them into a new identity as part of the community of God's people. Your "true north" discipleship target will involve a mix of Scripture, theological tradition, church history, and contextualized application. All of this will differ from church to church. Your approach needs to be holistic, but also simple enough to be remembered and shared.

In their groundbreaking book *Simple Church*, Thom Rainer and Eric Geiger give some suggestions for getting started:

> A simple church is designed around a straightforward and strategic process that moves people through the stages of spiritual growth. The leadership and the church are clear about the process (clarity) and are committed to executing it. The process flows logically (movement) and is implemented in each area of the church (alignment). The church abandons everything that is not in the process (focus).[11]

A clear, singular mission can lead to a beautiful array of supporting visions. Rainer and Geiger summarize the ongoing process of alignment and realignment this way: "Clarity. Movement. Alignment. Focus. All are necessary."[12] Other strategic planning approaches have surfaced in recent years to help churches define their discipleship target.[13] There is no single process that works for all churches, but Judges 17:6 gives leaders a time-tested recipe for *mis*alignment: ". . . everyone did as they saw fit." Regardless of how you seek alignment, stay focused and work together. Like paddling different directions in a canoe, if everyone is off doing their own thing, it will be impossible to keep the ministry aligned. Having a common mission focused on discipleship can help bring alignment to every aspect of your children's ministry.

A great place to begin is to check with the church leaders and spiritual overseers God has appointed in your congregation. Do you have a clear statement of faith? This statement provides guardrails for you and your team as you reset the ministry to have more of a disciple-making mission. The role of these overseers should not be bypassed or taken lightly. Don't fly solo! Jesus modeled the importance of following his Father's mission, seeking alignment with his heavenly Father before doing anything.[14] The early church lived by this prayer-saturated example as well. Before forging ahead with ministry initiatives or selecting and sending out leaders, they sought the guidance of the Holy Spirit and made sure they were aligned.[15] Adding a relational discipleship focus to your existing children's ministry will only strengthen what is already present.

Having defined your discipleship target and having sought common ground with leadership to make sure the children's ministry is in tune with the church's beliefs and mission, you are ready for the next crucial leadership step.

CLARIFY COMMON GROUND
FOR CONSTRUCTIVE CHANGE

I once heard the story of two sisters who came to an impasse over a piece of fruit. As they each reached for the last ripe orange left in the house, they exclaimed at exactly the same time, "It's mine!" The older sister, trying to claim her rights due to her age, said, "The Bible says to respect your elders." The younger sister replied, "It also teaches us to love others as we love ourselves." After a few rounds of "Bible judo," neither sister had gained the advantage. Seeing that the battle would not be won by superior biblical knowledge, the two sisters decided to compromise. The older one grabbed a chef's knife from the chopping block. The younger girl pulled out a cutting board and held the orange steady. The blade sliced through the middle of the fruit evenly. Each sister headed to a separate corner of the house with her half of the orange.

You will never find common ground without encountering some disagreements. That's where you'll need to practice the art of negotiation. We all come to the table with our own interests in mind, and we often lack an understanding of what others want and why they want it. It takes time to talk and listen and talk again and listen some more. But when we take time to understand others, we can often find consensus. We learn to appreciate the things that matter to others and why they matter. The goal is not for one person to gain at another's expense. It is for each part to gain and lose something, but to end up with something that brings unity to all parties involved. Psalm 133:1 reminds us, "How good and pleasant it is when God's people live together in unity!"

In the story I shared, compromise and alignment were certainly possible. The sisters just never got to the point of listening and understanding. The older sister was hoping to use the zest from the orange rind to make a delicious cake and frosting. She needed the outer rind to accomplish her mission. The younger sister, on the other hand, wanted the pulp for fresh-squeezed orange juice. She needed the inner fruit to accomplish her goal. They both needed the orange, but they wanted to use it in different ways. In this case, those goals actually complemented one another, rather than competing with each other. The two parties never made the effort to understand each other's perspective, desires, or goals. In the end, they were blinded by their competition and missed an opportunity to discover a win-win that would have benefited both of them equally.

I'm surprised by how often I find this same scenario played out in the church. Unfortunately, it's not always as easy as using different parts of an orange. It can involve making changes to long-standing practices, killing old programs, and changing staff structures. One of the most common disparities is when the church leadership reduces "church" and "children's ministries" to Bible-based events. The essence of the mission becomes the programming. Instead of seeing the ministry events and programs as pieces of the larger disciple-making mission, the worship service or the Wednesday night program becomes the top priority while other ministries exist to serve that program or event. What happens in the children's area (or any other sub-ministry) is valued as long as it does not disrupt the "main event."

This is something of a generalization, I realize. Most churches are at least somewhat aware of how each ministry fits into the whole and connects to its discipleship target. And yet the danger of drift is always there. Children's ministry leaders need to be intentional about this. Heart work is hard work. People need to be reminded of the bigger vision, the biblical motive for why we do what we do. Some will need to unclench their fists for the greater good. We will never be able to grasp God's love if we are holding tightly to something else.[16] Jesus modeled great humility by letting go of his rights and privileges as the Son of God to humbly serve those he came to save. When we follow his example, it leads to unprecedented unity.[17]

To get the most out of this next section, you may want to have a leader or decision maker in mind. Think of someone you can talk with about these four critical areas: aligning perspective, assessing priorities, activating plans, and achieving potential. There are four diagnostic questions you can ask this leader to help you find common ground between the mission of the church and the children's ministry. As you work through these questions together, remember it is only by prayer and in partnership with trusted people that God moves. Humble hearts and listening ears always precede honest dialogue. Where grace and truth are present, constructive change will come in time.

ALIGN YOUR PERSPECTIVE: WHAT IS TODAY'S REALITY?

Have you ever tried to watch a 3-D movie without the proper eyewear? The images are offset and blurry (kind of like the 13-inch black and white TV my mom and I had when I was a kid!). The 3-D imaging seemingly ruins the picture and makes the entire cinematic experience unwatchable. So while it can be awkward and even uncomfortable to wear the oversized glasses they hand out at the theater, the payoff is worth it. With the glasses, your vantage point shifts. Before it was blurry and weird. Now, with the glasses, you can enjoy a multidimensional picture leaping off the screen.

Humble yourself. Wear the glasses. Join the rest of the crowd. And have your vision aligned so you can see the story unfold.

Is your church mission and the mission of your children's ministry aligned? Are you on the same disciple-making trajectory? Ask the first question: "What is today's reality?" Is everyone looking in the same direction toward the same future with the same set of lenses?

PRINCIPLE 1: MISALIGNMENT SABOTAGES MISSION AND MINISTRY MOMENTUM

When you ask, "What is today's reality?" you are asking for an honest evaluation. Start by getting everyone at the table and asking, *What are your expectations? What are we trying to accomplish? What's our motive for doing what we do?* Be ready. This can be very, very discouraging. But it is necessary. You need to get a baseline assessment. Are your people and programs working at odds with the larger church vision? With one another? If so, this will kill your impact, especially when it comes to making disciples.

Have you ever seen those large maps at the amusement park or at a shopping mall? They show you the entire spread of stores and attractions. But seeing the big vision isn't all that helpful until you find those three words by the big red dot: "You Are Here." Locating your starting point provides context. Honestly assessing reality requires finding out where you are in relationship to where you want to go.

So before moving forward, you need to be clear about the mission of the church and the primary reason supporting ministries (like the children's ministry) exist. Find out where the mission and vision are not aligned, and dialogue about how things might change. Trust me—if you skip this step and don't have these conversations, what you build may end up crashing to the ground. Starting with an honest assessment of the current reality provides proper perspective and gets everyone heading in the same direction together.

Here is one practical way to get started. Gather five or six key leaders, half from the broader church leadership and half from the children's ministry. Grab a white board or a large pad of paper and some markers. Ask these questions:

- What is our church known for in the community?
- What is our children's ministry known for?
- What do we do well as a children's ministry? What do we do poorly?
- Where do the majority of our complaints arise from in the ministry?

The goal at this initial stage is not to come up with solutions. Don't go there. Just let people be honest. Let them share frustrations without becoming critical or attacking people. Remember, you want to know the truth. Ideas about how to change will come later.

ASSESS YOUR PRIORITIES: WHAT REALLY MATTERS MOST?

Values drive your priorities. What you value will determine your activity, your behavior. Test this out next time you go to someone else's home. Look around the different rooms (without being weird, of course). What kinds of pictures cover the walls? How is the furniture arranged? What's in the pantry and the refrigerator? As you talk with the person, what topics surface in your conversation? What, if any, questions do they avoid answering directly?

All of these things will give you a sense of what they value. What do they care about? What matters most to them? Here is the point: *what matters most to others is often in plain sight if you are willing to pay attention.*

Or, here is another way to get at this. If you really want to find out what matters to a person or an organization, look at how they spend their time and money. Your calendar and your bank statement reveal what you value. And here is the key focus of our examination: *does what I value match what I say matters to me?* The truth is, my time and money aren't actually mine. My life belongs to God, and every aspect of it is on loan from him for me to steward.[18] So it's especially important that my priorities and values as a disciple of Jesus are defined by the values of God. Do I love what God loves? Do I care about the things that God cares about? My day planner and my receipts may not always perfectly match my values, but my prayer and my desire is to reset my trajectory so I'm heading toward true north as I walk closely with Christ each day. "What really matters most?" is a crucial question to bringing about constructive change.

PRINCIPLE 2: ALIGNMENT BRINGS TOGETHER WHAT'S ESSENTIAL AND URGENT FOR GOD'S KINGDOM PURPOSES

After church and children's ministry leadership spend time honestly assessing the current state of the ministry and the mission, the next step is to decide what values matter most. If, as I've argued throughout this book, disciple making is essential and relationships matter more than events or programs, then your decisions and behaviors should indicate that disciple making is your priority. Again, you'll want to define this; flesh it out so it fits your particular tradition and cultural context. Being a disciple of Christ will mean looking to the example of church community modeled by the early church in Acts 2. It must include an element of multiplication, a commitment to expanding God's mission across the street, across town, and across the globe. It includes looking to Scripture to shape core commitments like grace, integrity, humility, reconciliation, truth, prayer, fellowship, stewardship, compassion, and outreach. These words are universal and biblical, yet they are distinctly contextualized to different ministry settings.

Early in my ministry experience, we prayed and determined we would set a five-tier priority pyramid. The bottom layer was God—our personal relationships with God through Jesus Christ. Working upward, the building blocks continued with Self, Family, Friends, and Life. The pyramid was helpful for me personally because it reminded me where to focus my attention and how to set my priorities. Too often, we invert the pyramid and try to balance all of life before relying on God. That is the opposite of what we should do. These five priorities provide a priority structure for the central values I hold closest to my heart. They work well at home, church, anywhere.

You and the community of leaders around you need to ask the question: "What really matters most?" Set aside some time with your key leaders and ask them to honestly share their dream and hopes for the ministry. Ask leaders to shout out or write down as many values for the ministry as they can think of. Once you have the list and everyone can see it, ask them to pick their top four or five and see where there is overlap. Ask questions like:

- What is the fruit of a children's ministry where everything is aligned with God's mission?
- What are the core values, the non-negotiables that we cannot and will not give up?

Spend some time comparing the core values you want for your children's ministry with the values of your church mission. Where is there resonance and dissonance? Try to find ways in which they can overlap. My prayer is that this process will unearth three to five simply stated values that uphold the priority of God's kingdom purposes in your community of faith.

ACTIVATE YOUR PLANS: WHAT IS OUR SHARED SUPPORT STRATEGY?

Many years ago, I led a children's ministry leadership team in an outreach-focused church. We welcomed people from all walks of life and invited them into a relationship with God through faith in Jesus Christ. When I began working there, our children's ministry was called "Children's Ministry." Catchy, I know. It was clear, but it was neither compelling nor creative. It did not help us articulate our mission, our vision, or our values as a ministry. After much deliberation and prayer, we changed the name of the children's ministry and landed on five purposeful statements that brought focus to what we believed God was calling us to do. These statements aligned with our church mission.

Discovery Kids

Discover God.
Invite Friends.
Serve Others.
Celebrate Christ.
Obey Him Together.

Discovery Kids was the name we chose, and each of our purpose statements highlighted the importance of evangelism, fellowship, serving, worship, and discipleship.[19] If you look closely, you'll notice the five statements form an unexpected acronym for a church ministry—D-I-S-C-O. It was fun and a little risky, but also incredibly practical. People remembered it. They could repeat back to me the five statements. Our posture in making these changes was to honor the past while preparing for the future. This meant holding to the unchanging truth of the Bible while bringing fresh creativity to our mission and keeping it simple and crystal clear. Before making these changes, we sought out collective input from multiple leaders across the church. What was our shared support strategy? As one of the sub-ministries of the church body, we knew we needed a *common language* to communicate our goals.

PRINCIPLE 3: EFFECTIVE CHILDREN'S MINISTRIES PURPOSEFULLY ALIGN WITH THEIR CHURCH'S CENTRAL MISSION

The mission, vision, and values of a church drive its support strategies, and everyone must work together to accomplish shared goals. But this can be harder than it sounds. How do you attract ongoing support from the rest of the church? How do you avoid being a lone ranger in ministry? Kid-influencers who chart their own paths apart from the body of believers will be frustrated when church leadership is not walking with them.

Any church that is grounded in God's Word will be committed to a handful of purposes and supporting strategies. Faithful evangelism, lifelong discipleship, biblical community, local serving, global compassion, and so on are all common goals. But what makes these fundamentally relational rather than programmatic? As a leader, you can influence this by implementing principles from this book. Invite co-leaders and colleagues to wrestle with the issues being raised. Present viable solutions based on what you're learning, trial and error, and personal experience. You can impact your church and children's ministry's lifelong discipleship trajectory if you get specific and stick with it.

Consider these ways to shift the programmatic pendulum toward a relational children's ministry model.

Off the Chart Child-to-Leader Ratios: We all struggle to find enough people to staff rooms in children's ministry. It takes a lot of people to ensure kids are engaged and safe. Relational children's ministries need to take it a step further. Rather than focus on "how few leaders will it take to keep the room open," how can you and your teams cast vision for as many kid-influencers as possible to be involved? Would it be so bad if you had leaders on a waiting list to mentor children and guide them in the faith? I don't just believe God can make this happen, I've seen it firsthand. A ministry director recently said to me: "I'm getting so many people applying to serve, I can't process the applications and background checks fast enough!" Imagine how children and parents would feel having not one, not two, but multiple people loving on them as a family as part of the church community. Raise the child-to-leader ratio bar and call kid-influencers to the plate.

Co-Create for Community Learning: Some teachers love to stand in front of a room and listen to themselves speak. It's certainly less risky than asking questions or sitting next to students to study together. In this information age, words are flying around all the time without penetrating minds and hearts. Relational children's ministry can change this by having kids and peers, kids and leaders, kids and parents all learn side by side. Disciple making happens best in relationship, not lecture halls. Kid-influencers need to find ways to break down traditional teaching paradigms. Increasing biblical literacy requires reading, study, discussion, application, reflection, and struggle. Knowing, loving, and serving Christ comes to life in the context of relationships. What projects, serving opportunities, Bible studies, and worship or prayer experiences can kids and adults do together instead of in their own corners of the church? How can you involve parents in your children's ministry instead of keeping them on the other side of the building? Providing co-learning opportunities will increase life-application across multiple generations. It can be fun to get perspective from older and younger disciples. You can help make this a reality as a relational leader.

Family First Ministries: Integrated is an overused educational term. It's crept into the church with every intention of building a discipleship bridge to homes. I'm not against the term "integrated," I just think it's not really working the way it's intended. Too many curricula provide "family resources" in the form of take-home worksheets that get tossed into the trash before parents get to the parking lot. Everything starts at church (and ends there too). Whatever gets sent home is viewed as "extra" in the eyes of children's ministry leaders and families. It's time for a shift. It's time for experiences to start in the home and be supported at church. Integration requires a full view and value of home *and* church in the creation of resources. What can you provide parents that can be done at home or with groups of families whether they attend church on the weekend or not? How can you build upon holiday weekends and special events to keep families together instead of providing age-specific offerings? Work with your church and children's ministry leaders to influence relational bridge building through family first ministry opportunities.

ACHIEVE YOUR POTENTIAL: WHAT DOES GOD DESIRE US TO DO?

At a leadership conference, I heard Dr. Henry Cloud say, "For the plan to work, you have to work the plan." It sounded too simple at first, but then God began using this simple phrase to soften my mind and strengthen my heart. Working the plan means faithfully persevering and not giving up, even when you don't see immediate results. If you have ever resolved at the turn of a calendar year to lose weight, eat right, pray with more focus, deepen friendships, read through the Bible, or get out of debt, please raise your hand. These are all good, godly goals. And often we assume that filled with the right motivation, we can effectively accomplish our goals in a reasonable time.

Wrong!

The sad truth is that having a full tank of gas in your vehicle won't get you where you want to go. You must act. To achieve your potential you need a plan of attack, and then you need to attack the plan.

By nature I loathe planning. People who know me well can attest to this. I just do not like doing it. Genesis 1–3 lays out the fact that humans were created in God's image to create and to care for the earth and each other, yet I find it difficult to establish a goal, develop tactics to reach the goal, and take necessary steps each day toward the goal. My preference is to go with the flow. Just lean on God. I will follow where God's Spirit and the wind take me. But that's not how God always chooses to work. I have learned over time that this approach is really just an excuse, a sloppy and lazy way of avoiding the hard work of prayer and planning.

The last question you need to ask yourselves as a ministry team is this: "What does God desire us to do?" And I'd even add to that question: "What does God desire us to do *right now*?" Where do we start? What comes first? Let's say your church and children's ministry leadership are aligned or actively engaged in becoming aligned. For the sake of children and families, you need to make sure you are stepping out in faith, keeping in step with God's Spirit and working for God's glory and his purposes.

PRINCIPLE 4: LIVES ARE TRANSFORMED WHEN CHURCH LEADERS INITIATE CONSTRUCTIVE CHANGE TOWARD ALIGNMENT

Just as working out and putting healthy stress on muscles increases capacity, the same is true in the church. Ephesians 4:11–13 makes it clear that there are leaders in the body of believers whose role is not to do everything but to equip others to do the work of ministry. Though the outcome is good, there will be some "growing pains." Some muscles have not been used before, and it will take some time and effort to develop new habits, to learn new skills. Don't give up! Push through the pain. Remember, work comes with weeds. Every ministry has programmatic pain points to rise above. Take time to talk with your fatigued leaders; don't give up when the budget is scarce. Complex programs won't change overnight. And even if you try to change the curriculum, you won't always escape the reality of shallow content or curriculum that doesn't work as you had hoped. Children's ministry leaders must set the mission, establish the values, and then do the hard work of actualizing the vision into sustainable ministry. Disciple-making communities in the way of Christ are not a given; they are grown over time.

You might be surprised what church and children's ministry leaders in your setting come up with when you ask the open-ended question: "Where is God leading us as kid-influencers? How does he want us to implement relational children's ministry?" I ask this question in trainings all the time. Most of the time there's a stirring to redirect or add to the current ministry. Here are some responses:

- We believe God is calling us to start up pro-bono legal services for families in need.
- Our children's ministry needs to re-focus on sharing the Gospel.
- The Lord is inviting us to reach out to an impoverished part of town.
- We'd like to start satellite children's ministries in our area.

- The foster care system needs our help. We're inviting parents to open their homes.
- Incarcerated parents have kids. We're going to host events to reach them for Christ.
- We were going to build a youth room, but the teens told us to build a preschool instead.
- Our kids care about the world, so they're raising money to help children in Haiti.
- No one is serving special needs families in our area. We're starting a new ministry!
- God is calling us to give food and school supplies to kids on the other side of town.
- Parents need a break. We're starting up a free childcare service on Saturdays.

Relational children's ministry is for kids of all ages. The family of God is comprised of biological and spiritual relatives who impact one another along the same journey of following Christ. For long-term success in your discipleship efforts, work with your church leadership to cast a vision that supports the disciple-making mission of the church with a relational ministry focus. Who knows? God may use your efforts with children to change the entire church! Remember that everything you do carries with it the potential to change the faith trajectory of future generations.

Still, don't make that your ultimate goal. Seek to be faithful where God has placed you. Pray for change in the entire church, and respect the process God works out through the leadership of your church. Our vision is not always God's vision, and our timing is not always the same as God's. Be faithful and patient.

> Truly intergenerational communities welcome children, emerging adults, recovering addicts, single adults, widows, single parents, teens whose parents are not around, the elderly, those in crisis, empty nesters and struggling parents of young children into a safe but challenging place to be formed into the image of Christ.
>
> **Holly Allen & Christine Ross**[20]

Our ultimate goal is to point children of all ages to God; to know, love, and serve people so they will increasingly know, love, and serve Christ. As we've seen in this chapter, this begins by asking the hard questions, *What is today's reality? What really matters most? What is our shared support strategy? What does God desire to do?* in order to engage in constructive conversations with leaders on your ministry team and with the broader church leadership. Find a place of common ground, a common language that unites your work with children to the mission of the larger church. Eradicate misalignment mayhem by setting out a clear discipleship target marked by mission and supported by ministry alignment.

QUESTIONS FOR REFLECTION & DISCUSSION

1. Are you more of a problem solver or problem avoider? Why?

2. What excites you and frustrates you most about leading people?

3. What do you hope will happen as a result of your faithful investment in the lives of children and families?

4. Describe a time when you experienced "misalignment mayhem" in ministry.

5. What steps do you take to bring people together when they are heading in opposite directions?

6. Do you agree or disagree that the church has one central disciple-making mission? Explain.

7. How have you experienced churches living out multiple missions? What impact does it have on people in the congregation and surrounding community?

8. Why is it hard to open up conversations for constructive change in your ministry setting? How can you help be a change agent in favor of a better future?

9. Who are the key leaders in your church and children's ministry that need to discuss the following questions:

   - What is today's reality?
   - What really matters most?
   - What is our shared support strategy?
   - What does God desire us to do?

10. How willing are you to implement relational children's ministry in your church?

11. What will it take to get church leadership and kid-influencers on board for this vision to become reality?

CHAPTER 12

RECONSIDER THE DISCIPLESHIP RESOURCES AT YOUR DISPOSAL

If I could relive my life, I would devote my entire
ministry to reaching children for God!
D. L. Moody[1]

Jesus said, "Let the little children come to me, and do
not hinder them, for the kingdom of heaven belongs to
such as these."
Matthew 19:14

©Studio-Annika/www.istock.com

CHURCHES OFTEN FORGET one of the most basic realities of children's ministry: *ministry to children can take place anywhere at any time.* Just look at Jesus. He didn't need big buildings and budgets to make disciples. He worked with what he had. He spent time with his disciples, teaching them through the daily events of life.

I once heard Pastor Harvey Carey challenge the unbiblical presuppositions of children's ministry leaders. He was speaking at a Children's Pastors Conference[2] and his words left a mark on me. Carey shepherds a thriving congregation in downtown Detroit, and while the Motor City is collapsing on so many levels, Carey is seeing God work in the midst of unemployment, poverty, drug trafficking, crime, and gang violence. As Pastor Carey spoke to a crowd of children's pastors and kid-influencers, he shared his journey from being a successful youth pastor in Chicago to following God's leading to plant a church in one of the toughest urban epicenters in America. His passion was remarkable.[3]

He shared about resource challenges, the difficulties of finding quality leaders, and several other pain points almost every ministry faces. Then he described the state of the neighborhoods in Detroit. Drug lords and prostitution rings. Dilapidated and condemned houses. Pastor Carey shared about the time his children's ministry decided to take kids and families camping. They located tents, sleeping bags, Coleman stoves, and the makings of s'mores. Obviously there is no good place to camp in downtown Detroit. Sure, there are some picnic benches, but most grass and trees have long since been replaced with concrete. And it's dangerous too. You won't find people camping out in front of stores even on Black Friday!

Their plan was to have a "camping" block party right in the middle of all the mess. With the gangbangers and drug dealers looking on, they set up tents and roasted their marshmallows. Seeing the sticky, chocolate-marshmallow-covered faces of children, moms, and dads was priceless. Kids singing around campfires on the street was a first, something no one could remember ever seeing in Detroit before. In the end, the family of God won the night, and the riff-raff moved out or moved on.

Pastor Carey's exuberance was contagious. His solution is not camping per se. He simply wanted people to wake up to the creative Spirit of God. Ministry doesn't need to be fancy or expensive to be fruitful. "If you have a Bible, you have a budget!" he said. He is right. Good ministry isn't a matter of large budgets or high attendance. All it takes is a willing adult, a child in need, and the Spirit of God.

INTERRUPTED TOWARD A NEW TRAJECTORY

Pastor and World War II martyr Dietrich Bonhoeffer says in his classic book, *Life Together*: "We must be ready to allow ourselves to be interrupted by God."[4] Bonhoeffer knew the high stakes of ministry and what he was up against as he stood against Hitler and the Nazi party. Standing firm to the end, Bonhoeffer demonstrated resolve and resilience, and his character compass consistently pointed to Christ. He believed God's free gift of grace came at an extravagant price. The debt of sin was cancelled, paid in full by the death and resurrection of Jesus Christ. Yet while salvation is free, the cost of discipleship is not cheap. Being a disciple means we work with God to change, to become like the one we follow. Bonhoeffer asserted, "Christianity without the living Christ is inevitably Christianity without discipleship, and Christianity without discipleship is always Christianity without Christ."[5] His vision was of the body of believers sustaining individual disciples in community as they walked in step with God's Spirit and one another. And at the center of it all was Jesus.

> Jesus Christ is the same yesterday and today and forever.
>
> **Hebrews 13:8**

When I began this book, I mentioned that many of my peers from my youth have walked away from the church and ministry, yet somehow, by God's grace, I'm still here. "You *almost* lost me" is a true statement. I've since come to understand that the disciple-making mission of the church matters more than the hurdles or hindrances caused by imperfect people that I've encountered along the way. The church is organized, but it's not an organization—it's organic. It is a living organism made up of real people who are saved sinners coming to know, love, and serve Jesus Christ, one day at a time. These are people drawn from different ages and stages of life. The old and the young come together in awe and adoration of the one true God of the Bible. Being in full-time ministry can be a struggle, but it is a good struggle.

I now work at Awana, a global evangelism and discipleship ministry impacting millions of children every week. Awana is the same midweek discipleship ministry that impacted my life deeply after I became a follower of Jesus as a young child. But Awana today is not the same Awana it was when I was a child. It has changed over the years, and in many ways that has made it an even more effective ministry in these challenging times for children's ministry. Ministry to children isn't the same as it was 65 years ago. It's not even the same as when I started writing this book! On the other hand, some things have not changed. As always, the core mission of Awana is to help all children and youth throughout the world come to know, love, and serve the Lord Jesus Christ.

I never planned to work in full-time children's ministry, and I certainly did not anticipate working for Awana. After graduating from Moody Bible Institute in 1997, I headed into youth ministry. My plan was to work with teenagers over the long haul, and never as a stepping-stone to becoming a senior pastor.

I hoped that I would be a "lifer" in student ministries. Then God interrupted my life, and I found myself managing a local coffee shop. I needed space and time for the Lord to recalibrate my heart. My family and I became participating members at Willow Creek Community Church outside of Chicago. Slowly, it became clear that God was calling me in a different direction. Graduate school at Wheaton College reset my personal discipleship trajectory and eventually I was hired at my home church, in the children's ministry at Willow Creek.

I knew something exciting was on the horizon. I was leading leaders of leaders serving kids. I was passionate about the children's ministry, but I saw how it fit into the larger mission of the church as well. One of my dear friends and ministry colleagues, Pat, took me under her leadership wing, and we served together in adult discipleship ministries for many years.[6] I was working with teams of volunteers, creating curriculum, and teaching regularly. It was thrilling work . . . until one day, God interrupted me again.

One of the hardest decisions I ever made was to walk away from my role as a discipleship pastor at Willow. I didn't have another position or a game plan on the other side of the door. I just knew God's Spirit was telling me, "Come home. Your work is done." When I told my friends, they presumed I was heaven bound. When I told my wife, she told me to get a job (just kidding). It became a season of searching and stumbling and looking for that next leg of the journey.

I returned to my roots, in one sense. I started teaching adjunct classes part time in the undergraduate program at Moody. Then, a full-time position opened up in the training department at Awana. It was the same ministry I had participated in as a kid and served at in high school. A year later, I was asked to become the Director of New Ministries and Parent Engagement. Today, as Director of Leadership Development, I am passionate about my work turning kid-influencers into communities of lifelong disciple makers.

The body of Christ is a divine mission lived out in human expression. Why do I tell you my professional testimony? Because I want you to know that the disciple-making mission, especially alongside children, is more than something I do; it's integral to my own lifelong discipleship and leadership. It's part of God's call upon my life and part of the work he is doing in the American and global church to transform our understanding of children's ministry to give it a relational focus on discipleship.

The founder of Awana, Art Rorheim, is one of the most genuine disciples and ministry leaders I have ever met. Art started Awana because the Lord used kid-influencers and disciple makers in his life to multiply the message and ministry of Christ. Art is committed to proclaiming the gospel of Jesus Christ in word and deed. His heart is saturated with God's Word, and it beats for kids of all nations. Awana exists today because Christ brought together a band of believers on an unscripted adventure to experience messy faith, unconventional community, life-transforming mission, and dynamic discipleship. From day one, Art followed Jesus and sought to reach kids and families with the gospel. Awana has a past—a strong, respectable legacy to lean on. Awana has a present—like any large ministry, it can be easily mis-understood and under-appreciated. And Awana has a future—opportunities to engage in reaching kids, equipping leaders, and joining God in changing the world are seemingly endless.

I believe you, like me, are in your ministry as a kid-influencer for a reason. The late theologian Robert Webber is famous for saying, "The road to the future runs through the past."[7] Your past, present, and future are working together to make you the person God uniquely created you to be. You have a mark to make on the ministry in which you serve, and on those with whom you serve. The faith community, church, or parachurch ministry you are part of today has a past, present, and future to be leveraged.

Whether you are leading a children's ministry, serving as a children's ministry volunteer, parenting your own children, or providing leadership to another area of your church or community, I believe God wants to bring fresh vitality to your ministry through a relational discipleship focus. Relational children's ministry has the potential to be a new paradigm for disciple mak-ing in the body of Christ.

EMBRACE CHANGE: RELATIONSHIPS ARE WORTH IT

School was out, it was a Monday, and I was stuck working, so Kate and the boys headed to the Museum of Science and Industry in Chicago. As we sat around the dinner table that night, Avery and Aaron talked all about what they saw, what they enjoyed, and what they thought was dumb. They talked about getting in trouble for goofing around. Then Kate chimed in. She mentioned an exhibit that showcased the progression of phones throughout history. As they walked the corridor, my wife pointed out several handsets that had been in her home growing up. She talked about when she first saw a cordless phone, and showed the kids the first mobile phone she could remember. The kids laughed at the size of the device. They walked and talked all the way to the last phone on display in the exhibit. One of our kids pointed and blurted out, "Hey mom! That's the same cell phone you have in your purse!"

Keep in mind, this is a museum.

For my wife, this was the shot heard 'round the world. She finally decided it was time to get a smartphone. It's not that she fears change; she simply dislikes the cost and the learning curve associated with new things. And since change is constantly happening at an unprecedented rate, it makes it difficult to keep up with all the new gadgets available. So she tries to avoid it.

We don't have that option in the church. If we refuse to adapt to the changing culture, we end up creating roadblocks that hinder people from hearing the gospel and coming to love Christ.

In the days, weeks, and months ahead, you can choose to do business as usual, or you can start moving toward constructive change. You'll need to talk with your church and children's ministry leaders. You'll need to look under the hood of your current discipleship approach. You may need to "reset" some older patterns and habits. And you'll need some good resources to help you do this.

LEVERAGE WHAT'S AROUND YOU

Cardboard boxes make great cars.

Okay, that's not true, but it's what I thought when I was a kid. My mom would bring home huge boxes from work, give me a pair of scissors and a pungent-smelling Sharpie, and let me create things to my heart's content. I turned those cardboard boxes into cars, busses, and tanks. Sometimes I made houses. I was bummed out when my mom changed jobs and she could no longer get me boxes (but it was time for me to head off for college anyway).

The best children's ministry leaders use what God has placed around them. Where some look at limited resources and see what they can't do, others see resources as gifts from God to grow and develop relationships. The relationship is the most valuable resource they possess—everything else is just icing on the cake. They can certainly use a larger budget and a nicer facility, but they don't need those things to do the work of ministry.

Relational children's ministries aren't too concerned with flashy presentations, the latest videos, or having cool lights and media. They want people who love children, who will share real life with them, and who love Jesus and God's Word. The lights will fade. The videos will be forgotten. But kids remember when an adult cares. When someone stops to pray with them. When you take the time to listen to their questions and show them how to look to God's Word for answers. Year after year, can you guess what is unofficially rated as the #1 toy of all time? Yep, the cardboard box. We don't need the latest gadgets to be relevant to our changing times. We just need to be willing to go with the flow, to be flexible in our relationships, and to focus on caring for children more than covering every point in the lesson.

Consider what the Apostle Paul writes in 1 Corinthians 9:19–22:

> Though I am free and belong to no one, I have made myself a slave to everyone, to win as many as possible. To the Jews I became like a Jew, to win the Jews. To those under the law I became like one under the law (though I myself am not under the law), so as to win those under the law. To those not having the law I became like one not having the law (though I am not free from God's law but am under Christ's law), so as to win those not having the law. To the weak I became weak, to win the weak. I have become all things to all people so that by all possible means I might save some.

Paul chose not to be boxed in to specific ministry models and methods. He kept the focus on Christ and built bridges with those he was trying to love and serve. Throughout the book of Acts, particularly in Athens (Acts 17) and before King Agrippa (Acts 26), Paul paid attention to his surroundings and studied the culture to open doors for spiritual conversations. For the sake of the gospel, and for the sake of people, Paul was willing to adjust as needed to relate to whomever God called him to reach. Like Jesus, Paul leveraged creativity and simplicity for the sake of eternity.

Every kid-influencer's situation and setting is unique, as are the people they desire to reach. So how do you get started?

HITTING THE ROAD TOWARD RELATIONAL CHILDREN'S MINISTRY

Start where you are. You may not know exactly where you are heading in children's ministry when you begin, but there is no better place to start than right where you are today. If you desire to head in the direction of relational children's ministry, you do not need to overhaul everything at once. You can make small changes. Gather your leaders together and study some of the examples of Jesus from the gospels, noting how he relates to people and what that teaches us about the way we minister to children. Encourage your leaders to be involved in a small discipleship group for a year, learning the basics of the faith and what it means to be a disciple of Jesus. Then, encourage them to try leading and discipling others. The things they learn in these settings will directly apply to their ministry with kids.

On the other hand, you may be ready for a complete overhaul. I've known some churches that grab on to the life-giving invitations of Jesus and shut down their children's ministry for several months to get everyone on the same disciple-making page. A six-month to year-long ministry detox might just be what the family of God needs to reset the discipleship trajectory of this and future generations.

Here are several key points you should consider if you don't have them in place already.

SET YOUR COURSE: WHAT'S YOUR PHILOSOPHY?

Feel free to adapt the principles in this book to construct a ministry philosophy that fits your passion, purpose, and personality as a faith community. Meet with other children's ministry leaders and pick their brains as well. However you go about it, you should develop a philosophy of ministry for discipleship with kids and families. This includes your mission, your values, and how they connect to your structure and programming. You can turn to this philosophy to guide you when decisions need to be made and when the journey gets tiring. There are many children's ministry providers—including denominations, publishing houses, parachurch organizations, conferences, courses, and training—that can help you figure this out. My purpose in this book is not to tell you what your philosophy should be. It's to encourage you to add a relational discipleship focus to whatever philosophy you adopt or create.

PICK A VEHICLE: WHAT PROGRAM WILL SERVE PEOPLE BEST?

There are a multitude of programming options available for children's ministry. Thumb through a resource catalog, check out options online, ask around, get sample materials from curriculum providers, and you will quickly learn that there is no shortage of ways to work with kids. Very little works "right out of the box," so learning to customize and tweak what you get is a necessary skill. Writing your own materials is a great way to ensure your content and community stay aligned with your mission. Figure out what will serve people best in your setting, and know that it will likely change over time. Try not to get it 100 percent perfect and you will probably be okay. Look for programs that provide integrated discipleship, but remember work comes with weeds. The work of ministry is never in the program; it's in cultivating the relationships. Guiding kids to know, love, and serve Christ is always worth the heartache.

GRAB THE SUPPLIES YOU NEED: WHAT PRODUCTS WILL SUPPORT YOU?

In addition to many different programs, there are countless products to assist you in ministry. Crafts, videos, curriculum, games—you can find a wide variety of resources all over the spectrum. Some take a deep dive while others are quite shallow. Some are simply entertainment while others are more educational. Some are expensive while others are not. Don't just default to buying "plug-and-play" options that require no leaders and no prep. They won't help you cultivate relationships with kids, and since relationships are where life-on-life interactions happen, you won't be engaging in biblical discipleship. Hastily scraping together a random selection of products and calling it "children's ministry" may sound silly on paper, but it's far more common than you might think. You and your team of kid-influencers can work together to figure out what products, resources, and tools will support your philosophy and programming best.

NOW IS THE TIME TO USE WHATEVER GOD PROVIDES TO REACH AND EQUIP KIDS AND FAMILIES

In life and leadership, the idea of sharing the last 10 percent is an important concept. It is the permission-giving commitment to tell that last bit of truth that may sting but needs to be shared.

> The Christian community needs a new mind—a new way of thinking, a new way of feeling, a new way of relating, a new vision of our role in the world—to pass on the faith to this and future generations.
>
> **David Kinnaman[8]**

What's the last 10 percent? In children's ministry it's letting go of "but this is how we've always done it." Over time, biblical principles get confused with community preferences and become systematized rules. It is likely that the approach you inherited in your setting is not as effective as it once was. Start by humbly going before God for redirection and renewed perspective.

Another step is to start looking around and listening to the kid-influencers around you, noting how they are gifted by God. Reaching and equipping kids and families in lifelong discipleship takes many people. Each of the chapters in this book ends with reflection questions that can be used to guide discussion among a team of kid-influencers. If you read one chapter a week as a leadership team and talk through your responses to the questions, it's a start. Use these times to model the kind of life-on-life discipleship you desire for kids and families. Encourage some parents or other church leaders to read this book and spend time discussing the questions with them as well.

It is my sincere desire that you will begin to see children and parents who cross your path as gifts directly from God. Proverbs 25:25 says, "Like cold water to a weary soul is good news from a distant land." As you serve the Lord, I pray you will be filled up and refreshed by the deepening of your own relationship with Christ. And as you are known, loved, and served by Jesus, you will be able to know, love, and serve others. Relational children's ministry can lead to a revival in your own life. That's how relationships work—they are contagious. Today, you stand at the threshold of a new opportunity to guide others as you follow in the way of Jesus together. Let the disruptive discipleship revolution of relational children's ministry begin!

QUESTIONS FOR REFLECTION & DISCUSSION

1. What challenges are you currently facing that hold you back from being as effective as you would like in children's ministry?

2. Who has God placed around you who can help you address the issues that are unique to your ministry setting?

3. In what way has the Lord interrupted you recently? How have the principles of *Relational Children's Ministry* impacted your thinking about what kids and parents need in discipleship?

4. As a disciple maker, what keeps you coming back so that kids and families will come to know, love, and serve the Lord Jesus Christ?

5. Change is happening all around us these days. What steps do you take personally to embrace changes in culture, technology, family, and church?

6. Inventory your church and children's ministry leadership. What resources has God placed in your vicinity? What spiritual gifts are present? What tangible tools and supplies around you can help kid-influencers guide children in the way of Christ-centered discipleship?

7. Have you taken time to build out your ministry philosophy as it relates to reaching and equipping kids and families in lifelong discipleship? What are some essential elements that are non-negotiable for ministry?

8. As you consider ministry programs, what models and methods are most aligned with your philosophy and particular church?

9. Even if you do not have an elaborate building or budget, what resources are unique to your ministry that can lead to lifelong discipleship?

10. How can you and the disciple-making community of kid-influencers you lead rise above the status quo in children's ministry for the sake of kids and families?

HOW CAN THE MINISTRY OF AWANA SERVE YOU?

Sometimes in the waves of change, we find our true direction.
Unknown

See, I am doing a new thing! Now it springs up; do you not perceive it? I am making a way in the wilderness and streams in the wasteland.
Isaiah 43:19

SURROUNDED BY SWELLS OF CHANGE

Change is a reality for everyone. It's inevitable. It's unsettling. And when it's widespread, it can be crippling. To be honest, today's churches, children's ministries, and parents are struggling to navigate the shifting tides. Culture, technology, media, and families are changing rapidly. It's difficult to keep a solid footing in life when the surrounding swells are so strong. Faithful parents, leaders, and decision makers in the children's ministry community provide candid perspective about what many are facing and feeling:

> Things are changing so fast, no one seems able to keep up! It reminds me of days at the beach when our kids were small. They loved the ocean but sometimes the waves came in so fast they'd be upended by one and they couldn't get back on their feet quickly enough to resist the next one. They loved the ocean and even the waves. But the relentlessness—not just the power—of the swells was just too much. A single wave—even a powerful one—would have been survivable; but they just kept coming and coming. . . . That's kind of how many of us feel these days. Workers, parents, and even professional children's staff all need help. We're just

253

overwhelmed. We need something; maybe something new and innovative, something custom-made for this current craziness.[1]

Amy, a seasoned children's ministry leader and mother of three

Is this perception surprising? Or does it sound familiar? Amy's sentiments give voice to what's going on inside the hearts of kid-influencers all over the U.S. and in many places around the world. God has placed men and women everywhere who love children and long for them to know, love, and serve Jesus Christ for life. They recognize that change is all around, yet they are not without hope. The apostle Paul's words in 1 Corinthians 4:8–9 resonate deeply with them: "We are afflicted in every way, but not crushed; perplexed, but not driven to despair; persecuted, but not forsaken; struck down, but not destroyed." While doomsday prophets may run around proclaiming the sky is falling, these devoted disciples are committed to reaching this and future generations with the gospel in personal and practical ways. What's most surprising is that, while change is all around, kid-influencers are asking for *even more change*. There's an outcry for relevant solutions that address the pressing spiritual needs of children, families, and churches.

CAN LEGACY MINISTRIES LEARN TO SURF?

For 65 years, Awana has withstood the test of time and the tides of change as a global children's ministry. Many who are familiar with days of Awana past are rediscovering it as if for the first time. The renowned club ministry that started in a church basement in Chicago has grown into an international movement. It spans more than 100 countries, involves over 300,000 leaders, and engages 3 million-plus children in weekly evangelism and discipleship ministry. Truly, God is reaching kids, equipping leaders, and changing the world through the ministry of Awana. Its legacy mission as an organization is stronger than ever:

> The global prayer of Awana is that all children and youth throughout the world will come to know, love, and serve the Lord Jesus Christ.

Awana's commitment to partnering with churches to reach and disciple children is resolute, yet in changing times, God-honoring change is needed for maximum impact. Churches across the country and around the world are finding fresh ways to bring the gospel into an ever-changing culture. They are adapting to address today's needs without compromising their convictions about Christ, God's Word, and the disciple-making mission. To reach more children for Christ, the ministry of Awana is adapting, stepping out to ride the waves of change alongside church and children's ministry leaders.

In 2013, the leadership of Awana took a bold step, asking difficult questions like, "How well is Awana listening to and serving churches? How do its current and past customers perceive Awana? What will it take to reach today's kids for Christ and engage them in lifelong discipleship? What needs to stay the same and what needs to change for Awana to partner with churches and children's ministry leaders in this mission?" As expected, we discovered some strengths as well as some shortcomings. What we found out led us to ask more questions of more children's ministry leaders and stakeholders. Not just for our sake alone, we needed to explore what *is* and *is not working* in children's ministry. So we conducted a follow-up study in 2014. It was our desire to hear directly from the children's ministry leadership community. What passion areas and pain points exist? Were the new solutions we were developing on the right track? The overarching research results are available in *The Gospel Truth About Children's Ministry: 10 Fresh KidMin Research Findings* (available at awana.org/thegospeltruth).

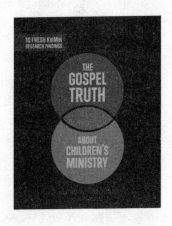

In *The Gospel Truth About Children's Ministry*, Awana lays out what nearly 1,000 children's ministry leaders and decision makers from across the U.S. long to see happening in the spiritual lives of kids. It also probes into their satisfaction levels about what's *actually* happening in their churches on their watch and from their perspective. As it turns out, there's a discipleship disconnect in today's children's ministry—a chasm between desired outcomes and reality. Evangelism, discipleship, and Bible teaching is foundational, yet running children's ministry programming and keeping it "entertaining" is hindering lifelong discipleship effectiveness. There's a clear desire for a bridge between church and home to be established so kids and families are working together with children's ministry. Culturally relevant, customizable, digitally accessible, and cost-effective curriculum solutions are desperately needed.

Nearly 50 percent of children's ministry decision makers are ready to change their programming in the next year, and 30 percent of those are most likely to change their curriculum first. It's time to get back to basics in children's ministry. The ministry of Awana is up for this challenge. We are riding the waves of change in order to serve churches and children's ministries all over the world.

SHIFTING TIDES, UNCHANGING MISSION

The God-given mission of Awana is to impact the global population of children and youth with the gospel and engage them in lifelong discipleship. This is an audacious vision, but we believe Jesus was serious when he commissioned his followers to make disciples of all nations (Matt 28:18–20; Acts 1:8). We also believe it was significant that he established the value of children and childlike faith in his Father's kingdom (Luke 18:15–17). The church really only has one mission: lead people of all ages to know, love, and serve Christ, and multiply them to do the same. No matter what may shift, Awana is wholeheartedly aligned with this unchanging mission, and is committed as an organization to locking arms with likeminded leaders and churches that are devoted to making disciples through children's ministry.

That said, in light of our recent research, we took a step back to identify pressing issues and innovate on behalf of children's ministry. We wanted to develop a new resource for churches, a curriculum solution in line with our longstanding mission that addresses the current realities children's ministry leaders are facing. We heard loud and clear that *less is actually more*: *less* complex, *less* moving parts, *less* expensive, *less* time-consuming, and so on. We also learned there are seven qualities that must be present in new children's ministry resource solutions:

- Strong biblical foundation
- Centered on the gospel and evangelism
- Focused on making disciples
- Highly relational
- Integration of church and home
- Appropriate leveraging of technology
- Flexible and adaptable programming support and curriculum[2]

If these focus areas don't seem groundbreaking, it's because they are foundational. These qualities were identified by children's ministry stakeholders like you as key factors for effectiveness in reaching and discipling kids. Yes, there's a need for fun and engaging experiences, but always with the unchanging end goal in full view: *make disciples.*

READY TO HIT THE WAVES?

Awana wants to serve you as you venture out to reach and disciple kids, families, and leaders. We're here to support you so you can live out the mission God has called your church and children's ministry to fulfill. You've read *Relational Children's Ministry,* so you know what's at stake and where our current trajectory is taking us. You also know, as we've learned at Awana, that there are two critical components (fueled by God's presence and power, of course) that bring children's ministry to life: high relational engagement and high Scripture engagement. Where these two overlap, it forms the sweet spot of discipleship. This "great connection" is the secret ingredient for maximizing ministry impact.

In a fast-paced world where kids, families, and leaders are always on the go, the need for deep connection with God, his Word, and each other is on the rise. This can't be done without concerted effort and timely support. Children's ministry doesn't need another turnkey program; it needs a revolution. It needs a renewed vision and resources that will reach and disciple this and future generations for Christ. This doesn't require changing our mission; rather, we must change our methods. There's a desire in today's children's ministry and in the hearts of kid-influencers everywhere to experience a renewed kind of disciple. For this to happen, Awana believes it's time for a renewed approach to discipleship. Any time you're ready to ride, we're here to serve.

AWANA RESOURCES FOR ESTABLISHING RELATIONAL CHILDREN'S MINISTRY

relationalchildrensministry.com

Go online for free ministry building resources, including videos, sermon outlines, and more.

God is changing the world through the Ministry of Awana by equipping leaders to reach kids with the Gospel and engaging them in lifelong discipleship.

ONE MISSION. MANY METHODS.

The ministry of Awana is customizable to meet the needs of your church.

MORE™ | awana.org/more

MORE is the global documentary of how the gospel is changing the lives of millions worldwide through the ministry of Awana. It's the story of caring adults investing time and reaching out to the global population of children and youth. Filmed over the course of five months, on location around the world, MORE is an inspiring and beautiful collection of stories of lives forever transformed by the power of the gospel. Visit awana.org/more to watch this free film and access additional resources for your church.

MOVE™ | moveyourchurch.org

MOVE is a dynamic church assessment for building healthy children's and youth ministries. The book and companion resources  equip you to evaluate your ministry, address current gaps, engage in constructive dialogue, and take simple strategic steps toward effective lifelong discipleship ministry. Go to moveyourchurch.org to learn more, get the free assessment, and purchase the book.

Awana Clubs™ | awana.org/clubs

Awana Clubs is a proven children's ministry for ages 2 to 18 focused on evangelism and discipleship. Each age-specific program incorporates sharing the Gospel, studying God's Word, memorizing Scripture, serving  others, and using at-home resources as part of lifelong discipleship. Children grow spiritually in the context of fun and engaging experiences, relationships with peers and caring leaders, personal engagement with God and his Word, and opportunities to live out evangelism and discipleship in the world. To learn more about our age-specific programming and curriculum, check out awana.org/clubs.

The Great Life™ | awana.org/thegreatlife

The Great Life is a Christ-centered integrated discipleship curriculum for use anytime, anywhere. It is a weekly relational experience that starts in the home and is supported at church so kids, peers, leaders, and parents will come to know, love, and serve Christ together. This small group curriculum is for children ages 5–11 and brings the Old and New Testament to life in simple, creative ways. Discover if this newest offering by Awana is right for you at awana .org/thegreatlife.

Awana Youth Ministries™ | awanaym.org

Awana Youth Ministries grounds middle school and high school students in a lasting biblical faith, equipping them to share their faith as they serve others in their churches  and communities. This is accomplished through proven resources, curriculum, training and partnerships for student ministry leaders, as well as ongoing access to Awana staff committed to supporting church youth leadership. Investigate all that Awana Youth Ministries has to offer at awanaym.org.

Mozo™ | awana.org/mozo

Ministry happens not just in big moments, but in small moments—moments that are too often lost when a leader is distracted by administrative tasks. It doesn't have to be this way. Your children's ministry needs technology tools with relationships in mind. Mozo, the new digital toolbox from Awana, streamlines the processes of Awana Clubs, turning those minutes to ministry. Learn more online at awana .org/mozo.

How can Awana serve you, your church, and your children's ministry best?
We're ready to connect whenever you reach out.

1 East Bode Road, Streamwood, Illinois 60107
Awana.org | 866-292-6227

NOTES

CHAPTER 1: ARE WE JUST SPINNING OUR WHEELS?

1. Francis Chan with Danae Yankoski, *Crazy Love: Overwhelmed by a Relentless God* (Colorado Springs, CO: David C. Cook, 2013), 97.
2. Matt. 28:18–20.
3. James C. Wilhoit, *Spiritual Formation As If the Church Mattered: Growing in Christ Through Community* (Grand Rapids: Baker Academic, 2008), 15–16.
4. Michelle Wright and Avril Guthrie, *The Magic of Mandela: Twenty Years of Democracy* (Raleigh, NC: Lulu.com, 2015).
5. David Kinnaman and Aly Hawkins, *You Lost Me: Why Young Christians Are Leaving Church—and Rethinking Faith* (Grand Rapids: Baker Books, 2011), 206.
6. Chap Clark, *Hurt 2.0: Inside the World of Today's Teenagers* (Grand Rapids: Baker Academic, 2011), 34 and 191.
7. Henry Adams, *The Education of Henry Adams: An Autobiography* (Cambridge, MA: Riverside Press, 1918), 300.
8. Brad Mathias, *Road Trip to Redemption: A Disconnected Family, A Cross-Country Adventure, and an Amazing Journey of Healing and Grace* (Carol Stream, IL: Tyndale Momentum, 2013), 79.

CHAPTER 2: MINDING THE DISCIPLESHIP GAP

1. Eric Metaxas, *Bonhoeffer: Pastor, Martyr, Prophet, Spy* (Nashville, Tenn: Thomas Nelson, 2010), 187.
2. Jon Tyson, *Sacred Roots: Why the Church Still Matters* (Grand Rapids: Zondervan, 2013), 36; Barna Group, "Six Reasons Young Christians Leave Church," last modified September 28, 2011, https://www.barna.org/barna-update/teens-nextgen/528-six-reasons-young-christians-leave-church#.U3IUWq1dUyv (accessed January 30, 2015); Barna Group, "Five Myths about Young Adult Church Dropouts," last modified November 6, 2011, https://www.barna.org/teens-next-gen-articles/534-five-myths-about-young-adult-church-dropouts (accessed January 30, 2015).
3. Gregory Carlson et al., *Perspectives on Children's Spiritual Formation: Four Views*, ed. Michael Anthony (Nashville, Tenn: B & H Academic, 2007), 2.
4. Barna Group, "Five Myths."

5. Ibid., 21.

6. Kinnaman and Hawkins, *You Lost Me*, 25.

7. Larry Fowler, *Raising a Modern-Day Joseph: A Timeless Strategy for Growing Great Kids* (Colorado Springs, CO: David C. Cook, 2009), 101.

8. Shared with permission.

CHAPTER 3: PAIN POINTS IN TODAY'S CHILDREN'S MINISTRY

1. Tryon Edwards, *A Dictionary of Thought: A Cyclopedia of Laconic Quotations* (Detroit, MI: F. B. Dickerson Co., 1908), 349.

2. Tyson, *Sacred Roots*, 33.

3. Shared with permission.

4. Shared with permission.

5. Tyson, *Sacred Roots*, 15–16.

6. The Epilogue at the end of this book provides you with more information about the global children's ministry of Awana. Visit Awana.org online to find out more about its ministry philosophy, programming and products, as well as its discipleship work around the world.

7. Matt Markins and Dan Lovaglia with Mark McPeak, *The Gospel Truth About Children's Ministry: 10 Fresh KidMin Research Findings* (Streamwood, IL: Awana, 2015).

CHAPTER 4: JESUS' DISRUPTIVE APPROACH TO DISCIPLESHIP

1. Dallas Willard, *The Great Omission: Reclaiming Jesus's Essential Teachings on Discipleship* (San Francisco: HarperSanFrancisco, 2006), 6.

2. Lauren Barlow, ed., *Inspired by Tozer: 59 Artists, Writers and Leaders Share the Insight and Passion They've Gained from A. W. Tozer* (Grand Rapids, Mich: Baker, 2011), 56.

3. There is no shortage of information on how kids rank in the world. Kid-influencers and churches can step up in so many ways. UNICEF's annual report, "The State of the World's Children," consistently reveals the ongoing plight of kids around the globe (http://unicef.org/sowc). In response to Christ's convicting call, faith-based organizations like Compassion International (http://compassion.com), World Vision (http://worldvision.org) and HOPE International (http://hopeinternational.org) are providing holistic and sustainable solutions in areas of greatest need. Additionally, global children's ministries like Awana (http://awana.org) and OneHope (http://onehope.net) strengthen the faith foundation of kids and families.

4. Herman Horne, *Jesus the Teacher: Examining his Expertise in Education*, revised and updated by Agnus M. Gunn (Grand Rapids: Kregel Publications, 1998), 23.

5. David Platt, *Follow Me: A Call to Die. A Call to Live* (Carol Stream, IL: Tyndale House Publishers, 2013), 37.

6. John Ortberg, *Who Is This Man? The Unpredictable Impact of the Inescapable Jesus* (Grand Rapids: Zondervan, 2014), 12.

7. Shared with permission.

8. Erwin Raphael McManus, *An Unstoppable Force: Daring to Become the Church God Had in Mind* (Loveland, CO: Group Publishing, 2001), 170.

9. Luke 6:27–32.

10. This program is no longer running, though many kids continue to face the effects of substance abuse in their homes. In 1986, I attended a camp through *Kids Are Special* that was chronicled by critically acclaimed reporter Emerald Yeh in a documentary entitled *Lost Childhood: Growing Up In An Alcoholic Family* (2004). If this issue is closer to your heart, visit the National Association for Children of Alcoholics website (nacoa.org/prods.htm) for a description or to order a DVD.

11. Shared with permission.

12. John 14:26; Acts 1:8.

13. Ps. 119:105; John 10:4; Gal. 5:25.

14. Keith Anderson and Randy D. Reese, *Spiritual Mentoring: A Guide for Seeking and Giving Direction* (Downers Grove, IL: IVP Books, 1999), 16.

CHAPTER 5: INVITATION 1: DRAW KIDS INTO AN UNSCRIPTED ADVENTURE WITH GOD

1. Catherine Stonehouse, *Joining Children on the Spiritual Journey: Nurturing a Life of Faith* (Grand Rapids: Baker Academic, 1998), 213.

2. Shared with permission.

3. Dallas Willard, *The Great Omission: Reclaiming Jesus' Essential Teachings on Discipleship* (San Francisco: HarperSanFrancisco, 2006), 107.

4. Walter Wangerin Jr., *Little Lamb, Who Made Thee? A Book about Children and Parents* (Grand Rapids: Zondervan, 2003), 104–5.

5. Catherine Stonehouse, *Joining Children on the Spiritual Journey: Nurturing a Life of Faith* (Grand Rapids: Baker Academic, 1998), 139.

6. Dr. Kara E. Powell and Dr. Chap Clark, *Sticky Faith: Everyday Ideas to Build Lasting Faith in Your Kids* (Grand Rapids: Zondervan, 2011), 85.

7. David Csinos and Ivy Beckwith, *Children's Ministry in the Way of Jesus* (Downers Grove, IL: IVP Books, 2013), 83.

8. Anderson and Reese, *Spiritual Mentoring*, 94.

9. Scottie May et al., *Children Matter: Celebrating Their Place in the Church, Family, and Community* (Grand Rapids: William B. Eerdmans Pub, 2005), 8.

10. Ibid., 16–22.

11. Barna Group, "The State of the Bible: 6 Trends for 2014," last modified April 8,

2014, https://www.barna.org/barna-update/culture/664-the-state-of-the-bible-6
-trends-for-2014#.VI3IJWTF—U (accessed January 30, 2015).

12. Barna Group, "The Books Americans Are Reading," last modified June 4, 2013,
https://www.barna.org/barna-update/culture/614-the-books-americans-are
-reading#.VI3PAWTF—U (accessed January 30, 2015).

13. 1 Cor. 15:3–4.

14. Check out legacymilestones.com and parentministry.net for rites of passage ideas,
training and support for children's and family ministry.

15. Robert E. Coleman, *The Mind of the Master* (Wheaton, IL: Harold Shaw
Publishing, 2000), 96.

CHAPTER 6: INVITATION 2: WRESTLE WITH MESSY FAITH TOGETHER

1. Powell and Clark, *Sticky Faith*, 46

2. Fowler, *Raising a Modern-Day Joseph*, 71.

3. Csinos and Beckwith, *Children's Ministry*, 38.

4. Shared with permission.

5. Robert Coles, *The Spiritual Life of Children* (Boston: Houghton Mifflin Co.,
1990), 100.

6. Anthony, Michelle. *Dreaming of More for the Next Generation: Lifetime Faith
Ignited by Family Ministry* (Colorado Springs, CO: David C. Cook, 2012), 23.

7. John H. Westerhoff, III, *Will Our Children Have Faith?* Third rev. ed. (New York:
Morehouse Publishing, 2012), 91.

8. Stonehouse, *Joining Children*, 150.

9. May, *Children Matter*, 43.

10. Clark, *Hurt 2.0*, 31.

11. Stonehouse, *Joining Children*, 63.

12. Ibid., 91.

13. Ibid., 135.

14. Ibid., 21.

CHAPTER 7: INVITATION 3: BUILD UNCONVENTIONAL COMMUNITY WITH FAMILIES

1. Mark Galli, "The Relentless Passion of Francis Chan," *Christianity Today* 56, no. 11
(December 2012), 46.

2. Shared with permission.

3. It turns out floor hockey carries spiritual significance. When I told Steve about
this section of the book, he sent me Isaiah 58:8, "Then your light will break forth
like the dawn, and your healing will quickly appear; then your righteousness will
go before you, and the glory of the Lord will be your rear guard." He said, "It was

funny how any kid felt invincible if I was their goalie. He would take on six other kids if it could be just that one kid and me. What if we went out with that same confidence, knowing that we had God as our goalie? We should go out expecting victory in the world knowing that his glory is our rear guard." Thirty years have come and gone. True disciples just keep on making disciples.

4. 1 Tim. 1:2.

5. Pew Research Center, "What Surveys Say About Worship Attendance—and Why Some Stay Home," last modified September 13, 2013, http://www.pewresearch .org/fact-tank/2013/09/13/what-surveys-say-about-worship-attendance-and-why -some-stay-home (accessed January 30, 2015).

6. Barna Group, "Americans Divided on the Importance of Church," last modified March 25, 2014, https://www.barna.org/barna-update/culture/661-americans -divided-on-the-importance-of-church#.VHIVoVfF-e8 (accessed January 30, 2015).

7. Ibid.

8. Carl Desportes Bowman et al., *Culture of American Families: Executive Report* (Charlottesville, VA: Institute for Advanced Studies in Culture, 2012), http:// iasc-culture.org/research_character_of_american_families_project.php (accessed January 30, 2015).

9. Barna Group, *Americans Divided*.

10. Will Miller and Glenn Grayson Sparks, *Refrigerator Rights: Creating Connections and Restoring Relationships* (White River Junction, VT: White River Press, 2007), 20.

11. To learn more about the ministry model of Fellowship Housing, check out fhcmoms.org.

12. Shared with permission.

CHAPTER 8: INVITATION 4: MODEL CHRIST'S LIFE-TRANSFORMING MISSION

1. Henrietta C. Mears and Earl O. Roe, *Dream Big: The Henrietta Mears Story* (Ventura, Calif: Regal Books, 1990), 151.

2. John 4:7–15; 7:37–39.

3. Shared with permission.

4. Wilhoit, *Spiritual Formation*, 29.

5. 1 Cor. 15:3–4.

6. Eph. 2:8–9.

7. Acts 16:31; Rom. 10:9.

8. Matt. 18:3.

9. May, *Children Matter*, 143–44.

10. John 15:13.

11. John 3:3, 16–17; 4:41–42; 10:10.

12. Coleman, *The Mind of the Master*, 94.

13. Wilhoit, *Spiritual Formation*, 126.

14. Gal. 5:22–23.

15. Anderson and Reese, *Spiritual Mentoring*, 132.

16. John 13:12–17.

17. Henry Cloud, *Integrity: The Courage to Meet the Demands of Reality* (New York: Harper, 2009), 6–12.

18. Ibid. 31.

19. Phil. 1:27.

20. Shared with permission.

21. Samuel D. Rima, *Leading from the Inside Out: The Art of Self-Leadership* (Grand Rapids: Baker Books, 2000), 27.

22. Much is being written about "reverse mentoring" these days, particularly in leadership circles. Earl Creps, *Reverse Mentoring: How Young Leaders Can Transform the Church and Why We Should Let Them* (San Francisco: Jossey-Bass, 2008) is a helpful starting point for church leaders on this matter.

23. Ps. 119:9.

24. Heb. 4:12.

25. Shared with permission.

26. Gal. 5:22–23.

27. There are many resources on spiritual disciplines, or practices, that point people toward fully devoted discipleship in Christ. Richard Foster's book, *Celebration of Discipline: The Path to Spiritual Growth* (San Francisco: Harper Collins, 2012), was originally published in 1978 and has become a modern day classic on this subject. I also highly recommend John Ortberg's *The Life You've Always Wanted: Spiritual Disciplines for Ordinary People* (Grand Rapids: Zondervan, 2002).

28. Explore the Epilogue in the back of this book or visit Awana.org.

CHAPTER 9: INVITATION 5: EQUIP CHILDREN FOR DYNAMIC DISCIPLESHIP

1. Frederick Douglass, "1855 letter," *My Bondage and My Freedom* (Lexington, KY: Seven Treasures, 2009).

2. Shared with permission.

3. Cheri Fuller, *The One Year Praying Through the Bible: 365 Devotions* (Carol Stream, IL: Tyndale House Publishers, Inc., 2013), 11.

4. Shared with permission.

5. John 6:63.

6. Rom. 8:14.

7. Anderson and Reese, *Spiritual Mentoring*, 43.

8. Matt. 13:16.

9. Walter Wangerin Jr., *The Orphean Passages: The Drama of Faith* (San Francisco: Harper & Row, 1986), 20–24.

10. Max Lucado does a great job of this in *God Came Near* (Portland, OR: Multnomah, 1987). Be sure to check out "Chapter 6: Twenty-Five Questions for Mary."

11. Luke 2:41–47.

12. Eph. 5:1–2.

13. Mark 12:30.

14. Josh 1:6–7, 9, 18.

15. Ex. 33:7–11.

16. Eph. 2:10.

17. Rom. 8:14–17.

18. Phil. 1:6.

19. Shared with permission.

20. There is an excellent chapter on "Healthy Friendships" in *The Seven Checkpoints for Youth Leaders* by Andy Stanley (West Monroe, La: Howard Books, 2001) that helped shape my thoughts on this many years ago.

21. Shared with permission.

22. Powell and Clark, *Sticky Faith*, 178.

23. Rom. 12:4–5.

24. Anthony, *Dreaming of More*, 91.

25. Shared with permission.

26. 1 John 2:6.

CHAPTER 10: RECOMMIT TO DISCIPLESHIP AS A WAY OF MINISTRY LIFE

1. Warren W. Wiersbe, *Be Courageous* (Colorado Springs, CO: David C. Cook, 1989), 20.

2. Gordon MacDonald, *Ordering Your Private World* (Nashville, TN: Thomas Nelson Publishers, 2007), 44.

3. I strongly recommend all leaders, especially those in ministry, take time to read *Courageous Leadership* by Bill Hybels (Grand Rapids: Zondervan, 2002). The principles are timeless and, if taken to heart, can realign you and your ministry trajectory.

4. Much is written on spiritual dry seasons; often referred to as "dark nights of the soul" or "the wilderness." In recent years, Jeff Manion's book, *The Land Between: Finding God in Difficult Transitions* (Grand Rapids: Zondervan, 2010), has proven to be a modern classic addressing this common experience.

5. Willard, *The Great Omission*, 94.

6. MacDonald, *Ordering Your Private World*, 76.

7. Luke 5:16.

8. Mark 1:35–39.

9. Willard, *The Great Omission*, 29.

CHAPTER 11: RECALIBRATE YOUR DISCIPLESHIP TARGET IN CHILDREN'S MINISTRY

1. Robert D. Larranaga, *Calling It a Day: Daily Meditations for Workaholics* (San Francisco: HarperCollins Publishers, 1990), 155.

2. "Rubik's Official Website," accessed January 30, 2015, https://www.rubiks.com/about/the-history-of-the-rubiks-cube.

3. Ibid.

4. Anthony, *Dreaming of More*, 59.

5. Michael Hyatt, "#015: How Leaders Can Create Alignment," transcript last modified June 6, 2012, http://michaelhyatt.com/015-how-leaders-can-create-alignment.html (accessed January 30, 2015).

6. If you want to stretch your leadership in this area, check out Simon Sinek's book, *Start With Why* (New York: Penguin, 2011), and resources at https://www.startwithwhy.com.

7. Peter Greer and Chris Horst, *Mission Drift: The Unspoken Crisis Facing Leaders, Charities, and Churches* (Grand Rapids: Baker Publishing, 2014), Kindle edition, 64.

8. Michael Hyatt, "How Do Leaders Create Alignment?," last modified February 24, 2010, http://michaelhyatt.com/how-do-leaders-create-alignment.html (accessed January 30, 2015).

9. Learn about what drives IKEA at http://www.ikea.com/ms/en_US/this-is-ikea/the-ikea-concept/index.html.

10. Shared with permission.

11. Thom S. Rainer and Eric Geiger, *Simple Church: Returning to God's Process for Making Disciples* (Nashville: B & H Publishing, 2011), 67–68.

12. Rainer and Geiger, *Simple Church*, 68.

13. Some examples for you to explore are *Becoming a Healthy Church* by Stephen A. Macchia (2003; http://www.healthychurch.net), *Church Unique* by Will Mancini (2008; http://auxano.com), *Advanced Strategic Planning* by Aubrey Malphurs (2013; http://www.malphursgroup.com).

14. John 5:19; 8:28; 12:49.

15. Acts 1:14; 4:23.

16. Eph. 3:14–19.

17. Phil. 2:1–4.

18. 1 Cor. 6:19–20.

19. Thank you to timely and strategic resources like *The Purpose Driven Church* by Rick Warren and *Purpose Driven Youth Ministry* by Doug Fields, which helped steer my thinking on this early on.
20. Holly Catterton Allen and Christine Lawton Ross, *Intergenerational Christian Formation: Bringing the Whole Church Together in Ministry, Community and Worship* (Downers Grove, IL: IVP Academic, 2012), 63.

CHAPTER 12: RECONSIDER THE DISCIPLESHIP RESOURCES AT YOUR DISPOSAL

1. Kenneth W. Osbeck, *Amazing Grace: 366 Inspiring Hymn Stories for Daily Devotions* (Grand Rapids: Kregel Publications, 2002), 79.
2. Learn more about the International Network of Children's Ministries (INCM) at http://incm.org. INCM's Children's Pastors Conference (CPC) is held annually to inspire and equip kidmin leaders from across the US and around the world.
3. Learn more about Pastor Harvey Carey and the church he leads at http://www.citadeloffaith.org.
4. Dietrich Bonhoeffer, *Life Together: A Discussion of Christian Fellowship*, trans. John W. Doberstein (New York: Harper & Row, 1954), 99.
5. Dietrich Bonhoeffer, *The Cost of Discipleship* (New York: Touchstone, 1995), 59.
6. Shared with permission.
7. Robert Webber, *Ancient-Future Faith: Rethinking Evangelicalism for a Postmodern World* (Grand Rapids: Baker Books, 1999), 7.
8. Kinnaman and Hawkins, *You Lost Me*, 13.

EPILOGUE: HOW CAN THE MINISTRY OF AWANA SERVE YOU?

1. Markins and Lovaglia, *The Gospel Truth*, 20.
2. Markins and Lovaglia, *The Gospel Truth*, 66.